A Playboy
Bunny
and
UCLA

Vikki Richardson

ISBN-13:
978-0997484502 (Vikki Richardson)

ISBN-10:
0997484500

PUBLISHER CODE: A19N281VDPM1CO

vrun4jc@hotmail.com

DEDICATION

This book is dedicated to all of humanity
for the wondrous ways we are connected,
regardless of continents or pre-programmed concepts
and beliefs about ethnicity, race, and religion.

Vikki Richardson

CONTENTS

ACKNOWLEDGMENTS

For proofreading and feedback on my manuscript: Barbara French, writing instructor, Joan Harmon, and fellow students, Tuesday writing class, Cypress, CA. Also, Mary Bussey, Rhonda Magasinn, Rachel Hinton, El Nora Willingham, Ruth Jordan and Bernard Schaefer. Line editor, Norah Sarsour, UCLA Alumni.

TECHNICAL SUPPORT

My wonderful husband, Kymmith Handy, and the Apple Store technicians, Brea, CA.

Vikki Richardson

INTRODUCTION

A Memoir - This book is about a baby girl who grew up battling many scary monsters and won.

Why did I write this book? I wrote this book because I have many friends who want to know the whole story, not just the segment of life that they know me from.

Furthermore, Oprah Winfrey has repeatedly stated and encouraged that, "We are not on earth by accident, and we each have a story to tell." Jose Silva, Gary Zukav, Zig Ziglar, Les Brown and many others have led me to believe that each human being is on earth for a good purpose. I believe that a major purpose is to love, share information, help, and encourage one another.

Undoubtedly, there are countless people who have gone through, or will encounter challenging situations and experiences, some worse than others. Hopefully, this book will be motivating and encouraging.

Our journey through life is constructed with obstacles. It is our responsibility to go through, around, under and over them, whatever it takes to bring positive end results. Regardless of who we are and where we are in life, there are conflicts and obstacles.

My story gives an account of abuse and brutality by family members and racial injustices by my fellow Americans. It exemplifies forgiveness and moving forward, rather than lingering over past negativity. Additionally, there are countless laughable moments beyond the tears.

Follow my journey from the cotton fields of Denmark, Tennessee, to having been labeled "uneducable," to Playboy Bunny, to topless Go Go Girl, to actress, to Silva Mind Control instructor and onward to academic excellence at New York University and UCLA. It took twenty years, but in June 1979, I graduated from UCLA with a B.A. Degree in English.

1

YUM! YUM!
A CHOCOLATE BUNNY

Voluptuous breasts and desirous derrieres sporting fluffy white Bunny tails were basic requirements for all Playboy Bunny girls.

Our costumes were tailor made to fit us individually. If Bunnies did not have a hourglass figure, the corset stays in our costumes gave everyone a tiny waistline, which brought adoring remarks from female guests. The pinched waist of the costumes pushed our breasts up to the very top of our Bunny suits, which made it easy for stuffed-in breast nipples to pop out, causing embarrassing grins from anticipatory men. The sides of our costumes were cut hip high, which gave all of us long, lean legs and round hips. The club provided our costumes with matching Bunny ears.

They came in a variety of jellybean colors and reminded me of my taste for those yummy candies. The club also provided the sexy black pantyhose, white cuffs anchored with Playboy cuff links, and the white collars with black bow ties, which caused customers to tease, "My goodness, what happened to the rest of your shirt?"

We had to pay for our own shoes and wigs. Just being a Bunny brought major discounts on shoes, makeup, wigs, and anything we bought. Most of the Bunnies had worn very little makeup, or none at all. Merle Norman Cosmetics provided professionals who matched our skin tones with the best shades for each of us. After my makeup was finished, including extended eyelashes and wig, I did not recognize myself.

The makeup artists also provided instructions on basic skin care and how to apply and remove makeup, which was needed since I had never worn any. Merle Norman gave us discounts on all of our skin care and makeup products. Bunnies brought business to local merchants, and we benefitted from the discounts.

After six weeks of intensive training, we had learned the Bunny dip and how to walk very fast in high-heeled pumps. While carrying a loaded tray of drinks, our fluffy white Bunny tails bounced around in preparation for the grand opening of the Cincinnati Playboy Club, September 1964. Keith Hefner, Hugh's younger brother, hired all Bunnies who worked the gala opening of the Cincinnati Club. During summer 1964, in the July issue, there was an ad in the 'Playboy' magazine that featured a pretty blond girl, wearing a two-piece swimsuit in an outdoor, sunny setting. The ad read something like: "If you or someone you know would like to be a Playboy Bunny, please fill out this card and mail it back with a picture."

Leading up to the life-changing event of becoming a Playboy Bunny, turning nineteen was also life-changing. I graduated from Shortridge High School and got my first "good job" with the State of Indiana. I worked as a receptionist in the Intangibles Tax Division. I became a nineteen-year-old bride to a very nice young man who turned out to have a "Doctor Jekyll and Mr. Hyde" personality, based on how much he drank.

By age twenty-four, knowing that I had nothing to lose except my life, by a disturbed, alcoholic husband, I responded to the ad. A photo studio near the newsstand was across the street from where I worked. For my Playboy glamour shot, I wore a black, short-sleeved leotard over long black opaque tights, and black high-heeled pumps. I also wore a happy smile. The sheer thought of mailing something to Playboy magazine in Chicago thrilled my soul, if nothing else. Sure enough, the shock of my life came in the mail a few weeks later from Playboy, informing me of the intended opening of the Cincinnati club. I immediately answered in the affirmative. After more correspondence and providing requested information, I received a confirmation letter and details that included date and time to arrive at the Sheraton Hotel in Cincinnati for a face-to-face interview.

I wore my little long sleeved, knee-length church suit, a bright tropical print of orange, red, white and yellow with a high neck white blouse, matching orange shoes and bag, and white gloves. I rode the Greyhound bus to Cincinnati and took a taxi to the hotel. The only person who knew about this was me. Certainly, I would have been discouraged, condemned and/or laughed at by anyone who would have known that I even dared to dream. I told Mother that I was going to a baseball game in Cincinnati with some friends from work.

Arriving at the hotel was an event within itself. This was the first hotel I had ever been in. Filled with fear and anticipation of the unknown, my heart pounded like a drum as I entered the hotel lobby. Awestruck by the size and splendor, I quietly prayed and remained calm. Apparently, everyone knew that Playboy was in town and hiring.

The lobby was buzzing with activity, people rushing around, places to eat and a bar, lots of talking and laughter. Seeing all of those beautiful "painted up" women wearing low cut dresses and big hair, I knew that I did not stand a chance. Anxiety made me want to run out of the hotel, but since the next Greyhound bus back to Indianapolis was leaving after my scheduled interview, I decided to go through with it.

When the young lady with the clipboard called my name, "Ann Summers," I nearly fainted, but I managed to get up from the chair, smile and follow her into the interview room, which turned out to be a hotel suite.

Keith Hefner warmly greeted me and thanked me for coming to the interview. Wow! He thanked me. He was very reassuring. My fears faded, and I found myself comfortably talking and laughing with him. It was further comforting that two training Bunnies were also in the room. As previously instructed through correspondence, I had brought my one piece swim suit. Keith asked me to step into the bathroom, put it on and walk around the room, which I did with ease and confidence.

When he said "Congratulations, you are now a Playboy Bunny," I ran across the room, turned a flip over the bed and landed on my high-heeled feet. Spontaneously, I jumped up and down like a cheerleader, clapped my hands and squealed with joy!

The other Playboy personnel in the room and Keith laughed heartily; he said that I was the happiest Bunny he had ever hired. If only he had known. Keith hired all of the plain, cute, scared and strong women who were willing to work hard, become transformed into Playboy Bunnies and maintain "The Bunny Image." To my surprise, he did not hire the sexy women with low cut dresses and big hair. From the hotel lobby, I remembered a scared girl sitting in the corner chewing her fingernails and another young lady sitting alone, wiping away tears; they were both hired.

At times, I had been very scared and wiped away countless tears along the dusty roads that took me to The Playboy Club. Getting to The Playboy Club was a most unlikely journey from Route 2, Box 3, Denmark, Tennessee, to St. Louis and Indianapolis. In Indianapolis, my good job in The Intangibles Tax Division did not provide the fun or adventure that I daydreamed about and longed for, but it did give me one astounding encounter in which I met a world leader.

Meeting President John F. Kennedy provided some fun and adventure that I could not have planned for. In October 1962, the President came to Indianapolis and boosted the senatorial candidacy for Birch Bayh, Jr.'s election to the U. S. Senate. As young Democratic campaign workers, six young ladies were selected to meet and greet President Kennedy upon his arrival, and we were ecstatic. When security arrived with the President, the six of us were waiting behind the speaker's platform. He arrived hungry, and I dashed off to get him a hotdog and a soda. He seemed to inhale it! He handed me his suit jacket to hold onto as he quickly stepped out on the platform.

Lightning has never sizzled through my body, but from what I have heard, holding the President's suit jacket felt like a bolt of lightning hit me. Never had I felt such a rush of energy and excitement! Without even trying, the other five hostesses and I formed a circle facing each other. They moved in closer to me so that all of us could inhale the aroma of cologne on the President's jacket. It was made from the most luxurious fabric we had ever touched. We giggled and gushed like the jacket was a cute puppy as we whispered our admiring comments.

After approximately twenty minutes, Mr. Kennedy's short speech was over. I handed him his jacket as calmly as possible. He graciously thanked each of us for our help and support. We could not believe how down to earth and friendly he was. Soon he was gone; our job was well done. However, two different 5x7 pictures of the hostesses remain in the Indianapolis Times newspaper dated October 10, 1962. The caption reads: "These young Democratic Party workers have the John F. Kennedy-Birch Bayh bandwagon rolling for the President's visit at Weir-Cook Municipal Airport at 4 p.m. Saturday." My family and friends were delighted to see my name, Ann Summers, in the newspaper. Meeting a President and holding his jacket was most unlikely for a little "Colored" girl from a backwoods farm in Denmark, Tennessee.

A year later, a splitting headache, upset stomach, agony and anger devastated me after President Kennedy's murder. When there were no more tears for me to cry, I slept three days with little food or water. Mother told me: "Even if you starve to death, it will not bring the President back to life."

Historically, that was a horrible time for our nation, in general, and for Negroes and minorities, in particular. President Kennedy gave us hope for civil rights and a better way of life as Americans. After the President's death, I felt numb and depressed. I desperately needed and wanted a positive change in my life, which included escaping from Larry.

I had divorced him, and we were not living together, but he constantly called me at work to remind me, "If I can't have you, nobody else will either." He frequently drove past my family's home where I lived, and everywhere I went, there he was. As a teenager, I did not know that I had unwittingly married a bipolar-type man who would be emotionally and physically abusive to me.

One Saturday afternoon he was drunk and in a fit of rage over his own guilt. He was angry with me because I found a love letter from his girlfriend and read it out loud to him. He snatched the letter out of my hand and accused me of cheating. Angry words flew from both of us like poison darts and contaminated our apartment. I screamed at him, "Since you already have a girlfriend, I'm going to get me a boyfriend."

While yelling and calling me names, he placed his loaded 45 revolver against my head. With the cold steel of the gun pressed against my left temple, he threatened to blow my brains out. I yelled back at him, "Shoot me mother-fucker. I would rather be dead than stuck with your drunk, stupid ass." Click! Click! Click! The gun did not fire. In anger, he forcefully threw the gun on the kitchen floor. It discharged a bullet into the wall, just above the floorboard. Then, he stormed out of our apartment, and he drove to Chicago to see his girlfriend.

On a different occasion, he punched me in my right eye so hard, he knocked me unconscious. A few hours later, I woke up on the living room sofa in the home of his alcoholic uncle. I was nauseated from the black eye and from the smell of a huge piece of raw steak on my face to supposedly cure my black eye.

My husband and his uncle had gone out to buy more liquor, and they continued drinking. While they were out of the house, the uncle's wife told me in hushed tones that my husband's father had murdered my husband's mother. With a long sharp knife, he slashed her throat from ear-to-ear. My husband's father died in prison and was identified as criminally insane. The uncle's wife had very fair skin that revealed deep purple bruises on her upper arms and back, as she lifted her top to show me her injuries. She whispered, "They are all crazy. You have to get away while you are still young, and before he kills you."

The meaning of her words knocked me unconscious again, and I slept until our husbands returned. Their loud voices and drunken laughter woke me up, but I did not move. The uncle's wife said, "Larry, just let her sleep. She will be all right." I slept on the sofa; he slept on the floor near the sofa. The following morning, the uncle's wife cooked a big breakfast, but I was not hungry. After breakfast, my husband drove me back to our apartment and made sure that I did not visit any of my family members. He did not want them to see my black eye, which was still swollen shut from the impact of his right fist.

Through careful planning, I eventually managed to get a divorce. I gave Mother my John Hancock life insurance policy and told her that I was going to get away, kill Larry, or she could bury me, because I could no longer live buried alive. The divorce terminated the marriage, but I could not terminate him. He became the sweet and persistent "Dr. Jekyll, but I knew that "Mr. Hyde" could leap out at anytime.

Prior to becoming a Bunny, my immediate escape was through reading various magazines, which I bought at the attractive and well-supplied newsstand and snack shop across the street from work. Along with monthly issues of 'Ebony' and 'Jet,' I also bought a 'Playboy' magazine. I enjoyed reading the articles and gazing at the colorful, jaw-dropping pictures of beautiful women spread out on the glossy pages. I wondered how they had the nerve to do such a thing. The Playboy dog always made me chuckle as I quietly turned the pages of my hidden magazine. The big Saint Bernard with the keg around his neck was a monthly feature.

The receptionist position in the Intangibles Tax Division situated me in the front section of the large office. Placing the 'Playboy' magazine in my middle desk drawer allowed me to take a peek between phone calls and people walking into the office. Thanks to reflective glass from the entry doors, I could see co-workers tipping towards my desk from the back of our office, trying to spy inside, but I quickly closed my drawer before they arrived. When I resigned from The Intangibles Tax Division, which was part of the State Office Building, I was earning approximately $350.00 a month.

When I filled out the ad in 'Playboy' magazine, I thought that making $350.00 a month would be much more fun in The Playboy Club. Moreover, it would create an escape hatch from Indianapolis.

The six weeks of Bunny training had been very difficult, and some of the Bunnies who trained us had been vicious. Therefore, I had memorized my Bunny Manual, which contained the Playboy creed of rules and regulations. It also contained the standardized method of placing cocktail glasses on the tray for drink orders. When a Bunny approached the bar, the bartenders automatically knew what kind of drinks to pour or mix by looking at the tray. Bartenders, busboys, room directors, wardrobe mistresses, Bunny Mothers and everyone involved had been trained in the Playboy methodology, a very efficient system. The Bunny Mother was there for us to cry on her shoulders. She also came into the club and observed us performing our Bunny duties and usually provided us with positive feedback. Good little Bunnies got merits, and there were numerous ways to earn them.

Although I was very shy and a nervous wreck, I volunteered to go on stage and introduce the entertainers who were performing in The Playboy Penthouse, for which I received 25 merits. Whenever a Bunny accumulated 100 merits, she received a Playboy reward of some sort. Adversely, 100 demerits delivered automatic expulsion from the club. A run or snag in our pantyhose brought demerits, but a straggly, frumpy looking Bunny tail was a much more grievous offense. We spent hours brushing and fluffing up our tails with a wire brush. After a while, most of us gave the wardrobe mistress generous tips to fluff out our tails for us, since it was a Playboy crime to take your tail or costume from the club, a sure way to earn demerits. However, whispered rumors in the Bunny dressing room alleged that Bunnies who were girlfriends of Playboy executives were immune to demerits and expulsion.

I, Bunny Ann, was determined to earn merits. Having grown up on a farm in Denmark, I was strong and agile, which enabled me to carry and serve a maximum of thirteen plates of hot food at once. I covered my bare arms with linen dinner napkins and balanced ten plates on my left arm. With three plates in my right hand, I carried them from the service area. To serve the food, I leaned back in the stylized Bunny dip and placed each plate on the table as the food was ordered. When they saw me approaching their table with my load, the customers exclaimed and automatically jumped up to help me. I responded with "Please don't touch me! You will throw off my balance." When the last plate was placed on the table, they cheered, whistled, applauded, and they left me a $100.00 tip! That was amazing for a little "Colored" girl, who had grown up up as "Little Miss Ugly Face" and labeled "uneducable" by my insensitive principal at Shortridge High School in Indianapolis, Indiana.

Becoming a Playboy Bunny was amazing, astonishing, and the most unlikely thing for me to do. As a Bunny, I was in a constant state of "I can't believe it." Having grown up in Denmark, St. Louis and Indianapolis, I had witnessed some ugly events, including drinking fountains and bathrooms marked "White only" and "Colored." I had been paid less money for doing the same job as a White co-worker in Indianapolis, while working as a receptionist in The Intangibles Tax Division.

Suddenly, it was profitable being "Colored." My life was immediately wonderful, in spite of the pain and agony of the Civil Rights Movements that were taking place at the time: The Free Speech Movement at the University of California at Berkley, the non- violent protests led by Martin Luther King, Jr., the more radical approach by Malcolm X. The Freedom Riders who endured powerful water hosing, biting dogs and death, created tension in our nation and conflict within me, as I embraced "The Playboy Bunny Kingdom."

Even so, The Civil Rights Bill in 1964 was an encouragement towards equality. The Playboy Club was an equal opportunity employer, and I was thankful. For the first time in my life, I was very proud to be a chocolate Negro, and I made more money because I was. Chocolate Bunnies were a premium, especially during the Easter season. There were four of us in the Cincinnati club of around thirty-something Bunnies, and I was the most chocolate one. Bunny Sandy was a lighter shade of brown, Bunny Elaine was a shade lighter than Sandy, and Bunny Jay-Jay had fair skin, blue eyes, and everyone thought she was White. As the most chocolate Bunny, I made bosoms and bosoms of money, especially around Easter. Bunny Jay-Jay tried wearing dark make up, but it did not match her boobs and arms.

A "High Roller" client who owned a local night club and a house boat, invited us to float up and down the Ohio river on hot summer days. Jay-Jay and every Bunny available loved going out on the boat, wearing swimsuits, stretching out in the sun and being served any and everything we wanted.

There was always an abundance of food and drinks on the boat, but what we wanted most was rest and relaxation before it was time to hop back to the club and stuff ourselves into our Bunny costumes. Since being a chocolate Bunny had perks, my sister Bunnies were determined to cash in on the chocolate factor. Watching them stretch out in the hot sun to get a tan was something I had never seen before. When they insisted that I join them, I did for a few minutes. Then I moved to a shady spot and teased: "I already have a tan."

Thoughts of being out in the hot sun generated flashbacks of my childhood years of chopping and picking cotton in that blistering Tennessee sun. At age ten, while chopping cotton for $3.00 a day so that I could buy my own shoes, I fainted and crashed to the ground, my face barely missed the sharp blade of the upturned hoe.

Late summer and fall brought cooler weather for picking cotton, but the trade off was not a desirable one. There were huge green worms with little horns above their black bulging eyes, a big, greedy mouth, and their entire prickly body was an automatic stinger. Green cotton leaves provided a perfect camouflage for the worms to hide and eat the leaves. They delivered a nasty sting when the picker reached for the cotton.

After so many stings, I was afraid to pick cotton. Mother told me to check the ground for droppings and shake the cotton stalk to knock the worms off. But the worms were smart enough to hide under the leaves without warning. The day I looked down and saw the biggest green cotton worm in the world walking up my chest was a day that "I had a fit." Although I was involuntarily shrieking and jumping up and down, my mother did not know that I was hysterical! She offered a whipping with a cotton stalk if I did not stop that foolishness and get back to picking cotton.

As the boat floated along, and I reflected on my past, I told my sister Bunnies: "I'll just stretch out in the shade and enjoy my lemonade, thank you very much," but they were determined to endure the sun.

Bunny Delores did not like her pale complexion. Her nickname was "Bunny White Roach." She said, "I'm Italian, and I can get very dark, believe it or not." Therefore, Delores and Bunny Bobbi bet money that they could get as dark as I am. Also born in Tennessee, Bunny Bobbi is the only woman I have ever known who dyed her natural blond hair black, to avoid being called a "dumb blond" or "Bunny Dumb-Dumb." Over time, Bobbi, Delores, Jay-Jay, and several other Bunnies tanned so well, they were advised by the Bunny Mother to stay out of the sun. One night several of the deeply tanned Bunnies were working The Penthouse. In the subdued lighting, all of us were "chocolate Bunnies." A key holder reportedly inquired if there were "any other Bunnies working the club?"

Bunny Hope was always working. Her nickname was "Bunny Great Legs." She and I lived in the YWCA and frequently worked double shifts, since the "Y" was just a block or so from the club. With curvy hips and strong shapely legs, Bunny Hope was one of the fastest moving bunnies in the club. She was definitely a show room bunny, which means that she and several of us were strong and fast enough to work The Penthouse and enjoy the entertainment, which always included a comedian, a band and a featured singer. We had to serve our customers drinks and food in the dim nightclub lights. Playboy supplied us with a small silver flashlight that looked like a ball point pen which provided enough light to total out checks for all of our customers. The calculations were relatively easy, since all basic drinks and food items were $1.50 in all Playboy Clubs. The challenge was getting in and out of the service area rapidly, carrying loads of drinks and food with out tripping over some tall guy's feet, naturally stretched out into the aisle.

The Penthouse was designed with a few steps for elevated seating and viewing. We had to carry our trays up the steps and gracefully do the Bunny dip. We called out each drink for every customer. "Your Johnny Walker Red on the rocks with a club soda back," as I placed a rock glass with ice cubes on the table in front of him and poured the shot over the ice. It required a highball glass with ice cubes and a glass bottle of club soda. Imagine a party of ten people! I served many groups of ten and more. The women usually ordered a one-glass drink like a whiskey sour, or some other mixed, blended, or creamed drinks. Fortunately, some men ordered a martini, brandy or other one glass drinks. Beer was a popular drink, which came in a glass bottle and was poured into a tall, frosty glass. We were trained to pour the beer with just the right amount of foam that made the men cheer for the perfect head we poured with their beer. And all of this took place in the dark while the comedian was telling jokes or the singer was singing.

The key to a smooth show turnover was to present the customers their checks before the bright lights came on. I used my pen light so that they could see what they were signing and where to write in the tip. Therefore, my station was always ready for seating customers for the next show, and there were usually three shows on weekends.

For those Bunnies who could not hop fast enough to work the Penthouse, there was the Party room, which key holders reserved for private events. The Playmate Bar was fun to work. It was decorated with glass covered framed pictures of recent Playmates in various provocative poses.

`The customers lined up at the buffet and carried their own plates to their tables, but Bunnies served the drinks and capped their ashtrays. Table ash trays were square, thin and orange; the design was a female figure with long hair. We were trained to cap an ashtray by placing a clean ashtray face down over the loaded one, pick them up, put the dirty one on the tray, and replace it with the clean one. When rapidly done, changing ashtrays looked like a magic trick.

The cigarette Bunny did not have to cap ashtrays. She had a uniquely designed boxshaped gadget that fit around her waist. The wide, flat, open box was filled with the most popular brands of cigarettes and cigars, and she carried a supply of Playboy matches and lighters. She slowly strolled through all of the rooms in the club, sweetly announcing, "Cigars, cigarettes."

There were gift shop Bunnies, and on rare occasions, I worked the gift shop. Even with my employee discount, I spent generous amounts of money buying Playboy jewelry and trinkets as gifts for family members and friends. Working the gift shop was the only time we had to see all of the Playboy items for sale.

The camera Bunny was in high demand with her Polaroid camera that produced instant black and white pictures. Customers generously tipped the camera Bunny for taking their pictures. They also gave the serving Bunnies bonus tips for being photographed with them.

Billiards Bunnies were very popular and made the most money for the least amount of physical labor. The manner in which the pool Bunny held her cue stick and scattered the pool balls made the men howl like wolves. Whatever position the Bunny placed her body in to shoot pool, it was tempting to the wolves. With big breasts barely contained, as she leaned forward to make a difficult shot, or upturned her tail to bank a shot, she caused amorous imaginations to soar unbridled. Some pool Bunnies were "sharks," and customers played hard to win.

One night I was called in to cover for the pool Bunny. I had never seen a pool table close up and personal. Initially, I held the cue stick like a spear and jabbed it into the colorful balls. Customers presumed that all pool Bunnies were "sharks," and their egos were highly inflated over beating my ears off on the pool table. That was my first and only shot at shooting pool, which I never learned.

There was no magic, but being a Bunny felt magical for most of us. We came from a wide variety of backgrounds and ethnic groups. I was intrigued and amused by Bunnies who spoke English with an accent. Bunny Cri-Cri was French, and Bunny Gabriella was German. They really knew how to pour on the accents and rake in tips. Actually, all of the Bunnies made more money than ever before, just because we were Bunnies and worked harder than people could imagine. Even so, we were happy that Keith hired us and gave us the opportunity to earn more money than most of our parents would ever make in a month.

Among my Bunny friends, I was the only one who got an interview by filling out the little ad in the Playboy magazine. Working as a Playboy Bunny allowed us to earn more money than we could imagine. I was twenty four years old and a great distance from my family and our poverty-stricken life in the log cabin. Working as a Bunny was amazing, but I could not prevent my thoughts from flashing back to my family.

2

MEET THE FAMILY

Our family members were our mother, Catherine Hennings Williamson, father, Othelder Williamson, and Mary Elizabeth Williamson, paternal grandmother. We called her Grandma Lizzy. My five siblings are Loretta, born January 1933, Robert - February 1941, Audrey - December 1945, El Nora - February 1947 and Kassandra was born in June 1949.

Grandma Lizzy never would have imagined that I would ever become anything, not to mention a Playboy Bunny, which was nonexistent at the time. After all, I am the one who grew up as "Little Miss Ugly Face," "Mule Lips," "Little Black Jap Gal" and "Squinty Eyes." Those were a few of the unwanted names that I was called as a young child. Where were my family members when I was being emotionally abused? They were the abusers. Grandma Lizzy was an original "potty mouth." Since my extremely short hair was sandy brown and stuck to my scalp like a sheep's wool, Grandma delighted in telling me, "Gal yo head look lak sheep shit in shallow water." She bragged that she had "good hair," and that she was part White and Cherokee Indian. Sometimes she would drift into a depressed mood, stare into space and clearly speak words that none of us understood. Perhaps she was speaking Iroquoian, language of the Cherokee, Tuscarora, Huron and Wyandot Indians. Whenever she was annoyed, which was most of the time, she would yell at us, "You lil black-assed nappy headed niggers ain't no kin to me." I often wondered why she was so mean. I did not ask to be born an "ugly baby."

Bloody water froze in mid air, when the midwife threw it out of the log cabin when I was born around 1:00 a.m in January 1940. It was not my choice to arrive in a backwoods log cabin during a blizzard. The dogs barked, sniffed, and licked the bloody ice, while howling the announcement of a new baby girl, Vessye Ann Williamson, but the Madison County clerk could not spell, so my birth certificate reads, "Vesa And Williamson." Reportedly, Mother's labor was long and painful. She was slender built, about five feet two inches tall. My passage from her womb was a ripping, splitting, tearing and tearful event as she struggled in strife, delivering me into life. Finally, my head popped out, feeling bigger than a basketball, causing a ripping sensation. Mother screamed! Then the birth of my shoulders felt bigger than my head, causing splitting. The midwife did what she could, but it was not enough to relieve the tearing pain for my butt being born, which felt bigger than my head and shoulders. Tears from pain and relief streamed down her face. The Negro physician, Doctor Meachum, had arrived earlier in the day and gave her a shot to dull the pain but could not stop the ripping. When my passage and afterbirth from her womb was complete, I weighed in just over ten pounds, "Looking just like a catfish."

Daddy was six feet and approximately two hundred pounds. He was not home during my birth. A couple of days later he stumbled home, smelling like stale whiskey and stinking from lack of soap and water. When he found out the baby was a girl, he cursed at Mother and stormed out of the house to drink more corn liquor whiskey. He was still angry with Mother because the first born child, Loretta was not a boy, and now another "got-dammed-nappy-headed gal." "Ah ought ta take it to da gotdammed pond and drown it! Lookin like a got-dammed catfish!"

As I grew up and Mother provided the details of my birth, she stated that during her pregnancy with me, she took her faithful dog O'Patsy and walked about a mile to fish in cousin Lawrence Bond's pond. She caught a bucket full of catfish but had to keep them swimming in the water bucket until it was their turn for dinner.

My parents did not own a refrigerator, which would have been useless without electricity, which we did not have. They did own a very old-fashioned ice box, which required a fifty pound ice block. But by the time my drunk daddy would make it home from Jackson, the ice block was just a large ice cube. Relatives within a couple of miles from us owned nice homes with electricity, and some had running water and indoor bathrooms.

We had an outhouse located some distance from the house to avoid smelling the stink, especially on hot summer days. It was too dark and scary to trot to the outhouse after dark. The solution was a slop jar, which Grandma Lizzy referred to as "the piss pot." It was a white galvanized bucket with a matching lid, trimmed in red. Scatological humor was common in the country and set to a country blues beat, one of our favorite, toe- tapping tunes was:

Sittin on the slop jar
Waitin for by bowels to move,
Well I ain't constipated, but
I got those slop jar blues.

Emptying the slop jar was my first chore of the day. If the pot contained only urine, I dumped it in the field near the house. If it contained more, I emptied it in the outhouse to prevent our dogs from eating the contents.

One morning I took the slop jar to the field to empty it as usual. When I removed the top, there was a small amount of fecal matter floating in the urine, and a monstrous white tape worm, about ten inches long, slithered up, its head wiggling beyond the slop jar. My endless series of piercing screams split the air, as I kicked the slop jar over, trying to get away. My body bolted backwards, and my feet spun in the same spot as I tried to run backwards. I could only jump up and down in the same spot, where I tripped and fell on the ground. My eyes were transfixed upon the worm as it coiled and stretched around the slop jar.

With all of the creepy-crawly things on the farm, worms were one of my most feared. Worst yet, I fully realized that this worm had come out of somebody's body! Lord have mercy, Jesus! Hysteria prevailed! Robert, Loretta and Mother came running! The dogs were barking, snapping and growling, the same way they did when facing snakes. My barefeet were actually flying and spinning out dirt, arms flapping frantically, but my body was not moving away from the slop jar. When my family came running into the scene, they all hollered and jumped back when they saw the long white worm. Realizing where it came from made them scream again. Mother yelled at Loretta, "Run get a Mason jar."

Loretta yanked me up off the ground and ran me back to the house, but I stayed with her. She ran to get a big glass jar with a lid. Mother placed the jar in the worm's path as she rotated the slop jar to prevent it from slithering out. When the worm crawled into the inescapable jar, Mother closed the lid, took the captive back to the house. She removed the lid and filled the jar with water. Then, she covered the jar with white cloth so that the worm could breathe but not slither out.

When I saw the wiggling worm in the jar on top of the doorless china cabinet with no china, screams automatically rushed from my throat, and I felt sick to my stomach. Nightmares were frequent as millions of huge white worms stretched and slithered through my stomach. Realizing my fear and anxiety, Mother put the monster inside a brown paper sack and hid it until she could get to Jackson and show it to Dr. Meachum. Mother had explained that whoever did "number two" in the slop jar during the night had passed the worm. Thank God it was not me. Otherwise, I probably would have died from acute constipation before subjecting myself to the possibility of another worm.

Finally, Mother took the monster worm to Jackson for Dr. Meachum to observe, and she brought back anti-worm medication, that actually tasted good, unlike foaming castor oil. She told me that the doctor said bigger kids don't get tapeworms, because we had outgrown the tapeworm stage. I was approximately eight years old. The doctor was obviously a good "child psychologist." Many years later I learned that people of any age can and do get tapeworms and other parasites from meat, fish, produce, air and water. At the time, I did not know that microscopic parasites are everywhere, but I was thankful to learn that most of them are not deadly.

Furthermore, I learned that parasites travel into the body through pores on the bottom of barefeet and grow into horrifying, internal creatures. Some parasites come from animal feces. Even when the fecal matter is gone, parasites remain. This information triggered thoughts of when I accidentally stepped in warm chicken poop that squished up between my toes, which evoked nausea and sent cold chills down my spine, as we were barefoot most of the time.

I suspect that Mother and the doctor created the story that "Older kids don't get tapeworms," so that Robert, Loretta and I would not go crazy wondering how many were living inside of us. Audrey and El' Nora were too young to understand, and Kassandra was not yet born. Nonetheless, after the doctor's story and medication, waves of relief surged through my body, and the millions of worms stopped crawling around inside my stomach. Possibly the monster tapeworm came from pork, our main source of meat, which my family cured with salt and hickory smoke. Consequently, everyone went right on eating pork, but there were no more worms in the slop jar. I was paranoid and feared emptying the slop jar, but I still had to do it. The worm in the slop jar did not prevent hogs from being slaughtered.

Hog killing time was horror in sight, sound and motion. It came immediately after the last bale of cotton was picked and sold. Five or six hogs were designated for slaughter, placed in a pen and overfed into fatness. The night before that fatal day arrived, the designated hogs began squealing and moaning their impending doom. They knew that death lurked near. Perhaps it was the boiling water in the big, black pot that they would be scalded in later. Or maybe they sensed themselves hanging head down on the scaffold, structured expressly for them. It could have been the sound of knives being sharpened that made the hogs know that this was their last day of life. Whatever it was, they knew.

Around 7:00 a.m, four or five neighbor men, carrying tin tubs, arrived for the kill. All of them wearing boots, the most agile man with strength and hog holding know-how, jumped in the pen and brought out the first squealing victim. The remaining pigs huddled in a corner and groveled in low, desperate oinks. The men flipped the hog on its side and bound the feet with twine. Three or four men held the hog down while another swiftly slashed the throat. A final shriek, blood gushed, and I ran screaming on behalf of the hogs.

One time the men did not tie a hog's feet securely, and Daddy did not slash the right spot because the hog moved. The long sharp knife stuck in the hog's throat, as it dashed away, running frantically, spurting blood and emitting high-pitched squeals.

Everyone thought the pig would soon fall down dead; it did not. The hogs waiting to be killed were hovering in horror, as the bleeding pig ran around. The ground was bloody. The dogs were yelping, and the kids had to keep the dogs out of the way. After several minutes of life and death chaos, Mother aimed the rifle at the center of the hog's forehead, fired one shot and relieved the hog from agony. Soaked in its own blood and without another sound, it dropped dead on the ground.

During one particular rainy season, a mother pig and three piglets drowned in the flood that resulted from so much rain. There was one female survivor. We called her "Lil Piggy." I placed the tiny piglet in a box and fed her cornbread and clabbered milk. She was like a puppy, and we became very attached. As she grew bigger and stronger, she was placed in the pig pasture with the other hogs. But she always escaped and came back to the house for a piece of cornbread or whatever we could find to give to her. She was very intelligent and oinked responses when we talked to her.

As horrible as Daddy was, I thought he would not kill "Lil Piggy." The following year I fell apart with sorrow and hated Daddy with a passion when he also killed her at hog killing time. So, in my mind, I knocked Daddy to the ground, face up, and repeatedly stabbed him with my pitchfork from his head to toes, with blood gushing out of his body like the bleeding hogs. If I could have hated him any more, I certainly would have. After the hogs were slaughtered, they were dipped in the big black pot of scalding water, which made their hair loosen and easy to scrape off.

Our water supply came from an old well in our back yard. A very long and sturdy rope was attached to a three-foot-long cylinder bucket. The rope was attached to a big round, wooden wheel with a metal handle. The wheel looked like a jumbo spool of thread. The long rope wrapped around the jumbo spool, until we lowered the bucket into the well. Then, we pulled up the water by turning the handle, which wrapped the rope back around the spool. That was a heavy and difficult job for two little kids, but extra water was needed at hog killing time, and we were mandated to do it.

After the hogs' hair was scraped off from the boiling hot water, they were suspended by their feet on the scaffold, head near the ground, eyes open, tongue hanging out, teeth glaring, and there they waited to be gutted. A round tin tub on the ground was placed under the hog's head. A long sharp knife was plunged into the hog's belly, near the hind legs. As the knife slit the belly wide open, internal organs, blood, guts and gagging odors swooshed and slithered into the tub. All internal organs were cut out and put in their individual organ tin tub. Intestines, still warm from the hog's body heat, and stuffed with fecal matter from over-feeding, were put in their own tin tub for me and Robert to clean with our bare hands.

We squeezed all of the excrement out of the guts, and it plopped on the ground as if the pig pooped. Brown, stinky stuff was packed under our finger nails, wedged between our fingers and splattered on our feet and legs. Cleaning hog intestines was the most revolting job in the entire world and made me sick in the pit of my stomach, but I did not have an option. After we squeezed out all of the waste, an adult cut open the intestines, and Robert and I swished them through a tub of cold water. By the time the last gut was washed, the water was brown fecal soup, but they were washed and washed until the water remained clear. Mother seemed surprised that I covered my mouth, choked, gagged and carried on at the thought of eating "chittlins." Not on your life, not in a million years or more! Several years later, I learned that they were spelled "chitterlings."

Mother did not have to squeeze the poop out of hog intestines when she was a young child. Hog killing was done by her papa and other men in the community. They teamed up and went from one farm to the next, until all of their designated hogs were slaughtered and cured. But not Dad, he was some kind of different, and many, many years later when I saw the TV show, I realized that we were born in and endured "The Twilight Zone."

Mother was not born in "The Twilight Zone." She was born in a nice home in June 1910. Her parents, Mamie Jones Hennings was born March 1, 1887 and Robert Walker Hennings was born August 20, 1885. Mother's parents and grandparents were prosperous landowners. They built and lived in beautiful homes, and Granddad Walker owned a Model-T Ford. The Williamsons were replete with land and fine homes also.

When Daddy asked Mother to marry him and told her that he owned land and a house, she was pleased. They were married in the home of her parents, and she did not see Daddy's house until she was moving in. Passing hundreds of acres and several nice homes along the way, Catherine smiled confidently as newlyweds do, but her smile faded going through the woods on a dusty dirt road in June 1930. Shock and disbelief gripped her entire existence, and time stood still when she arrived and gazed upon her hew home, a falling down log cabin with added-on rooms, which were also decaying. Something told her to whack those horses and guide that wagon back home to her parents. She did not heed the warning, because Daddy put his arm around her shoulders and said, "Aw don't worry bout dat, um gonna build ya ah brand new manchon."

Daddy was actually living with his parents, Anthony Swift Williamson and Mary Elizabeth Theus Williamson. They were both aging, in poor health and needed Mother to cook and help care for them. Surprise! Surprise! Daddy was born in January 1907. With his mother's light brown complexion and wavy hair, he was born good-looking. When he was around nine years old, he fell asleep on a chair in front of the fireplace, fell off the chair into the fire and burned his right eye. At some point in his childhood, his older brother Walter Lee, tricked him into grabbing the tail of a young colt that kicked him in the mouth and chipped his four upper front teeth. His teeth were never repaired and slowly deteriorated as thirty years flew by.

As a married man and drunk adult, he fell off of a chair while nodding in front of the fireplace and dangerously burned the same eye, but he was not at home. His mother said that he had been sneaking and drinking her homemade wine when he fell in the fireplace as a child. He had adequate vision in his right eye, but it always looked raw and red. He could not close his eye because there was no skin on the lower lid. When he slept, his right eyeball stared blankly into space.

He was scary looking, and I was afraid of him. Over six feet tall, he was 200 plus pounds of muscle, with a big behind like his mama, but his abdominals were flat. He feared and deeply respected his mama, because when she said, "Boy, brang yo blak ass here," he came running. I witnessed her whacking him with her walking cane. No wonder he was such a mess, dipping snuff, chewing tobacco, smoking and drinking since childhood, like his mama.

Grandma dipped snuff, chewed tobacco and smoked corn cob pipes, which she made to her own specifications, but she did not drink. When I was approximately five years old, I asked her for a piece of chewing tobacco since she seemed to be enjoying it so much. She told me it was sweet chewing tobacco, and she gave it to me. I chewed and swallowed an ample bite. A few minutes later I was staggering around, tongue burning with the nasty taste of tobacco, stomach churning, and I went spinning to the ground, whining and moaning. I can still hear Grandma Lizzy's witch-like cackle, as she delighted in my misery. Mother came running! When she found out, she told Grandma that she should have known better. Still laughing, Grandma said, "Bet she won't ask for no mo," and I never did. Knowing the tricks of Grandma, I should have remembered.

When I was around four-years old, I asked Grandma if she could bite, since she did not have any top teeth, and her remaining bottom teeth were worn down. She said, "Hare gal, stick yo fangar in there and see," and she opened her mouth. In went my little right index finger. She bit down very hard, broke the skin and left tooth marks. Screaming from pain, I jumped around trying to rescue my finger from Grandma's mouth. Mother was furious, as Lizzy Williamson laughed until she cried.

In the log cabin, I cried a lot but not from laughing. Vicious beatings by

Daddy caused tears, pain and injuries. I also cried when Daddy beat Loretta. She was seven years older, and my only brother, Robert Anthony, was two years younger than I was. Grandma Lizzy manipulated all of us. She antagonized my mother and condemned her dark skin, even though Mom was beautiful with shoulder length hair. If we did not do whatever Grandma wanted us to do, she would say, "Uma make Othee beat yo ass." If she was not in agreement when Daddy was about to beat one of us, she would say, "Othee, you hit that chile, and I will kick yo ass," as she hobbled her fat body towards him and shook her cane in his face. Her height was less than five feet.

Daddy was sneaky. He would beat us in the field or the barn, knowing that Grandma could not do anything about it after the fact. In general, everyday life with Daddy was a nightmare. He would beat us anytime for the slightest offense, or for unfounded assumptions. At one time or another, he has beaten us with the following terrifying weapons: a razor strap, leather belt, bullwhip, a tree branch switch, rope and his hands. Having endured beatings from all of those weapons, the cracking bullwhip that whisked away my skin and fragments of clothing with every crack was the worst, but all of them caused burning pain and physical injuries. Daddy practiced barbarity without any sign of remorse. Surely he must have known how brutal and cruel he treated his children and the animals that he beat with the whip, ropes and two-by-fours. His brain was sizzled and segmented by too much white lightning whiskey, which he made in the backwoods near the pond bank. As a young child, I knew that he had problems, but it is not the child's job to figure out and fix a parent's problems. I thought one of his problems was his inability to read and write.

When I was in first grade, he attempted to read "The Three Little Pigs." My sister Loretta was very smart in school, and she taught me to read when I was five-years old. Learning the alphabet was serious, because if I got one wrong, she whacked the back of my hand. She used the same method for reading. I knew every word in "The Tree Little Pigs," and I knew that Daddy was looking at the pictures and making up words, and I told him, "That's not what's in the book." That was the one and only time he ever showed any interest in my education. He did not know all of the letters in the alphabet. He signed his name, "O. T. Wmson," because he could not spell Othelder Williamson. I do not know how far he could count.

Dad's language did not have any subject and verb agreements, and he only spoke "curse." He used God's name in vain to begin each sentence. All of his words were profane, and none of them were profound. His mama spoke the same language but with more authority. Like all children, I spoke the language of my parents, but I was slapped in the mouth for my language skills, which filled me with internal rage. If it's so bad, why do you say it all of the time? The standing answer for all of my parent's wrong doing was

"Cause u'm grown." That statement always made me want to choke my parents and slap some sense into them. I could not wait to get grown so that I could get away from those people, but that would take quite some time.

Time had passed slowly until I was finally grown and free to work as a Playboy Bunny. Daddy never did build Mother a "manchon," but I did visit the Playboy Mansion in Chicago with Bunny Peggy. She was a tall buxom blond who was happy-go-lucky and loved having fun. Her nickname was "Bunny Big Peg." She was six feet tall in her spike heels. In spite of her strong looking statue, she claimed that her wrists were weak, and she could not carry a loaded tray. Therefore, she worked the gift shop and knew everybody in the club. I did not know everyone in the club and did not know the latest buzz on whatever was going on at the time, but I had a few good buddies, and "Big Peg" was one of them. She was from The Chicago Club and transferred to Cincinnati. Being able to transfer from one club to the next was a bonus.

By some good fortune, Peggy and I had the same days off, and she invited me to Chicago. She said, "I know Hef, and we can stay in the Playboy Mansion." For real! We piled our bags in Peggy's little blue VW, and she drove to Chicago. Sure enough, we were welcomed into the Playboy Mansion.

The guest area looked just like a little Playmate Bar, complete with glossy colored pictures of recent Playmates. There were booths and dining tables, a bar and of course, a bartender and a chef, just like a Playboy Club. But unlike The Playboy Club, there was a swimming pool, and I met the sauna for the first time. The sauna was way too hot for my wig, so I sat on the side of the swimming pool, wearing my conservative swimsuit and splashing my feet in the water. Hef's bartenders seemed very surprised that I did not drink or smoke, and they were delighted to keep me supplied with orange juice with grenadine, that sticky, sweet syrup made from pomegranates, and all of the sugar sweet, red, bar cherries that I could eat.

While I was sitting at the bar eating cherries, Hugh Hefner came downstairs to greet us. He was wearing pajamas, house slippers, and a robe. He held an unlighted pipe in his mouth. He shook my hand and warmly welcomed me. When he asked, I told him how much I loved being a Bunny. He said, "Thank you," and wished me success. After a few minutes of pleasant conversation with us, he went back upstairs, and I did not see him again during the remainder of our visit. Was I dreaming or what? I just met the "Bunny Father!" I expected him to be some big, tall, flashy guy, but he was "average" and appeared quite shy, not nearly as energetic and outgoing as his brother, Keith.

After meeting the "Bunny Father," my big delight was hanging out with and petting Hef's big brown-and-white Saint Bernard dog, the one who was featured in the monthly 'Playboy' magazine. I felt like I knew the dog from the magazine. It was like meeting an old friend. Hef's affectionate dog made me think about the best dog I ever knew. When I was a young child in the log cabin, we had a wonderful black-and-white dog named Trixie. Southern custom dictated that "Ole" preceded the name of all animals, some people, and things. I cannot confirm or deny the origin. Perhaps "olde" trickled down through slavery from the British infantry. It could have been, "Old, Ole, or Ol," but in our house it was "O" for all of the animals. So, O' Trixie was a Collie and something mix. His mother was O' Patsy, and she was Mother's faithful dog. Trixie was my everything. He would bring the cows home. He was a great hunter, and I felt safe with him everywhere I went around the farm, fields, and into the woods. Blackberries grew wild in the woods, and Trixie cleared the path of snakes and critters when we went berry picking. We loved the adventure of picking berries, because Mother made, pies, jelly and jam.

Trixie would follow us to school if he could, but we always yelled at him to go back home. Coming home from Neely Elementary, Robert and I walked through the field as we always did. Daddy did not allow us to walk the hard packed dirt road with our cousins and schoolmates, because it took longer than cutting through the field, and we had to rush home to do chores.

Daddy did not care that taking the short cut was dangerous due to the threatening mule, O' Jack. On more than one occasion, Robert and I barely rolled under the barbed wire fence before the angry mule caught us. O' Jack would hide behind a bush and come charging after us with his ears pinned back against his head, his eyes glaring, big brown teeth, lips quivering, snorting, stomping his feet and making scary sounds. Mother did not help ease our fear when she told us that some children must have teased the mule when it was little, and that's why it did not like kids. She said, "If you don't run, it won't chase you." Not only that, there were snakes to worry about in the field.

One May afternoon Robert and I were walking through the field, on our way home from school. We had just crawled under the barbed wire fence when a Blue Racer snake started chasing us! The snake raised her upper belly. Her wavering head was straight up in the air, tail on the ground, and she slithered towards us like a lightning bolt! Mother never told us what to do if chased by a snake. Horrified, our screams split through the air as our feet cut a fresh path through the weeds and grass, barely avoiding the snake. Both of us were screaming and running. Without conscious effort, Robert veered to the right and I veered left. The snake slithered straight ahead but turned back to get us. By the power of The Holy Spirit, Robert and I ran together, split off and ran back together, thereby avoiding the snake until Trixie intercepted.

Barking and growling, Trixie pounced and caught the back of the snake's neck with deadly determination. With the snake firmly between Trixie's sharp teeth, he viciously shook his head side-to-side until the snake was dead. The shiny dark blue snake lay dead, scaly white belly pointing towards the sky. Robert and I fell down on the ground, hugging and kissing our wonderful dog, as he barked and licked our faces. Then Robert picked up a big "Y" shaped stick, scooped up the snake and took it home for all to see. The snake was a huge monster to us, probably five or six feet long. Mother and everyone for miles around heard us screaming, and they were anxious to know what happened. Robert and I talked at once, reenacting the horrifying incident. Trixie barked his point of view and wagged his tail proudly.

Trixie took pride in everything that he did. He was a dependable herder and sent straying pigs squealing back into their pens. He truly enjoyed rounding up the cattle. One command of, "Go git the cows Trixie," sent him dashing to bring them back to the barnyard. Trixie could count. I knew this because if he did not have all of the cattle, he would bring in the majority and run back to the pasture for the stragglers.

When I was around eight years old, the cows did not come home one day, and Daddy sent me alone to find them. He made Robert do some other chores and prevented him from going with me. I ran up the lumpy, dusty road, into the pasture, but I did not see or hear the cows anywhere. In desperation, I ran home and told Daddy that the cows were lost, and I could not find them. He said, "Uma find yo ass wid dis whip if you don't git bak out dare and brang dem gotdammed cows home." By now, the huge, orange, evening sun was sinking swiftly and so was my heart. I flew towards the pasture, determined to outrun the sinking sun. Again, I looked high and low for the cows, but they could not be seen or heard. O' Betsy was wearing a big iron cowbell around her neck, but it remained soundless.

Fear gripped my heart, and my stomach fluttered, as mental pictures of a huge wolf leaped from the woods to gobble me down. Anger, pain, fear and sorrow always caused a huge lump to pulsate in my throat. The lump was so large, I could hardly swallow, and my mouth was dry. I was gasping from out running the sun and realized that I was totally lost in the woods, in an area I had never seen before, but the cows were not there. The thought of Daddy waiting in the barn with the bullwhip was more dreadful than being lost. I stopped dead still, looked all around, listened and called the cows, "Sookie-sookie-sookie, com'on O' Betsy."

Instead of the cows, Trixie came dashing through the thickets, anxiously wagging his tail. The cattle became oblivious as I chased after Trixie, but I could not get close enough to put my hands on him. He ran swiftly ahead of me. Then he would stop and wait, but when I reached to stroke him, he ran ahead. Onward he dashed through the woods, up a hill and down an embankment, which led straight to the cows. There they were, all eight of them, lying on the ground very close to each other, quietly chewing their cuds. O' Betsy was chewing like dignified ladies chew gum in church, and her bell did not even tinkle. They had heard me running and calling them. When Trixie led me to them, they seemed to be smiling and smirking, enjoying the prank they had pulled on me.

I was not amused and picked up a big stick to whack them and call them every curse word that Grandma Lizzy and Daddy ever used! This caused the cows to scatter and run helter-skelter. Trixie brought them back together and drove them home. I could not catch Trixie but grabbed O'Betsy's tail, wound it around my right hand and held on tightly, because I did not know my way back home. By then, they were running like a stampeding herd! That cow dragged me through the bushes, down the gullies and over every rough spot she could find. Trixie kept all of them on track, and the cows ran into the barnyard after sundown but before dark. Robert flashed me a big smile of relief as worry and tears faded from his six-year-old face, but he did not see Trixie, as I told him about the cows.

After milking and feeding the cows, we carried the bucket of milk home, and Mother asked where did I find the cows? I told her that Trixie found the cows for me and drove them home. She said, "That dog been dead for two years, and he ain't never coming back. I don't know why you can't get that through your head." I painfully realized that the dog was dead, and I did not attempt to explain the unexplainable to my mother. Robert believed that I had seen Trixie and regretted that he had not. I didn't care what Mother said, I was thrilled to see my dog, who came back and saved me from a bullwhip beating.

On the day of Trixie's death, my ear shattering screams had brought everybody running! I had found him hanging in the barn. After yanking the rope from around his neck, I tried to pick him up like baby, but he was too heavy. Robert was immediately behind me. I had barely outrun him to the barn in our search for Trixie. Now, everyone was hovering over us cursing and yelling at the same time, and the barn started spinning. Daddy scooped up Trixie, ran out of the barn and laid him on the dusty ground. Crying and scrambling, Robert and I desperately tried to stand Trixie up, but he plopped on the ground with his mouth open and tongue hanging out on one side. Air gushed from his throat like a faint cough. In my hopeful heart, the gush of air told me that Trixie was breathing, and he was going to wake up... We waited in total silence for Trixie to take that next breath. He did not.

I had a spasm but was not beaten or threatened for my involuntary convulsive movements, as I thrashed around on the dusty ground and hyperventilated. No one noticed me, because the family huddled around Trixie and wept broken-heartedly as they stared in disbelief at his dead body on the ground.

O' Trixie was dead, and my cousin Junior had killed him. I was angry with him and hated him for killing my super dog. Even so, I felt sorry for Junior because he did not intend to harm the dog, and everybody was outraged at him. Daddy cursed at him, called him names and threatened to beat him with the bullwhip.

Junior had tied up Trixie in the corn bin, which was a small room separated by a partition. We did not know what a dog leash was. Therefore, Junior tied a rope around Trixie's neck and tied the rope to a hook on the wall. When the dog jumped over the partition, the rope was not long enough for his feet to touch the floor, and he could not jump back to the other side. When I ran to the barn and encountered Trixie facing me, he appeared to be standing upright on his hind legs, holding up his front paws, but since his feet could not reach the floor, he was hanged by the short rope.

Junior tried to explain that he tied up Trixie in the barn because he thought that would make the dog hunt better. Stupid city kids! Trixie was a great hunter, and we never tied him up. Normally, I was thrilled when my paternal cousins, Junior, Willie and Delores, from Indianapolis, came down to spend the summer when school was out, but Trixie's death changed all of that. Junior was a year or so older than Loretta. Willie was four years older than I, and Delores was a year older than Robert.

There was no joy to be found among us as we sadly prepared for Trixie's funeral. A sack that was used for picking cotton was placed in the wheelbarrow. They picked up Trixie and gently laid him in the wheelbarrow. Grandma Lizzy's claim to fame was her ability to grow pretty flowers, which we freely picked and placed them around Trixie. Then we wheeled him to his grave site, which was a corner in the vegetable garden. Robert preached a tearful farewell to the best thing that ever happened to us while living in the log cabin: the love and devotion of Trixie. The lump in my throat was choking me. Tears leaked while agony and anger gripped my soul. My mind whirled, wondering why Daddy had not died instead of Trixie.

My thoughts brought me back to Hef's lovable Saint Bernard dog who had triggered some traumatic memories, but my happy recollections of Trixie were comforting. Nevertheless, my fairytale visit to The Playboy Mansion had come to a happy ending. Peggy and I had to get back to work in our Cincinnati Club.

My Bunny room popularity increased as inquiring minds wanted to know what went on in the Playboy Mansion. Did I meet Hugh Hefner, and what was he like in person? They were surprised when I told them, he was not flashy. He was just a regular nice guy, clean shaven, with a very short hair cut.

However, some of those Playboy Club key holders and their dates were very flashy. Especially the women, wearing high fashion hairstyles, movie star makeup, with low cut dresses, showing off their diamonds and jewels, all purposed at putting us hard-working Bunnies to shame. Meanwhile, we bounced our fluffy tails in and out of the service area, filling drink orders, where their every wish was our command.

One busy Saturday night I was working The Playmate Bar, which was seated to capacity. The trio of musicians -- piano, guitar and drums -- were jamming, and the club was rocking. With a loaded tray to serve a party of eight, I went speeding out of the service area and skidded in a puddle of water on the floor where scattered ice cubes had melted.   My feet flew forward, like I was on run away roller skates. I landed on my left side, heels in the air. My pointy Bunny ears leaned far to the left, desperately clinging to my wig, which was cock-eyed but still firmly anchored to my corn-rowed hair underneath. My little black bow tie flew through the air, and my left breast popped up out of my Bunny suit. The left side of my pantyhose was ripped, and my left elbow was skinned from sliding on the floor. Spontaneous screaming from me and people who saw me fall, and the loud crashing sound of breaking glass caused a major scene in The Playmate Bar.

A dozen hands quickly lifted me from the floor, everyone nervously asking, "Are you all right?" No, I was not all right, as burning embarrassment engulfed me. The room director came running to assess my injuries and escort me to the Bunny room. Falling and the fright of breaking glass was indeed disconcerting, but I was not injured. Even so, my psyche experienced temporary terror when my memory produced a flashback of shattering glass from childhood. Accidentally, I had broken a water jug on my way home from the cotton field.

It was a warm day in August, and I was seven-years-old. Robert, Daddy and I were going home from chopping cotton, and Daddy had been plowing the cotton rows. It was referred to as "laying by the crop," which was the final plowing before the gestation period. After the final plowing, cotton blossomed beautifully, and all too soon became cotton balls for us to pick. Robert was carrying two empty gallon water jugs, which had been filled from a clear running, natural spring that bubbled ice cold water on sizzling hot days. I was carrying the three hoes across the back of my neck, with arms stretched out on the handles. The farther we walked towards home, the heavier the hoes became on my neck and shoulders. Attempting to balance the load, I traded Robert one hoe for one jug.

During the exchange, I swung the hoes into a jug. Glass shattered! Fear gripped me! Daddy and the mules, O' Bob and O' Sue, were in front of us, because mules walk faster going home. Daddy spun around and yelled "gotdammit!" Then he grabbed a plow line from the mules.

I was wearing shorts and a short-sleeved shirt. Both of my small fists were cupped to my outer thighs. The first lash came like roaring fire. I could hear the rope whistling through the wind before connecting to my skin. Another lash, then another until my hands were numb and blood trickled down my thighs. I stood with clenched fists, glaring up at him. I would not give him the satisfaction of making me cry, which infuriated him, and he beat me until he ran out of breath, clutching his chest, gasping and coughing. I was praying that he would choke to death, drop dead in the dust, and the mules would stomp him into the ground.

Each time Daddy struck me, my mind repeatedly saw him face up on the ground, and I imagined viciously stabbing him with a pitchfork from head to toe, blood spurting out of him like water from a sprinkler system. Tears quietly poured down my brother's face as he dug his hands in the dust, picked it up and sprinkled it on my wounds to stop the bleeding. I did not shed a tear until hours later, after all of the night chores were done and I was in bed with face buried deep into my pillow.

Sore hands, bleeding thighs, raw welts all over my body, wounded spirit and all, I still had to get up early the next morning, milk the cows and do more chores before going out to work the fields.

My thoughts reeled forward and returned me to The Playmate Bar, as I quickly regained my composure. Yes, I had fallen on my left side and shattered glasses while working in the club, but I was not bleeding from a beating. When co-workers picked me up from the floor, I rapidly adjusted my costume, ears and tail, then assured the room director that I could make it to the Bunny room on my own. As I walked through the club, customers cheered, whistled and applauded, causing further embarrassment, but it made me smile and wave. Within twenty minutes, the wardrobe mistress had fluffed up my tail and helped me regroup. New pantyhose, a different color costume and shoes, fresh collar and cuffs, fresh makeup, wig on straight, ears pointing upward, I strutted back into the Playmate Bar and resumed serving my customers, who applauded my return. That incident made me a popular Bunny, the one who crashed in the Playmate Bar and was dubbed "Bunny Klutz."

3

A BUNNY PARTY
AND FLASHBACKS

Even "Bunny Klutz," was included in special events as Bunny popularity increased in Cincinnati. Riding in a limousine was always new and exciting when we did promotional work, such as working auto shows and country clubs where men of means played golf. One night after we had finished working, "Mr. High Roller" took us to an after-hours night club. It was an exciting ride over the tall, lengthy, frightening-looking steel bridge that connected Cincinnati to Kentucky. There were three carloads of us, Negro and White, male and female Playboy employees. All dressed up in fashionable party clothes, we looked forward to a rare night out for fun. Regardless of popularity, some Bunnies and male employees from Playboy were not allowed in some clubs in Kentucky.

The big, burly, red-faced bouncer, working the entry door, stepped forward, folded his arms across his chest and said, "No Nigras allowed."

"Mr. High Roller" told the big tall bouncer, "You will be sorry! These beautiful ladies are Playboy Bunnies." Without further dialogue, we piled back into the cars and drove away from the location. "Mr. High Roller" took some affirmative action over the incident, and news of it spread very quickly. Headlines screamed and radio disk-jockeys announced, "Negro Bunnies and other Negro personnel from The Cincinnati Playboy Club denied entry."

A few weeks later, the Kentucky club owner contacted "Mr. High Roller" and offered his apologizes. The Kentucky club did not do well after the incident, so the owner rolled out the red carpet and welcomed all of us.

Reportedly, his newly integrated club became "the in place" without further incidents.

Going out and attending parties was new to me. Working nights and many shifts did not allow much time for frivolous activities. I felt relieved that I was not subject to "Dr. Jekyll and Mr. Hyde" handsomely dressed in a hat, suit, white shirt and tie, promising me the world to take him back, with a gun drawn under his jacket I was free to enjoy the party people, who were gay with happiness, optimism, and upbeat attitudes, long before 'gay' alluded to homosexuality. We were nightbirds, working night clubs, bonding together by being up all night and half of the day, never getting enough sleep but always having plenty of energy to work the next shift. Even when I felt tired, walking into the club and transforming into my "Bunny Image" was energizing and fun. Therefore, I was tickled to party with my eager friends on those rare occasions.

During such an occasion on a warm summer night in 1965, we were having a blast in a White friend's home in an upscale area of Cincinnati. Furniture had been moved to the side in the living and dining rooms. A bar was set up with a variety of drinks, and delicious food and sweets were close at hand. The new hot hit, "Wooly Bully," was blasting, and we jumped up and down to the fast beat. White people couldn't dance, and neither could I. But that did not deter us from making loud joyful sounds, clapping our hands and laughing loudly at everything. When more party people pounded on the door around 4:30 a.m, the host flung open the door to the beat of "Wooly Bully."

There stood the Cincinnati Police, staring in at us. The approaching officer appeared to be seven feet tall and three hundred pounds of solid brown mass. With a voice like rolling thunder, he said, "Turn that music down," and three people dove on top of the record player. "You all know what time it is?" All of us simultaneously responded like a chorus, "No sir." He went on, "Folks trying to get some sleep around here so they can get up and go to church in the morning. Y'all don't know nothing about that you?"

The uninvited police ended our party, and the big, tall Negro officer made me think of Daddy and how he never went to church, except for funerals, and my thoughts digressed. Grandma Lizzy would have gone to church, but she did not have transportation. Her physical abilities were limited, but she was quick to holler "Oh Lawd, hep me," when her joints ached. She cursed more than she prayed, and she definitely was not a modest woman, neither verbally nor physically.

Whenever she took a bath, there was no place to hide her naked, fat body and endless breasts. She was short, but she weighed a ton. On those rare occasions when Grandma took a bath, Robert and I were her chief assistants. We had to bring in the round tin tub, make a million trips with the tin bucket, fill up the tub with warm water that was heated on the wood burning stove. When the weather was warm, Mother instructed us to fill up the jumbo black pot in the backyard with water so the sun could warm it. Whenever Robert and I would have a chance to play hide and seek, that big, black, cast iron pot was one of our favorite hiding places. When hot sun light warmed the pot, that was our hot running water, but Robert and I did all of the running.

With the tin tub full of warm water and placed right in front of Grandma's chair, Robert lifted one of Grandma's feet and put it in the tub, and I lifted the other one. She used her cane to stand up and, with our support, she eased her fat self into the water, which spilled over when she squatted down. With knees sticking up as she squished down in the tub, she looked like a fat roasting hen in a pot, and where the sun didn't shine, her body was just as pale as a roasting hen.

As time progressed, she could no longer squat in the tub, but we still put her feet in and helped her stand up. After we got her walking cane stabilized to support her weight on one side, and with her holding on to the back of a chair on the other side, we washed her back, arms and legs. Her breasts were huge and sat on her double stomach, even when she was standing. Robert and I each held up a breast so that she could wash under them. We had to squat down and use the palms of both hands to push her breast up over our heads. Then we had to stand up to hold them while she washed with one hand and held on with the other. We were small children, and big, heavy, soapy breasts were difficult to hold on to.

One time the breast Robert was holding slipped out of his little hands, plopped on the top of his head and knocked him down on the floor. Grandma said, "Boy git up offa yo blak ass and hold this," pointing to her fallen breast that was bigger than my little brother's head. I laughed so hard, her other breast slipped out of my hands and bounced on her stomach. After much giggling and cussing by Grandma, we finished her bath. Then we poured a bucket of warm water over her body to rinse off the soap. Her chair by the tub was covered with an old sheet for her to sit on and for us to dry her body. Mother cringed and verbally discouraged Grandma's uninhibited behaviors. Grandma said, "Gal if ya see any thang God didn't gimme, tho yo hat at it." For our efforts, she rewarded us with a stick of Doublemint gum, which she kept locked in her old trunk, with the key on a string, tied around her neck.

Even though Grandma Lizzy was mischievous or downright evil at times, she was our source of amusement and a great story teller. When we lived in the log cabin, on warm summer nights, we sat out in the front yard around an old worn out tin tub with smoldering rags. The burning rags made smoke to keep mosquitoes and other insects away, while she told spine tingling ghost stories that made us afraid to move from her side. They called them "haints" and "hainted houses," which turned out be "haunted" years later. She told us about some old lady who told family members not to remove her piano and other items from her home, after she was dead and gone. Some time after the lady passed away, family members decided otherwise and attempted to remove her piano. The piano reportedly weighed like lead and would not yield to moving. When the movers brought in more manpower and started to roll the piano from its accustomed spot, the piano reportedly groaned and blood leaked from the piano keys on the movers hands and dripped down on the floor, causing them to flee in terror!

Grandma claimed that one time she and Grandpa Anthony were coming home after dark from visiting relatives. A headless man jumped in the buggy and rode with them for a few minutes, but he jumped out and disappeared before they got home.

Grandma and Grandpa Anthony reportedly witnessed a woman in a long white dress and matching bonnet frequently walking down the road, past the log cabin. The lady always appeared in the same location with her back towards them, and they never did see her face.

Reportedly, a big red light appeared and floated around above the yard several times until Grandpa Anthony shot at it, and it did not re-appear. She told us about the dead man who came back to life. When she was ten years old in 1887, a male relative died in his home. A family member went to town and bought a casket. The deceased was reportedly bathed, dressed in his best suit and placed in the casket. A wake was held in his home, and relatives and friends brought food and sat up with the body for a couple of nights, which was customary. On funeral and burial day, the casket was placed in a horse drawn wagon and driven to church.

In the middle of his farewell sermon and eulogy, while relatives and friends were weeping and wailing his demise, the dead man opened his eyes, sat up in his casket and asked, "What's going on here?"

Weeping turned into screeching! People ran all over each other getting out of church, with the preacher leading the way! Mourners unhitched their horses, jumped in their wagons and buggies so fast, they drove off, leaving family members screaming and running behind them in the dust that the horses kicked up. Within minutes, the only person left behind was the dead man. He had to remove himself from the casket and walk a very long distance back to his home. In reality, the man probably lapsed into a coma. Fortunately for him, there were no funeral homes, and embalming was not a common practice, which allowed him to wake-up at his own funeral.

Unfortunately, his remaining life was drastically altered. People feared and shunned him, and he became known as "Dat walkin dead man."

Grandma also spoke about Cherokee Indians, slavery and the Civil War. Although she was born in 1877, fourteen years after the Emancipation

Proclamation was issued by President Lincoln on January 1, 1863, she still witnessed the impact of slavery.

There was a faded blue-gray Civil War uniform hanging in the attic of the log cabin. Grandma Lizzy said it came from "The gotdammed Yankees." There were no stair steps leading to the attic. So, Robert and I crawled up the bannister to get up there. The house was so old and in such disrepair, the bottom stair steps had decayed, fallen apart and were completely gone. The last four steps onto the attic floor were still in place.

The attic floor was creaky, but Robert and I knew how to walk on the beams. It was amusing and fun, looking through the holes in the attic floor, down into the room we had just crawled up from. Gazing out at tree tops from the attic window was thrilling. Boundless treasurers and wonders waited for us to investigate them: old shoes, boots, hats, clothes, a warped trunk full of stuff, broken furniture and other items of interest. About half of the attic floor seemed stable, and Robert and I ventured across it.

We peeled off spider webs, slapped away spiders and other critters, so that we could put on the Civil War jacket and cap. We delighted in marching around laughing and holding the huge sword. The long, heavy, silver sword lived in an old weather beaten leather case. The sword's handle was ornate and shaped like a big fancy "C." It was too heavy for either one of us to lift up with one hand. Using both of my hands, I would pick up the sword, lean back to hold it against my stomach, and march around playing "Soldier." Then it was Robert's turn. He really looked funny in the uniform, which swallowed him up. The sleeves swept the dusty attic floor as he marched around. He still managed to pick up the sword and have his turn at playing "Soldier." Anything I could do, he could do also. He was my little "big" brother.

My thoughts returned to Cincinnati. The following day I went to work, and my only brother, the log cabin, the attic and the Civil War uniform all seemed like a distant dream, as I strutted around The Playboy Club, did the Bunny dip and made great tips. We also received a weekly paycheck from The Playboy Club. I cannot quote an exact amount of hourly wage, but it was not substantial. However, the small checks still added to our weekly income, which was beyond substantial. Working nights and sleeping days, weeks would fly by before I could get to the bank and deposit cash into my savings account, which I opened upon arrival in Cincinnati. I just threw my tips and paychecks in a dresser drawer, under some clothing. When I finally got up early enough to get to the bank, I would count and recount my paychecks and cash, put the money in a big brown paper bag, write the total on the inside of the bag and walk to the bank. The bank was right around the corner from the "Y."

The first time I took in my brown paper sack with $2,300, the White male teller behaved like I was robbing the bank or had already robbed one.

There were no Negroes working in banks at the time, certainly not in that bank. I was whisked into an office where I was questioned, and my money was counted two or three times by many people. I said, "I'm a Playboy Bunny. We work very hard and make great tips."

"Playboy Bunny" was whispered to everyone working in the bank. With deposit slip in hand for $2,300, I accepted their apologies and left. Everyone gawked at me like I was only wearing ears and a tail. I was conservatively dressed, no make up. My hair did not look like a wig, even though it was, and I was wearing sunglasses.

Working the club and taking money to the bank was always fun and so were the promotional activities. My first limousine ride was head spinning! Me in a limo! As I rode in the limo's splendor, up from the rickety wagon that was pulled by aging mules, I could not restrain smiles and laughter. I remembered lying face down on the wagon floor, hiding so that none of my cousins or school mates would see me when Daddy drove us a few miles to Mr. Jimmy Lee Williamson's country store at Neely Station. Mr. Jimmy Lee was White but probably related down the line. Maybe his family had owned my family during slavery? Maybe his family had fathered some of my ancestors? At least he was kind. On those rare occasions when we went to the store, he patted us on top of our heads and always gave us a treat. Cheddar cheese was my favorite.

In the wagon, I was hiding because I was ashamed of the way Daddy looked, dressed and smelled. I was also ashamed of the mules. O' Sue limped on her crippled right front foot. I felt very sorry for her, especially when Daddy beat her with the bullwhip or a two-by-four. My relatives living near Neely Station lived in nice homes with electricity, and their parents drove cars or trucks, and they farmed with tractors.

Nonetheless, as the long, black, shining car transported us to the promotional location, those memories faded. We arrived at a golfing range and were well received because we were Bunnies, but our promotional gear was not sexy.

Bunnies, and the viewing public, did not like our promotional outfits: Black Bunny ears, black T-shirts with Playboy Club printed with white letters on the front, white knee length pleated shirts, black pantyhose and black pumps. Spectators wanted to see us in our Bunny suits with ears and tails, but the only place we ever wore them was inside the club.

As I flitted around, served drinks, smiled at the fancy cars and limos, I could not stop my mind from revisiting the log cabin. The only long black shining car I saw from the log cabin was the one that drove Grandma Lizzy to church for her funeral in May 1947. Grandma had frequently said, "I'll be glad to git to glory." I did not know where "glory" was or how to get there, but she had spoken of it frequently. Prior to her death, she had been moaning a lot, and she was agitated. Robert and I lingered around her bedside to get whatever she needed.

On one particular morning, she did not wake up. She was not moaning, and we could not shake her awake. We went running and calling Mother. She came and explained that Grandma had passed on. I asked, "What grade did she pass to, and where is her school?"

Daddy looked broken and sad as he climbed up on our prized black stallion, O' Hal. Granddad Walker gave him to us when he was a colt. He was powerfully big and beautiful, with a white patch of hair in middle of his forehead. Hal galloped through the dust, carrying Daddy to notify the undertaker, who was located in Jackson. Daddy probably rode up to Neely Station, hitched the horse, and a relative drove him the 13-miles into Jackson.

Grandma remained dead in bed all day, and I stayed by her side talking to her and examining her. I opened and closed her eyes, gazed into her unmoving eyeballs, pinched her nose together and stuck my finger in her mouth to see if she would bite it. Although they were heavy, I raised and dropped her two-ton arms, that fell down on the bed with a clump.

I tickled the bottom of her feet and blew in her ears. I expected her to say, "Lil' old nappy-headed gal, long as yo asshole points towards the ground, don't you never do dat again." She had frequently said that to us, when we had gotten on her last nerve. Bewildered by the phrase, one time I innocently asked, "Grandma what other way can it point?" She called me a "Lil' nappy head heffer," and whacked me on my thigh with her walking cane for being sassy. But this time, she did not move. She did not make a sound.

Nighttime came, but Daddy and the undertakers did not. The following afternoon they arrived on horseback. After some preparation, the undertaker and Daddy slid Grandma out of bed onto a stretcher. Still wearing her nightgown, they wrapped her in a white sheet, strapped her on the stretcher and put her face up on the wagon's floor. They had to transport Grandma out in the wagon, because the road to our house had washed out, and cars could not drive up the sand ditch and deep gullies that led to our home. About a half mile from us, the hearse was parked in cousin Leon Williamson's yard. He was one year older than Robert and our nearest playmate who had real toys.

The little kids rode in the wagon with Grandma, and the rest of us walked behind. When we arrived, Leon and his family were waiting by the hearse. They placed Grandma inside the black shining car and secured her. We gazed into the vehicle and "oooohed" over every angle. After he spoke some comforting words, the undertaker drove off with Grandma Lizzy.

When I saw Grandma Lizzy again, she was in church, beautifully dressed and looking very peaceful on the rose pink satin inside her coffin. She looked so pretty, I did not recognize her and wondered what they did to her. All during service, I confidently waited for Grandma to open her eyes and sit up, like "That Walking Dead Man." She did not. Worry set in when they closed the coffin. My heart pounded when they lowered the huge box into the grave, threw all of that dirt on her and packed it down.

After her burial, there was a festive atmosphere as long lost relatives and friends talked, laughed and enjoyed delicious food that various families had brought to church. I especially enjoyed meeting and visiting with so many pretty cousins, who seemed very happy to see me, as we ran around and played together. Sadness of her death came rushing back. Laughter trailed off, and people drove away in their cars and trucks or on horseback.

In the late afternoon when we returned home to our log cabin, it looked caved in and sadder than ever, but all of our relatives from up north made it look better. Naturally, I ran to Grandma's room which was cold and empty, but not for long. Since her room was the nicest and best furnished, everyone flocked in. I don't know who or how many slept in her room, but I'm sure it was packed.

Viney and William could have been among many cousins who all slept there. Their Grandmother Fanny Mae, was Daddy's sister, and she had been stabbed to death by a jealous lover when William and Viney were young children, and Grandma had been especially fond of them. They had come from Indianapolis with Dolores and family.

Grandma's death was sad, but all of those relatives brought zest and laughter into the house, and some of them brought cigarettes and liquor, and Daddy drank more than his share. Too soon, all of the relatives were gone and what a tremendous let down it was, saying goodbyes and watching them leave.

Nonetheless, the cows, hogs and chickens did not leave. They did not know or care that Grandma Lizzie "passed." Farm and field work was endless, but I still found time to go to Grandma's room every day.

Approximately a week or so after her funeral, I ran to her room and found her sitting in her rocking chair, rocking back and forth. Jumping for joy, I asked, "Grandma, what took you so long?" She did not answer me and continued rocking. I reached into the chair to touch her, but my hand only connected with air and space. Although I had been looking and hoping, her return truly amazed me! I was so excited! "Grandma, show me how to do that. How did you get here? Where did you go?" A million rapid questions, and she did not answer any of them. After a very short time, she stood up and walked out through the door. I ran behind her, but she disappeared from the front porch. I ran back in her room and waited, but she did not return until the following day.

I was only seven years old but realized that Grandma's coming and going was so unusual, that I knew better than to tell anybody, except

Robert, who also saw her. She came to visit every day for about a week. Even though she never spoke, I was thrilled and enthralled with her apparitions.

Late one afternoon, we came out of her room to find Mother and Daddy standing near the door with puzzled expressions on their faces. Wide eyed, Daddy asked, "Who wuz y'all talkin to gal?" I gave them descriptive details of Grandma's visits. Mother said, "Child, Lizzy Williamson is dead, buried and gone, and she ain't comin back." Daddy looked scared and admonished, "Stay outta dat gotdamed room or I'll whup yo ass." The following day, when I saw Grandma, I told her what Daddy said, and she never came to visit again, not until several years later. I stared at Daddy in anger and rolled my eyes at him behind his back, as he nailed her door shut.

The door was not nailed shut for long, because the "nicest" room in the house was needed for our growing family as time flew past, and the last born child, Kassandra, arrived in June 1949. Jean was two years old, Audrey was three, Robert was seven, and I was nine years old. Sixteen-year-old Loretta had graduated from Denmark High School and escaped to St. Louis to live with Aunt Vessye so that she could pursue a career in nursing. The log cabin was literally caving in. The roof above the front porch had fallen on the floor, blocking the entry to the other rooms where we slept. Daddy cut some poles from small trees to prop it up, but that was also dangerous.

The kitchen was on the other side of our sleeping rooms. Grandma's room stood alone on the opposite end of the porch. When snow fell, it had to be scooped away from the door so that we could get out, walk across the porch, through the other rooms and into the kitchen. There were so many holes in the roof, rain poured inside our house. Rain water froze on our dining room floor, where Robert and I delighted in running and sliding around on the ice. Like the rain, snow also floated through holes in the roof and gently piled on the floor in the dining room. Snow created an illusion that made the log cabin shimmer beautifully. Every winter I wished that the snow would stay forever.

One winter Saturday when Loretta was still in the home, Daddy went to town to buy some much needed supplies. A few scattered snow flakes were falling as he walked towards the main road to catch a ride into Jackson. A few hours later we could barely see each other through the rapidly falling snow. Daddy did not return home that night. Mother said he probably spent the night with his brother John Anthony, who lived in a "big o' pretty house" in Jackson. Loretta said, "I sure hope he's dead."

The following morning Loretta, Robert and I filled the yard with snow replicas of ourselves, our baby sisters, Mother, her parents and Grandma Lizzy. With Daddy gone, we experienced total blissful joy, throwing snowballs at each other and rolling jumbo balls to make heads, breasts, bellies and bottoms for our snow family. We laughed out loud while pointing at the huge snow breasts that we had attached to Grandma Lizzy's snow woman. As the light of day dimmed into darkness, our snow family glistened in the moonlight, and Loretta, Robert and I chattered delightfully over our happy snow family. The following day, Daddy came home, cursed at the snow people and kicked some of them down.

During winter, conditions of the house made it necessary for all seven of us to sleep in Grandma's room. That room had come to be known as "the house," after Grandma died. Mother said "the house" was the original log cabin, which was still solid and built better than the added on rooms, which had decayed.

Unlike the rest of the home with bare plank floors, "the house" had faded linoleum on the floor, which blocked some of the cold wind that blew in through the cracks. Three faded cherries in a cluster formed patterns on the loose wall paper that sagged in the corners and along the wall.

We were scared and amused by mice that made the cherry clusters move when they scampered over the wall, underneath the wallpaper. Mother was an expert at smashing them against the wall with the palm of her hand, neatly slitting the wallpaper with a razor blade, lifting the mice out by their tails and tossing them into the fireplace. The burning hair and guts from the mice made me sick to my stomach, as Mother smoothed down the wallpaper and went after the next wiggling cherries on the wall.

Mother was a very creative cook, and she fed us delicious soup, stew and other meals from the small black cast iron pot, that hung from a hook over the fireplace. I learned how to wrap sweet potatoes in collard green leaves, bury them under the hot ashes to bake without getting grit on the potatoes. Gritty sweet potatoes were nasty, but we ate them anyway. Therefore, I was very careful. Fried corn cakes in the black cast iron skillet over the hot cinders were a treat with crunchy edges. I also learned how to "bank" a fire by covering it with enough ashes to put out the blaze, but would start the next morning when the ashes were stirred.

Before daybreak, after Loretta had moved to St. Louis, early one August morning when all seven of us were still sleeping, something stirred in my parent's bed, and Daddy woke up to a huge black lizard walking up his chest, more than a foot long from head to tail. Daddy automatically hit the thing moving up his chest. He leaped out of bed and hollered curse words that made us wake up scared.

The lizard fell from bed to floor, and Daddy stomped after it with his barefeet. He grabbed the fireplace iron and hit the lizard as it ran under some furniture. The tail broke off, bolting and looping around the floor, seemingly searching for the lizard. Daddy grabbed the shotgun and let the dogs inside to flush out the creature as he flung furniture, trunks and boxes.

Pandemonium erupted! I sat on top of a flat trunk that Daddy had moved to the middle of the floor. I held my three baby sisters, while Robert and the dogs, O' Patsy and O' Flash, searched for the lizard. I was horrified by the lizard's wiggling tail, but Daddy just picked it up with one hand and threw it outside on the ground, where it continued wiggling, for I don't know how long.

Daddy referred to the lizard as a "wood bitch." I can not confirm or deny if "wood bitch" was the colloquial name for that type of lizard or just Daddy's angry expression. He said that those lizards lived in logs and wood, and that's why they were called "wood bitches." With the house caving in upon us, and wood bitches crawling in bed, Mother knew she had to get us out before fatality struck one of her children.

Therefore, she wrote an explanatory letter to her parents, Mamie and Walker Hennings, and scraped up three pennies for a first class stamp to mail it. They wrote back and told her that she and the five of us were welcome to come and stay with them. Oh my God! Heaven on earth! I was getting away from Daddy before I actually stabbed him to death with my pitchfork. Furthermore, Mother had written to Daddy's brother, Walter Lee, who lived in Indianapolis and worked at LinkBelt. Daddy was going to live with him and hopefully work for LinkBelt also.

Mother wisely kept this information a secret from us until it was almost time to start packing; it was September 1949. Arrangements had been made, and Granddad Walker had loaned my parents a horse, O' Lou, a beautiful white mare, who was also O' Hal's mother. There was no furniture to pack. Even if there had been, it would not have fit in the wagon with the seven of us. Mother took her most valuable possession, her Singer sewing machine. She also took two trunks, some cardboard boxes and cotton flower sacks stuffed with clothes and sundry items.

Finally the wagon was loaded. O' Lou and O' Hal were hitched to the wagon and waiting. Mother carefully placed all five of us in the wagon, and I was holding the baby. Mother went back into the house to get one last item. Before she reached the wagon, Daddy yanked the ropes on the horses, and they started moving forward. Mother yelled, "Othelder, wait a minute!" He yanked the lines to make the horses go faster, but the heavy wagon prevented them from galloping down the rugged road. Mother easily climbed into the slowly moving wagon, but she was obviously angry with Daddy, as she sputtered under her breath.

Certainly, I had looked forward to this day all of my life and was beyond happy to be finally leaving, but as I sat in the wagon facing backwards, my heart sank. The log cabin looked sad and lonely. I felt sorry for it as tears welled up.

O' Patsy was limping along behind the wagon. I asked Mother if we could put her inside, so that she would not have to walk all the way to

Granddad's house. She said, "Patsy has to stay here. Papa already got his own dogs." Mother waved her hand and told Patsy to go back. The dog halted, but she did not turn back. Soon she was limping along, trying to catch up. Once again, Mother waved her hand and told Patsy to go back. This time, Daddy stopped the horses and wagon. He grabbed the bullwhip, jumped off the wagon, cracked the whip at Patsy and yelled, "Git you ass bak up dare!" Running towards the dog, cracking the whip and cursing, Daddy scared Patsy back up the dusty road to the empty log cabin. She did not attempt to follow us again. She sat down on her hind legs, waving her front paws, yelping and begging not to be left alone. Finally, she stretched out on her stomach, head on the ground between her front paws. Patsy whimpered and moaned as the wagon slowly rumbled down the dusty road. Looking back towards the log cabin, I watched until Patsy disappeared into the distance.

I was choking from the huge lump in my throat as hot tears tumbled down my face and dripped on the wagon floor. Robert and Audrey were also weeping silently, but El' Nora Jean and Kassandra were too young to experience the horror. Daddy also left O' Bob and O' Sue to starve to death. Later on, I learned that O' Flash and the few younger animals had been sold or given away long before we moved.

Living in the log cabin had been tension filled and painful. Moving from it was joyous and agonizing, but I could not wait to live with Grandma Mamie and Granddaddy Walker in their beautiful white house, trimmed in green, which matched the grassy yard surrounding it.

4

FROM THE LOG CABIN
TO GRANDPARENTS

Slow and steady, the horses pulled the wagon and all of our worldly goods closer to Grandma Mamie. The distance from the log cabin to Grandma's was approximately eight miles, but it felt like a hundred in the loaded wagon that took forever to get there. Over the years, we had attended very few family reunions with our maternal grandparents, their twelve children and countless grandchildren. Finally, from a distance down the road, the steeple on St. John Number-2 Baptist church came into view, and I knew that we would soon turn left on the private lane that led up the hill to my grandparent's house, and I physically jumped with joy and anticipation.

Still seated and guiding the horses with the long ropes attached to them, Daddy whirled his body around towards me and with a punitive voice and eyes, he stuttered, "Se-se-set yo ass down gal." I was so happy and excited to be moving in with my grandparents, knowing that Daddy was moving to Indianapolis, I did not care what he said. He could not kill my joy, and I could not contain it. As their house came into view, my heart raced much faster than the wagon was moving.

Granddad's barking dogs had sounded our arrival. When I saw my grandparents standing in the yard, waving and smiling at us, Robert and I automatically leaped out of the moving wagon and dashed into their waiting arms. We knew that we were safe from Daddy on the property of our maternal grandparents. Of course, Daddy would show his best behavior in their presence, which rendered us safe from a brutal beating. Daddy unloaded the wagon, and Granddad helped him carry our belongings inside. He and Grandma Mamie had moved furniture around and made space for us in the L-shaped guest bedroom. Daddy stayed overnight, but I knew that he was anxious to get to his brother John's house in Jackson, so that he could smoke, curse, and drink, because Granddad did not do any of those things. From Uncle John's, Daddy would take the Greyhound to Indianapolis and stay with his brother, Uncle Walt. Robert and I rejoiced over his departure and wished that it had come sooner, like before we were born.

Robert and I would run around the yard, run up the front porch steps, run behind the swing and jump off the porch, roll on the ground, jump up and do it again, and again. Audrey was big enough to run behind us, but El Nora Jean was a tumbling toddler, and Kassandra was an infant. From our perspective, our grandparent's house was huge, but it only had four large rooms. Except for the kitchen, all of the rooms could be entered from the front porch.

Our grandparent's bedroom contained two full-size beds, Grandma's Singer sewing machine and two rocking chairs in front of the fireplace. A small reading table held a large dictionary and a huge blue globe that Granddad used to teach us geography. A big walk-through nook connected their room to the kitchen. Aunt Vessye had bought a refrigerator for them, but Grandma refused to give up her trusty wood-burning stove for an electric range. She was suspicious that the electric stove would not slow cook her food as she desired.

Grandma's pantry had a door and three windows; the space was bigger than some modern day kitchens. All of the pantry walls had built-in floor to ceiling shelves that were loaded with home canned produce in glass jars - vegetables, fruit, jams and jellies. She had separate barrels for her flour, cornmeal and sugar, and there was still enough space for us to play around and hide in.

There was more hiding space on the big back porch, which was fully screened. Typically, it functioned as the bathroom. There were shelves, benches, hooks and racks for wash basins, towels and toothbrushes. There was a large tin tub hanging high on the wall and a slop jar in the corner for nighttime emergencies.

Moreover, Grandma owned a double-tub washing machine. It had an automatic wringer with a drain pan. When a load finished washing, we put the wet clothes through the wringer. The water drained back into the wash tub, and the clothes went through the wringer into the rise tub. After the rinse cycle, we put them through the wringer and they dropped into Grandma's big laundry basket. Then we carried them out in the back yard and hung them on the line with clamp-on clothespins. Wow! No more scrubbing clothes clean on a washboard in the tin tub and boiling them in the big, black pot like we did in the log cabin. She also owned an electric iron.

A door separated our L-shaped bedroom from the kitchen, where the washing machine was kept in a corner. Our room contained two full-size beds, one twin size and a fold-up, rollaway bed. On the other end of our room, a door also separated us from the parlor, the only room that we did not play in. It was reserved for distinguished guests, like Reverend Nelson, the pastor at St. John Baptist Church.

The parlor was magnificent with a modern black wood burning heater, black leather davenport (a pull-out, sofa bed), stuffed chair, an oblong table in front of the sofa with a silver tea pot and four cups. An electric lamp and some "whatnots" were placed on a round table in a corner of the room. But the centerpiece of the parlor was a full-sized bed covered with a white chenille spread that had the design of a huge peacock in the center. I spent every possible minute staring into that room, admiring everything and gazing at the dazzling colors that created the peacock, the prettiest thing I had ever seen. Not only that, a beautiful black piano with a matching bench caused me to sneak in, sit on the bench and wiggle my fingers in the air above the keys, like I was playing the most melodious music in the world.

Startled by Grandma's appearance as she stood in the door way watching me one day, she asked, "Would you like to learn how to play the piano?" "Yes ma'am," I uttered while hopping off of the piano stool. She told me that cousin Willie Margaret, the church pianist, would probably be willing to teach me. She did, and eventually I learned to play, "Mary Had A Little Lamb," "Jesus Loves Me," and a boogie-woogie.

Meanwhile, Greer Elementary School was starting, and Robert and I looked forward to meeting our new teachers and schoolmates. School was approximately a two mile walk from home, but we had cousins to walk with, because Granddad's brother, Uncle Charlie and Aunt Carrie lived nearby, and they had several grandchildren in our age range living with them -- Blondell, Lester, Marvin and Marjorie. Blondell was the big sister, but she was on her way to Denmark High School.

Other than playing at home, Uncle Charlie's was our next favorite place to play. He had built a carpenter's shop where people came and placed orders. He sawed wood and made beautiful furniture, sturdy lawn chairs, tables and other items. Blondell's mother, Marilyn, cooked delicious food and fed all of the kids who came to play on Sunday afternoons -- ten to fifteen children.

Mother and Grandma Mamie also cooked tasty meals and fed us when all of the kids came to play at our house. Our playmates especially enjoyed coming to our house because we owned a unique toy.

Aunt Wilma had given us an old 8mm movie projector and one movie of the Lone Ranger, but not the same one that made me scream in the

Jackson movie theater. She also included one cartoon of "Porky Pig." At the time, movies were made on long strips of film that rolled through the projector from reel-to-reel. Granddad hung a white sheet on the wall in our room, and that was our movie screen. Robert quickly learned how to run the film backwards and fast-forward, which made us squeal with laughter. With every showing, Robert would point the projector into a corner in the room and set it on fast-forward. The projection angle made the characters speedily crash into the corner, as we collectively howled with laughter and rolled on the floor every time. No matter how many times we viewed the movies, all of us could not wait for the next showing. One time Grandma said, "Y'all laugh like it's the first time you ever saw those silly movies." We tried to explain that it was funny because every time, we saw something different. Well, grown folks just didn't get it.

Whether adults got it or not, our grandparents were saints. Grandma Mamie was the first adult who hugged and held me in her lap. Her endearing name for all of her grandchildren was "Totem." We did not know or care about the origin or meaning, but whenever she called out, "Come here Totem" every grandchild within hearing distance went running to answer her call, but she had another name for all of us when we got on her last nerve.

It took some extreme measures to annoy Grandma Mamie, but we managed to do just that during the family reunion in 1950. By dusting and neatly arranging jars in the pantry, Roann inconspicuously filled two quart jars with Grandma's bubbling blackberry wine, which was kept in the pantry. She had the fermenting wine in two huge stoneware crocks, covered with cheesecloth. The jars resembled two ladies with scarves tied around their heads. Roann lifted the cloth from one crock and submerged the jars until they were filled.

Then she put the lids on tightly, wiped off the jars to prevent drips and handed them out of the pantry window to me. I had two tin buckets waiting to transport the jars to our secret hiding place. They were gallon buckets with lids and metal handles, which made them easy to carry.

When the coast was clear, we retrieved our stash and dashed into the nearby cornfield. Robert, Rochell and Conwell were our lookouts, and they motioned our swarm of cousins towards the corn field, toddlers included. Perhaps there were sixteen kids involved. We huddled in a circle. Roann and I took the first big gulps of the tasty substance and passed the jars around. Wide-mouthed, eager toddlers also gulped down the sweetness and smacked their lips for more.

We happily raced from the corn field and around the yard, giggling, falling down and rolling on the ground, running back in the corn field until all of the wine was gone. Our mothers yelled at us to stop acting so silly and settle down, but Grandma recognized the cause of our jubilant behavior and yelled, "You lil' cabbage-head Negroes better stay out of my wine."

Otherwise, Grandma Mamie did not use foul language, nor did she endure it from anyone else. The first time she heard Grandma Lizzy's vulgar language roll off of my nine year old tongue, she offered to wash my mouth clean with lye soap. I explained that Grandma Lizzy and Daddy said those words all of the time. She said, "I know, but that don't make it right." None of us liked the name Grandma Mamie called us, but Rochell was the only one who cried over it.

I snickered and thought, "That's nothing; he should have heard Grandma Lizzy." All of us preferred being called "Totem," and we usually behaved accordingly. Roann and I got away with a warning and the promise of a keen switch on our bare legs if we ever smuggled her wine again.

My grandparents actually had thirteen children, but one son died of pneumonia when he was three years old. Their remaining children thrived and produced several children of their own, but as adults, most of them only saw each other during family reunions.

Family reunions always brought a yard full of grandchildren, and we squabbled over whose turn it was to sit in Grandma's lap. Frequently, she was completely covered by children as we piled on top of each other in her lap and all over her chair. That's when she would stand up and laugh as we fell in a pile on the floor, giggling and crawling over each other.

My grandparents, their seven daughters - Catherine, Wilma, Vessye, Audrey, Ruby, Effie, Mary and five sons - Ted, Ed, Ivy, Clyde and Rudy - stayed connected by having a family reunion every two years on the even years, starting in 1938. Family reunion 1950, when we drank the wine, seemed like a dream, because we were living with our grandparents and did not have to return to the log cabin.

As years flew and children grew, some reunions were celebrated around July 4th, but my grandparents preferred the third week of August, because that was revival time at St. John Baptist church, and they wanted to make sure that all of their family members "got saved." With all of my uncles, aunts, spouses and children, there was always somebody who needed to "get saved."

August 1950, excitement had been difficult to contain when aunts, uncles and cousins arrived. We were thrilled to see Loretta, who had become "a city girl."

Roann, was the only child of Aunt Audrey's, and they lived in Ohio. Roann came to Tennessee every summer to stay with her paternal uncle in Jackson and work in his store. During those summers I had the privilege of visiting overnight, and helping out in the store. Roann and I had permission to eat all of the candy, drink soda pop, or consume anything else that we wanted in the store, which was stocked with a wide variety of sundry items, groceries and some hardware items.

It was a sizable, prosperous, local neighborhood market in "the Colored" section of Jackson. But Roann looked forward to staying with our grandparents on weekends and attending St. John Baptist church.

Rochell and Conwell, Aunt Ruby's only two sons, lived nearby, and we saw them every weekend. Robert and I shared more time with those three cousins due to geographic location and age proximity.

Grandma Mamie called us her little stair-steps, because I am one year younger than Roann, one month older than Rochell, and Conwell was one year older than Robert. Looking back, I realize that we were the welcoming committee, and we jumped with joy as more aunts, uncles and cousins arrived. We were especially happy to greet Uncle Eddie's only son, Bernard. He was a year older than Roann, but I barely knew him, because he rarely came to Tennessee. For the same reason, I did not know Uncle Ted's eight children. There were so many family members, it was necessary for most of them to sleep over with other relatives and friends due to limited space in our grandparent's home. In spite of that, all of the kids wanted to stay with Grandma, and we slept three kids at the head our beds and three at the foot, and pallets covered every inch of floor space.

My five uncles loved driving their shiny new cars from St. Louis, Chicago, Detroit, or wherever they were. Happy to see each other, they talked, told jokes, clowned and laughed loudly, especially after they had consumed a few drinks. They knew how to hide their liquor from Grandma, and she never saw them take a drink, but they could not hide the liquor's impact upon their behavior. When impact exceeded Grandma's tolerance level, she would yell at them, "Don't come in here acting like you lost yo salvation." She was also quick to go after them with a stove wood stick. As growing children, watching our very chubby, buxom, four foot Grandmother chase after our tall uncles made all of us scream with laughter.

My uncles made everyone laugh, including Grandma, even when she tried to keep a straight face. My six aunts also laughed and interacted with my uncles, but they were more interested in talking about things going on in their lives, plus they were busy preparing delectable foods for every hungry one of us. Aunts and uncles went shopping in Jackson and brought extra delights for us, such as Kool-Aid, marshmallows, cookies, candy, raisins and bananas.

Food was abundant. My grandparents grew a fruit orchard, vegetable garden, chickens, beef and pork. Time brought about change in the way animals were slaughtered and preserved. When fresh meat was needed Granddad took chosen animals to the local slaughter house near Jackson, which eliminated the gathering of men to hand-slaughter each other's animals.

Granddad's' nephew, Curtis, owned a pick-up truck and willingly transported him and the animals where butchers prepared the meat for consumption and stored it in Granddad's rented freezer. It was common practice for Granddad to pay a small fee for renting a freezer locker to preserve fresh meat. For reunions and big events at church, the butchers prepared the meat, and Granddad brought it back home for roasting. For the August 1950 reunion, Granddad and Curtis (Uncle Charlie's son) delivered a big hog to the butchers. Prior to delivering the hog, Granddad and his sons had begun digging the barbecue pit in the back yard, a safe distance from the house and the woodpile.

We were intrigued with Granddad's roasting pit, which was big enough to roast a whole hog or a side of beef. It was a rectangular hole about four-feet in the ground, maybe four-feet wide and five-feet long. Dimensions were irrelevant to us, but jumping across the hole without falling in was of utmost importance, because the child who made the most jumps was declared winner until some safety-minded adult made us stop, which only temporarily suspended our game. We had to run fast and jump quickly during every sneaky opportunity, before it was time for Granddad and my uncles to prepare the pit for cooking.

Watching Granddad build the pit was a unique adventure. Moreover, he let us help. The brick pile was across the yard from the pit. Our job was loading bricks into the wheelbarrow and rolling them to the pit. Roann, Rochelle, Conwell, Robert and I ran around like busy little squirrels. We offered each other rides in the wheelbarrow for the fun of dumping the rider on the ground. After loading several bricks in and out of the wheelbarrow, we were ready to finish before the job was complete. Therefore, we piled bricks in the wheelbarrow until they stood taller than we were. The load was so heavy we could barely move it. With two kids pulling and three pushing, the wheelbarrow promptly toppled over, and most of the bricks fell on the ground. We learned that it was smarter to move fewer bricks and make more trips.

Granddad covered the bottom of the pit with bricks and used more bricks to line the pit walls. He covered the pit floor bricks with hay and twigs before he piled on several wood logs. We never witnessed Granddad igniting the pit fire. Lighting the fire was some magical thing that Granddad did in the middle of the night while all of his grandchildren were sleeping.

Pit cooking was a lengthy process, and after several hours, the wood logs burned into red hot coals, which was the desired cooking temperature. The whole hog, with head attached, had been throughly seasoned and wrapped in chicken wire. Mother made the barbecue sauce. She used Daddy's formula, which tasted much better in his absence. Mother, her six sisters and Grandma cooked an overwhelming amount of mouthwatering chickens, greens, other garden fresh vegetables, home baked rolls, pies, cakes and homemade ice cream.

Homemade ice cream was a rare and royal treat. Turning the hand-crank on the manual ice cream freezer was a privilege that the children lined up to perform. Our uncles brought several blocks of ice, and they chipped off small pieces and placed them around the ice cream bucket with lots of rock salt. Although there were several little hands waiting to turn the crank, it still took forever and longer than that, before we could finally devour our hand-cranked sweet treat.

Granddad had borrowed extra tables and chairs from church for the official gathering and eating on Saturday, and nearby relatives with children came bearing more food and joined our reunion. Surrounded by tasty food, love and lots of cousins, Robert and I spoke of our good fortune of living with Grandma Mamie and Granddad Walker. We realized that we were living on top of the world, and we marveled over so many shiny cars and trucks parked under shade trees around the yard and on the roadside leading into the yard. My thoughts temporarily flashed back to the crumbling log cabin where roads were practically impassable, and my heart rejoiced that we did not have to leave this happy place, as we skipped away to play hide-and-seek in truck beds, behind cars, in trees, behind trees, bushes, other objects, and in the cornfield.

Why is it that happy events always end sooner than miserable situations? Reunion day flew by, and the setting sun seemed to have sent a signal that the gathering was ending. All of the attendees owned cows that had to be milked, and all of the animals had to be fed and watered.

Moreover, everyone was looking forward to attending church on Sunday, except some of my heavy drinking uncles. They avoided Sunday school. Nonetheless, my uncles and their hangovers went to eleven o'clock service in obedience and respect to their parents.

The fourth Sunday in August was significant because it was the beginning of "The Big Meeting," which was revival week at St. John Baptist Church Number 2, where Reverend Leonard Nelson preached the gospel. For this occasion, church was packed, and most of us were related, but several visitors also came from neighboring churches. Whether they came for the message or the food, there was plenty of both.

Grandma and her daughters prepared two large corrugated boxes of food and desserts. Every family brought more than their share, and the church kitchen overflowed with more delicious food.

The church was built on a slight hill. The kitchen was in the basement, but the basement was above ground. A kitchen door opened into the church yard on the south side of the church. Some people walked down the steps from inside, others walked out the front doors and down the hill to tables and chairs that Granddad and his sons had returned and set up just outside of the kitchen.

There were tin tubs of ice with different flavors of soda water and orange juice, tables filled with homegrown, sugar sweet watermelons, cantaloupes and ruby red tomatoes. Children were always served first, and there seemed to be hundreds of us standing in line, starting from smallest to tallest. We ate hurriedly like growing, energetic children, so that we could play some more before it was time to go.

Regardless of our energetic efforts, we had not played enough before it was time to leave our extended relatives and new friends from church. Some of my uncles and aunts were in a hurry to leave church so that they could drive back to their homes up north. Roann, Rochell, Conwell, Robert and I were sad to see them go, but glad that all of them did not leave immediately after church service. We were especially thrilled that Aunt Mary would stay a week and allow us to play with her adorable baby boy, Andy.

Aunt Mary was Mother's baby sister, just a few years older than Loretta, but she was very bossy. Even so, she looked forward to revival week and bragged that Leonard Nelson was the most intelligent preacher ever. He was big and tall, about six feet five inches, with a dark chocolate complexion and perfectly aligned white teeth that sparkled through his contagious smiles and laughter. Aunt Mary claimed that Reverend Nelson did not whoop and holler and run all around the pulpit, because he was well educated and held a Master's Degree in Theology. He was indeed articulate, spoke formal English and used polysyllabic words, which he defined in his messages.

Therefore, as young children, we understood when he said, "We should be thankful that we serve an omnipresent God, a God who is everywhere at the same time." "Every- where at the same time" told me that God was the wind, because the wind is everywhere all the time, but the sun and moon disappear and return. One time Grandma chuckled and commented that, "Reverend Nelson be using such big words, I wonder if the Lawd nows what he be talking about."

I believed that Reverend Nelson knew what he was talking about. In his sermons, he frequently stated, "Whatever you do in life, learn to do it right, because God is watching you." Every time he said that, he appeared to be staring directly at me from the elevated pulpit, which made him a convincing giant in my world.

Monday night was the first night of revival, and Roann, Rochell, Conwell, Robert, and I made our way to the mourner's bench, which was the front pew, reserved for sinners. The pew was filled with people in various age ranges, but we were among the youngest who wanted to accept Jesus as Lord and Savior.

Reportedly, the Holy Spirit moved among sinners, and they jumped around and shouted for salvation. By Thursday night, the Holy Spirit had not moved among the five of us. Therefore, eight year old Robert poked a sharp safety pin in my right thigh, which made me groan and jump up, and so did all of my cousins. Our elders hugged us and thanked the Lord for our salvation.

During the end of service when Reverend Nelson held my small hands and looked down into my teary eyes, my heart fearfully pounded. I thought he was going to say that God was watching when Robert poked me with the pin. To my heart's relief, he asked, "Do you accept Jesus Christ as your personal Savior?" I stammered, "Yes Sir," and just like that, I was miraculously saved, the easiest thing I had ever done.

Moreover, I believed St. John 3:16, "For God so loved the world that he gave His only begotten Son that whosoever believeth in Him should not perish but have everlasting life." After accepting Him, all of us converts had to be baptized by submersion. I knew that we would be baptized in Uncle Charlie's lake, and I wondered how that water could become so Holy after the cows were doing stuff in it every day.

The following Sunday, we were scheduled for baptism, and the lake was directly across the road from church. All of the newly converted wore white frocks, and the girls and women also wore white head wraps to keep our pressed hair dry. Reverend Nelson wore some water-ready clothes under his white robe, and all of us were barefoot. The choir and congregation stood on the lake's bank, and there were a few chairs for elders. After some singing, praying, and blessings upon the lake's water, Reverend Nelson waded in knee-deep. I was very concerned, because that was the exact same area where I had watched Uncle Charlie's cows wade into the water.

There were probably fifteen or sixteen to be baptized, starting with the youngest child. Very soon, it was my turn to be submerged. The instant that water covered my face, I experienced a visual image of cows in the water, pooping and peeing in the exact spot where I was being purified. Such imagery caused me to grab hold of Reverend Nelson's robe, which ripped as I bolted up from submergence, wiping imaginary cow dung from my face and mouth.

Everyone presumed that I was just a child who was afraid of the water. Later on, Mother scolded me for acting so foolish and ripping the preacher's robe. When I told her about my image of the cows, she laughed and said, "Lord have mercy."

Although I was happy to be saved, I asked several questions at home. How come Jesus did not love us as much as he loved White people? How come White people lived in those big beautiful homes along the highway to Jackson and Coloreds did not? Since White people were so mean and evil to us, how could I trust a White Jesus? Are there "White only" and "Colored" signs in heaven? Endless questions without answers...

Nonetheless, Granddad explained that "Jesus is the son of God. God is good and almighty. All you have to do is trust in Him." He further explained that all White people are not evil, and if it had not been for good

White people, like John Quincy Adams, who fought long and hard to abolish slavery, "Negroes would still be slaves like my Papa was." Years later I learned that John Quincy Adams was the sixth president of the United States from March 4, 1825 to March 4, 1829, and he was a leading opponent to the "Slave Power."

Granddad told us that his father, Leonard Henderson Hennings, fondly known as L.H., was the last generation born into slavery. I was ten years old, and it was riveting to know that my great-grandfather had been a slave, and I cried for his hardships, even though he had passed on long before I was born. L.H. was born May 1, 1850 in Madison County, Tennessee on the Hennings' plantation. His father was sold when L.H. was an infant. It was a turbulent era, and during the Civil War, L.H. and his mother Narcissus, and many other slaves hid in the woods, hoping the soldiers would not find them. His mother gave him a $20-dollar gold coin to hold on to. The slaves were inadequately dressed for the cold weather, and his mother consequently died from pneumonia. L.H. was ten years old (my age), and I cried harder.

In 1865 the Civil War ended and so did overt slavery L.H. was fifteen years old when he went searching for his father, but he found a half-brother that he did not know existed. He never found his father who was reportedly re-sold to a plantation owner somewhere in Mississippi.

However, L.H. met Mr. Crittendon. a White man, who was very impressed by his intelligence. He took in L.H. and made him his protege. Mr. Crittendon's kindness made L.H. a loyal servant. In return Mr. Crittendon taught him to read, write and count. He also taught him furniture making, blacksmithing, farming and many other skills. With the help of Mr. Crittendon, six years later, L.H. was able to buy his first ten acres of land in the Johnson Grove Community, in Denmark. He was twenty-one-years old. With the passage of time, L.H. sold that land and bought several acres in the St. John Community, in Denmark, where he and others established Greer Elementary school.

Mr. Crittendon changed L.H.'s opinion, and he experienced that all White people are not evil. With good business skills learned from his mentor, my great-grandfather bought more than a thousand acres of land, some of which he sold to struggling Negroes who did not qualify for conventional bank loans.

Therefore, L.H. bought the land they wanted and sold it to them with affordable terms. L.H. was very prosperous and highly respected. He and his pretty wife, Great-grandma Mary Etta, and their eleven children lived in a fashionable home and were the first ones in the community to obtain carbide lights. He was the first Negro in West Madison County to own an automobile, even though the auto dealer refused to sell him a new one, which he could easily afford.

No wonder Granddad and his siblings were successful land owners and farmers. When they became young adults, L.H. gave each of them a plot of land, which they had worked hard for as they were growing up, and they bought more land for themselves as time went on. Granddad owned one hundred twenty-five acres. He knew how to make furniture, sharpen saws and other cutting blades. He could fix anything, and everyone brought their horses to him for horseshoes, including respectful White men. He was also known as the best molasses maker in the area.

Granddad owned a transportable sorghum mill press. Farmers grew sorghum cane, which looks like sugar cane. When the cane crop matured, it was cut down, stripped of leaves and stacked in neat piles on the ground. One time Granddad took me and Robert to a molasses job site. We felt privileged to go help Granddad. We freely expressed our excitement, and he delighted in our joy. He loaded the sorghum mill and big black pot into his wagon, which was pulled by two of his magnificent horses, O' Hal, our black stallion and O' Scott, a handsome reddish-brown stallion.

Upon arrival in the cane field, Granddad set up the mill and hitched a horse to the long pole-like device that was attached to the center of the mill. That device directed the horse to walk around the mill in circles. Granddad worked each horse for a couple of hours so that neither horse became exhausted or dizzy. As the horse walked around and around, it turned the mill, and Granddad let me and Robert help him put canes through the press, which looked like putting clothes through Grandma's washing machine wringer.

Cane juice did not gush out, but it consistently dripped into a large container, placed directly under the mill's spout. After so many hours of slow dripping juice, there was a large amount, and Granddad would begin the cooking process in the big, black pot that we brought from the log cabin. Granddad's formula was his preferred cooking temperature and the right amount of cooking time, which produced a repeatable method for perfect molasses, based upon syrup consistency, color, and taste.

Considering the community spirit and barter system at the time, Granddad was probably paid little if any money for grinding sorghum cane, but he was always given gallons of molasses. By the end of the process, he would have accumulated an eye-popping amount of molasses, which he carefully stored in his smokehouse.

During the late fall season, Grandad transported a few gallons of molasses to Jackson. Customers were waiting, and Granddad earned a profit on his tasty molasses. Therefore, sorghum cane was one commodity that he never had to cultivate. He also sold ears of corn fresh from the stalk and other produce. He was not a truck-farmer, per se. He simply sold any seasonal excess produce, including strawberries.

Grandma Mamie also made money in Jackson by selling farm-fresh eggs, butter and cream. One time while she was rolling her profits in a handkerchief and stuffing it deep under her big bosoms, she smiled at me and said, "Totem, as you grow up, make sure you always have your own egg money stashed away." She used part of her "egg money" to buy soft burgundy velvet and other materials to make clothes for me.

My grandparents made some profits in Jackson, but there was always a generous amount of commodities set aside for our hot lunch program at Greer Elementary, where all parents contributed meat and fresh food.

Our school cook, Ms. Maggie Lou, whipped up delicious meals. Their tasty smelling aromas floated through our three classrooms and totally distracted us and our three teachers from our daily studies. Ms. Maggie Lou's cooking was not her only distraction. Her behind could not go unnoticed by even the most Godly. She was busty and "stout," but her behind made the rest of her body appear smaller by comparison. She was easily moved by the power of the Holy Spirit, which made her jump and shout during Sunday morning service, as many women (and some men) did. Any children in church (and some adults) could not control their spontaneous laughter when she shouted. We used our hands to hide our faces so that we could peek through our fingers and watch her behind bounce up and down, which looked like there were two short people with huge heads hiding under her dress. Our bodies shook with silent laughter, and we squirmed in our seats.

Grandma Mamie knew that Ms. Maggie Lou's shouting was amusing, but after service she emphasized that we go to church to learn God's word instead of laughing when others feel it, and learn we did, every book in the Bible.

I memorized all of the books from Genesis to Revelation and recited them for one of our annual Children's Day Programs. St. John's annual Children's Day program was celebrated like Mother's and Father's Day.

For several generations, Granddad's sister, "Aunt Sissy," was a dedicated teacher for the salvation of children. She was especially kind and loving to kids, and she taught Children's Sunday School and the Sunshine Band. Mother and all of her siblings had been her students. The Sunshine Band was not a musical group. It meant that all kids through age eleven were in that group for Sunday morning, Sunday night and Wednesday night services. Children age twelve and older were in the Baptist Young Peoples Union group, fondly known as The BYPU.

Our lives were centered in church, and I loved the activities, especially the well organized Easter egg hunts with straw baskets. Additionally, there were more activities at home since Uncle Eddie moved back from Chicago to live with us in late fall.

The children did not know that during the family reunion Uncle Eddie made a plan to move back and help Granddad and Mother with farm work.

Robert and I were thrilled because Uncle Eddie was patient and kind. After the family reunion was over, he drove Bernard back to Chicago where he lived with his mother. Uncle Eddie had to "tie up some loose ends" before he could move out of Chicago. With him moving in with us, there was only one place for him to sleep and that was in my precious parlor with the cherished piano. Even so, I still had time and privacy to practice my piano lessons.

After Uncle Eddie moved in, he allowed me and Robert to ride on the tractor with him. I carefully watched and memorized every move he made. When the tractor was parked in the shed, I would sneak off to visit it and mentally practice driving around on it. While sitting in the seat, I made vocal tractor sounds and turned the steering wheel. Granddad already owned his modern green tractor and a stylish beige 1946 Buick when we moved in. I loved the chrome on that car, and it was my privilege to help polish and make it shine "like new money."

Granddad had been using the tractor to work his fields and to haul running water from church. Robert rode with him to transport water, but I did not. Uncle Eddie let both of us ride along. While riding with Uncle Eddie, I knew when it was time to shift gears, especially when driving uphill with a load in the tractor's trailer.

Consequently, the next time we needed water from church, my entire family was delightfully shocked when I backed the tractor out of the shed and drove it to the front yard and yelled, "Let's go get the water." With much pleading and reassuring of my abilities, Uncle Eddie allowed me to drive to church, but he drove back. Of course, Robert could not wait for his chance to drive the tractor to church for water.

The following summer was very hot, and water in lakes and ponds was receding from drying up. The water level in Uncle Charlie's lake receded, but it did not totally dry up. Water receded in Granddad's big pond in the pasture, but it did not dry up either.

However, the smaller shallow pond in the barnyard's lot was quickly drying up, and small fish that lived there were swimming in the middle of the pond where half of the water remained. Robert and I were intrigued by the dry, curled, cracked and flaky dirt that had been recently covered by pond water.

Therefore, one hot Saturday afternoon in July, Robert and I were running around the pond bank and thought it would be easy pickings to wade into the remaining water and grab up the little white belly fish with our bare hands. Excited by our adventurous idea, we tried to outrun each other as we raced from the pond to Granddad's tool shed for two of those tin buckets with handles, the wine transporters. We flew back to the pond and filled our buckets with water, so that we could keep our fresh catch alive until the day Mother decided to clean and fry them for dinner.

With buckets at the water's edge, Robert and I removed our shirts, took off our sandals, rolled up our shorts and stepped into the pond. The water reached just above Robert's knees. With cool mud squishing through our toes, we churned the water with our feet, which made the little perch and catfish surface. We used both of our hands to grab the fish so that they could not slip from our grasp.

Robert caught the first one, about five inches long; he dropped it in his bucket and smiled proudly. With all of the churning, fish surrounded our legs, and we could not pick them up fast enough. Bubbling with confidence, I reached in to pick up another little fish with both hands, but when I lifted it from the water, I screamed in terror. It was a huge catfish, big gaping mouth, long wiggling whiskers and bulging eyes staring up at me. It twisted and bolted against my body trying to free itself from my death-grip. My repeated high pitched screams echoed in my ears. Robert was hollering and trying to take the fish out of my hands. Fear caused my hands to lock onto the fish, and I could not let go. The fins were thrashing painfully against my muddy abdomen. Pain was intense, like a sharp knife when you cut your fingers slicing apples. Still, I could not let go. My family came running with Uncle Eddie leading the way.

I was out of the pond, jumping around in circles, screeching beyond control, with Robert running around trying to catch me and take the fish. Uncle Eddie ran to us and attempted to snatch the flapping fish from my hands, but he could not get a grip. He was hollering, "Let it go! Let it go!" Audrey and El' Nora Jean were hollering and crying because I was. Granddad caught me and held on to my gyrating body, while Uncle Eddie individually lifted each of my fingers from the fighting fish.

Mother and Grandma offered words of comfort while toddler Kassandra helped us cry. After they rescued me from the catfish, everyone caught their breath when they focused on my bleeding abdomen. Uncle Eddie carried the bolting fish home and put it in a tin tub by itself. The pond monster was approximately thirteen inches long.

Granddad said that we were lucky that we did not pick up a water moccasin snake with our bare hands, because they live near water and frequently go swimming. He said that some of them are harmless and some are not, but he did not know "which was which," so, "Stay away from all of them." I nearly passed out when he told us that!

Mother used rubbing alcohol to clean the mud and blood from my abdomen. The burning sensations from the alcohol made me jump up and scream anew. There were three nasty open cuts and several bloody scratches from holding the catfish against my stomach.

After a soothing, warm bath and shampooing my hair in a tin tub, mother applied some soothing Sayman Salve to my injuries and covered them with a piece of cheesecloth. Grandma brewed a pot of sassafras bark tea. My siblings and I used a generous amount of molasses to sweeten ours. The hot tea was delicious and comforting. Afterwards, I crawled into bed and took a nap. When I woke up, I wondered if the scary catfish ordeal had been just another one of my wild dreams. Nightmares had frequently plagued my dreams when we lived in the log cabin, but the wounds on my abdomen verified that I had not been dreaming.

Further confirmation came when we went to church on Sunday. I found out that my cousins at Uncle Charlie's (and others in our rural community) heard me screaming, and they were anxious to know what happened. Each member of my family told their version of my catfish saga, which caused an uproar of laughter to all who heard it. My family claimed that they had to rescue the catfish from me! Actually, my anti-heroic event was embarrassing. I thought, "If it had rained the pond would not have dried up, and we would not have been picking up fish with our bare hands in the first place."

I wondered, why it did not rain before everything dried up? At other times, why did it rain too much, flood the land and drown animals? No point in asking Granddad. I already knew the answer, "It's in God's hands."

Nonetheless, Robert and I experienced sheer delight playing in the rain. It was awesome watching the dust fly when huge rain drops fell on the ground. Sometimes we outran the rain by running up the steps to the front porch. Frequently, we ran to the rain by dashing down the steps and running towards it until we were soaking wet. Audrey and El' Nora Jean also loved playing in the rain, as they giggled and chased after me and Robert.

In June, when I was ten years old, there had been a thunderstorm. The rain waited until Robert and I helped Granddad finish milking the cows and feeding the animals. When we left the barnyard with our milk pails, rain was drizzling. Sounds of thunder rumbled around us, and occasional streaks of lightning danced through the dark blue, foreboding clouds. By the time we finished eating supper, the weather patterns were intermittent.

I washed dishes and cleared all items from the table so that we could use it to prepare our homework. We were distracted by the sounds of rolling thunder and fascinated by lightning and how it appeared to cling to the kitchen windowpane. The rain called me and Robert, "Come out and play." Watching lightning on the windowpane encouraged me to capture some for ourselves.

Therefore, we ran out the back door with a plan in hand. We each had a quart jar in one hand with the metal lid in the other hand. We ran towards each bolt of lightning and tried to catch it in our jar and put the lid on before it could escape. We were accustomed to catching lightning bugs in our jars, so we thought that catching lightning would be even better. Lightning appeared to flash through our jars, but we could not get the lid on fast enough to keep it inside. We were determined to catch some lightning, until we witnessed it strike a tree and set it on fire while we were chasing it under that exact tree. Audrey and El' Nora Jean had been chasing us, but they did not have any jars.

When lightning struck the tree, all of us yelped and ran up the steps to the back porch. We were soaking wet and totally astonished to witness a burning tree in the pouring rain. How could that be?

Mother had been doing chores and sewing in our room, and our grandparents had been reading the Bible in their room. They did not know that we had eased out to play in the rain and chase lightning until they heard us hollering and running up the steps. They appeared equally shocked when we excitedly spoke and pointed to the burning tree in the rain.

Even so, Mother scolded us and threatened to whip me and Robert with an extension cord, and she blamed me for letting my little sisters play in the thunder storm. Granddad defended us and argued that we had learned our own valuable lesson. No one had to tell us that lightning was dangerous, and it is not a good idea to catch it in a glass jar with a metal lid.

5

A MAGICAL CHRISTMAS
AND DEATH

November 15, 1951 was the next occasion where I found myself running in the dark during a thunderstorm, but I was not trying to catch flashing lightning. The sunny day had begun with a cool breeze and some scattered blue clouds.

Robert and I had enjoyed walking to and from school with our cousins. Unlike walking home from school while living in the log cabin, we ran, played tag and giggled all the way home. Having fun walking home made the distance feel shorter. Robert and I frequently told each other how happy we were to get away from Daddy and the caved-in house.

Moreover, we loved school. A little country store was across the playground from school. The store was well stocked with an abundance of penny candies. An eight ounce glass bottle of soda pop cost five cents, and we had plenty of pennies and nickels. When Audrey and Jean started school, twenty five cents was enough to cause a generous amount of tooth decay for all of us.

The solution for tooth decay in rural school children was mobile dentistry. Once a year, a dentist came to our small three classroom school, where Mrs. DeBerry was the principal, and she taught seventh and eight grades. Mrs. Whiteside taught fourth, fifth and sixth grades. Mrs. McGee taught first, second and third grades.

The dentist and his assistant set up the big examination chair and equipment in Mrs. Whiteside's classroom. A floor to ceiling, sliding partition separated Mrs. McGee's classroom from that of Mrs. Whiteside. For graduations and special programs, the partition was rolled back, which created one big room, and that became our transformed Greer School auditorium.

All of us kids were excited over the big chair, the bright dental light and the many implements. My fifth grade classmates and I were proud that the dentist was set up in our classroom, and the fourth and sixth graders were equally proud.

This procedure would take about a week, and the dentist started with the youngest students. Excitement turned into fear and screams when the dentist started drilling cavities and extracting rotten teeth that were beyond repair. With the dentist set up in our classroom, Mrs. Whiteside taught fourth and fifth grade in a corner of Mrs. McGee's room, and sixth grade joined Mrs. DeBerry's class.

In an effort to calm and reassure the younger children, the dentist decided to save them for last, and he started working on the oldest kids, which compelled them to be brave and set a good example. Working down the age scale, soon the dentist was ready for eleven year old me. When the dental assistant called "Vessye Ann Williamson," my heart skipped several beats, and I was scared, but I kept telling myself, "Daddy is a lot worse than this."

The dentist drilled and filled three cavities with some nasty tasting, silver metallic substance. Through it all, the loud drill was the worst. I kept my eyes tightly closed. I did not scream or cry and was praised for being brave and setting a good example. Every child was delighted to receive a brand new toothbrush and a tube of toothpaste. My family had been brushing their teeth with baking soda for generations.

Not only did our school provide a mobile dentist, they also provided an annual visiting doctor and nurse, and all of them were nice White folks. Since the doctor did not have a noisy drill, children were not frightened by loud sounds, but they squirmed and yelled from the pain of penetrating needles.

We were injected with medications to prevent whooping cough and diphtheria. I watched the doctor prick the skin on my upper left arm. It caused a sore and left a permanent scar; that was my vaccination against smallpox. Having endured bloody beatings from Daddy made me and Robert brave children who did not cry from dental or medical applications. Living with our grandparents made dental drilling and medical injections seem easy. Everything was easier with them. There was less to endure and more to enjoy.

Wearing beautiful clothes that Grandma made for me was indeed an enjoyable experience. I could hardly handle the joy whenever Grandma gently turned me around and said, "Hold your arms out to your side, Totem" and she measured me. That meant she would cut out a pattern and sew something pretty - skirts, blouses, dresses, suits.

Robert wore store-bought suits from Jackson like Granddad and Uncle Eddie. Grandma also helped Mother sew pretty, colorful dresses for my three little sisters. Some of the dresses were made from beautiful material in the twenty five pound bags of flour that Granddad bought for the pantry's flour barrel.

Comfortable, fashionable clothing made life wonderful, especially my first pair of store-bought, step-in panties when I was nine years old. They were pink and soft with white lace on the bottom front and two tiny, pink satin-type bows in the lace. Something so beautiful had to be shown, but trouble would certainly find me if I lifted my dress to show-off my fancy panties at church. Therefore, I casually turned a couple of fast cartwheels while running and playing around after service one Sunday. All of my peers looked and howled, "Ooooh weeeee, look at those fancy panties."

In addition to pretty clothes and fancy panties, as time progressed I also had several pairs of shoes, including black patent leather slippers for church. One Saturday night I used lard to give my shoes extra shine. Lard was like a magnet for all of the church yard dust that stuck to my shoes and totally covered them. My shoe wardrobe had come a long way from the day when I had no decent shoes in the log cabin.

My mind flashed back to the log cabin and a pair of white leather slippers. They had become old and dirty brown. One fall morning I did a good job of scrubbing them white. My seven year old mind thought it was a good idea to dry them in the stove's oven.

I imagined that they could dry fast when Mother lit a fire in the wood-burning stove to cook breakfast biscuits. Then Loretta and I dashed to the barnyard to milk the cows before school. I anticipated that the shoes would be dry, and I could wear them to school.

I had almost finished milking the second cow when I suddenly remembered that I forgot to tell Mother about my shoes. Panic-struck, I told Loretta and sprinted back up the path to the house. I ran into the kitchen, yanked open the heavy oven door, and billowing smoke rushed out. I reached in and grabbed my hot shoes. They had shrunk from the heat, which caused the toe area of the shoes to separate from the sole, and that made them look like two little dead, open-mouthed, dried-up animals. Devastation rushed over me. Mother had been looking after her babies in the bedroom, which was a substantial distance from the kitchen. When she heard me, she came running, asking a million "Why," questions and fussing at me for putting the shoes in the oven, especially without telling her.

Panic seized my entire being. Mother and I knew that Daddy would beat me bloody if he found out about the shoes. Hurriedly, Mother wrapped the shoes in an old tattered sheet, dipped some water from the bucket, poured it over my shoes, rolled them tightly in the sheet and hid them securely.

I flew back to the barnyard, scared that Daddy would beat me for running to the house, but he did not know, because he was inside the barn feeding the mules and shoveling manure to one side. I was heartsick and very angry with myself for destroying my only shoes. Now I had to wear the worn out, mismatched shoes that I wore to milk the cows and to work the fields whenever I was not barefoot.

Nonetheless, when we returned from the barnyard, Mother found some solid brown fabric in her sewing pile. She told me to dust off the mismatched shoes and stand on the material. Then she measured and cut two pieces of fabric to fit over the old shoes. She gathered the fabric over the shoes and around my ankles. She also cut some long strips from the fabric, wrapped them around my ankles and tied them like bows on a Christmas present, and those were my school shoes until a box arrived in the mail a few weeks later.

Aunt Audrey mailed me several items of clothing that Roann had outgrown, including a pair of barely worn, Buster Brown hightop shoes and a pair of black patent leather slippers. Mother said, "Thank you Lord" when she opened the box as all of us stared inside. Moving out of the log cabin and living with our maternal grandparents made it possible for all of us to have brand new Buster Brown high-top shoes, which we happily wore to school.

On November 15, 1951, walking home from school was like walking home on any other school day, and we arrived hungry, but rushed into Grandma's room to give her a hug. To our surprise Cousin Lizell had come to "sit a spell" with Grandma. She lived up the hill from church but had gotten on her cane and walked up to see "Sweet Mamie." She and Grandma were having a good time talking when we burst in and excused ourselves.

Grandma was resting in bed because the doctor had told her to stay off of her feet for awhile, until her high blood pressure became normal. She gave each "Totem" a big hug and told us to change out of our school clothes, as she continued talking and laughing with Cousin Lizell.

To ward off hunger until supper time, Mother gave us cornbread and buttermilk. We crumbled the bread in a bowl, poured in buttermilk and ate it like cereal. After our snack, Robert and I grabbed our little cotton sacks and ran to the nearby field to help Granddad and Uncle Eddie pick cotton.

Robert and I did more playing than picking. My little brother knew that I was afraid of the big, green sting worms that lived on cotton leaves, and he made me flinch and run around by threatening to drop one down my back. Granddad looked back and said, "Alright, settle down back there," as Uncle Eddie turned around and shook a finger at us.

Maybe a couple of hours after Robert and I arrived in the cotton field, we heard Mother calling, "Papa, Eddie, y'all need to come home," and we could see her waving arms beckon us homeward. It was close to quitting time anyway.

Robert and I gathered up our almost empty cotton sacks and vowed to outrun each other to the house. Carrying their cotton sacks over one shoulder, Granddad and Uncle Eddie walked faster than usual. Mother was waiting in the backyard with a worried look on her face. She said, "It's Mother." Robert and I dropped our cotton sacks in the shed, flew up the steps, kicked off our dusty shoes on the back porch, dashed through the kitchen and into Grandma's room. Mother was right behind us. Grandma was sleeping peacefully on the edge of her bed with an endearing smile on her face. Cousin Lizell said, "She is in God's hands." Robert and I gave Grandma a hug, but she could not hug us while sleeping.

Immediately, Granddad and Uncle Eddie were hovering around her bed. I knew that Grandma was alright, but I wanted to know why Mother called us home so fast. Granddad sat on a stool beside the bed. He placed Grandma's left hand between both of his hands and held it for an unknown length of time. Finally, he said, "She's in God's hands now."

Mother explained that Grandma had gotten up to to use the slop jar. She and Cousin Lizell were helping her get back into bed when Grandma fainted. Mother said it took all that she and Cousin Lizell had to prevent Grandma's chubby body from falling on the floor, and that's why she was sleeping on the edge of the bed. When Granddad moved out of my way, I placed my left ear on her chest. I could not hear her heart beating. I could not feel her breathing, but she was warm and smiling.

Granddad, Mother and Uncle Eddie were having an intense, low volume conversation in the kitchen. A few minutes later Uncle Eddie had cleaned up and changed clothes. He was in a big hurry to summon the doctor, but he had to drive Cousin Lizell home first.

As Uncle Eddie was driving away, Robert and I went to help Granddad milk the cows. Daylight would soon disappear as dark clouds covered the sky and thunder rolled in the background. I was anxious to return to Grandma's bedside, but helping Granddad would give her more time to sleep and recover from fainting. Meanwhile, a gusty wind had begun making its presence known by tossing around bits of hay, twigs, and dust. I quickly milked one cow. Fear of the unknown propelled my feet back to Grandma's bedside. Granddad would bring all of the milk home.

I prayed that she would be awake by the time I got there. After all, I was saved, and Jesus was there to answer our prayers and watch over the little children. She was still smiling and still warm, but she seemed to be sleeping harder than ever. Jesus would certainly answer my prayers. I thought, "Now is the time to walk by faith." Uncle Eddie and the doctor would be back any minute now.

It felt like forever, but I do not know how much time elapsed before Uncle Eddie and the doctor arrived, but it was late night for country folks. It was dark and windy with drizzling rain. Thunder rumbled loudly, and colorful lightning patterns danced through the stormy looking clouds.

Uncle Eddie arrived first, dashed out of the car and ran up on the porch. A long black car backed up until the back bumper touched the front porch. Two well-dressed Negro men scrambled out of the vehicle and hopped up on the porch. Granddad, Mother, and the five of us were waiting on the porch in front of our grandparents' bedroom. Mother rushed us out of the way and told us to stay in our room, but we could not.

We ran from our room, through the kitchen, to the doorway of their bedroom. Grandma continued sleeping with that sweet smile on her face.

My siblings and I leaned forward and stared into the room. Granddad, Mother, Uncle Eddie and the two men were standing around her bed talking. One of the men removed a stethoscope from a bag to hear Grandma's heartbeat. He moved that round, silver, flat device all around her chest area. He appeared to be holding his breath while measuring Grandma's vital signs.

My heart was pounding so loudly, I could not hear what the men were saying, but I sensed anguishing terror had come upon us. The enormous lump in my throat caused me to gasp for air, and volcanic tears boiled down my face. Robert was weeping like rain, and our little sisters were crying because we were.

The man put his instruments back in the bag while the other gentleman went to the vehicle and rolled in a stretcher. Grandma was wearing a nightgown, but they wrapped her in some white material and used some to slide her face-up from bed to stretcher. Surely this was one of my crazy nightmares that I would wake up from. We ran back through our room to the front porch and watched them carefully roll Grandma out of her room, across the porch, and into the hearse. One of the men took out a big black umbrella before they buckled Grandma in, secured the stretcher, and closed the double doors on the back of the vehicle.

After some consoling words to the family, the two men walked down the front porch steps and climbed in the front seat of the hearse. Ever so slowly, the vehicle pulled away from the front porch and moved through the yard and down the road.

Ear-damaging screams escaped my throat without my permission. I was jumping around hollering, "Granddad don't let them take Grandma!" He did not attempt to stop them from taking her. In that moment, it felt like the wind lifted me into the air and I leaped towards the ground, but Uncle Eddie caught me. I was kicking and screaming, "Don't take my Grandma." Granddad told Uncle Eddie, "Just let her go," and I flew down the steps, sprinting towards the red tail lights of the hearse.

The heavy clunk sound of the hearse doors slamming shut seemed to have triggered the vicious storm. Thunder clapped, lightning flashed, the sky opened up, and rain poured like never before, and the wind's power blew the rain around. Lightning seemed to be following the hearse, which made it easy for me to see, but I could not catch it. Robert was running after me yelling, "Ann, come back here." The red tail lights faded into the darkness. I dropped to the muddy ground on my knees, looked up in the lightning-filled sky and screamed obscenities at God! I was outrageously angry with God! How could He take Grandma Mamie and leave Daddy on earth?

Robert insisted that we should go back to the house. I stomped my feet in the muddy road and screamed for lightning to strike me dead. I saw no point in living without Grandma Mamie. Everyone was waiting for us on the front porch. Six-year old Audrey, four-year-old Jean and two-year-old Kassandra were scared and crying. Our parents looked sorrowful, especially Granddad and Uncle Eddie, but Mother appeared stoic.

Mother fussed at me for chasing after the hearse in the storm, "Like you don't have good sense." She said, "Your grandmother is dead, and she is not coming back." She further fussed at us to hurry around to the back porch, and get out of the storm and those muddy clothes. Hysteria had claimed me. I could not stop hollering, and my body was shaking itself.

Robert and I shared bath water in the round tin tub. I washed up first, but I could not control my emotions. The minute I emerged from the back porch in my pajamas, Mother gave this hollering child a warm cup of milk, laced with some of Uncle Eddie's hidden brandy. I found out about the brandy later, but I did not remember anything after drinking the milk.

When I woke up the following morning, I felt numb, and my throat was sore. My heart and chest hurt, and my entire body felt heavy and achy. My mind played back scenes from the previous night, and I still hoped that it was all just a bad dream. Mechanically, I got dressed and went to the back porch to brush my teeth and wash up. As I walked through the kitchen to the back porch, Granddad was sitting at the kitchen table drinking black coffee. The painfully sad expression on his face confirmed Grandma's death. Mother was making biscuits and cooking breakfast. My little sisters were getting dressed and playing around. Robert and Uncle Eddie were tending the animals. I helped the girls get dressed. Then I helped Mother with breakfast and set the table for the five of us. The girls had their own cute little table with four chairs in a corner of the kitchen.

I was not hungry for breakfast, and I felt queasy. Mother fussed at me to "Eat something." I told her, "My appetite went with Grandma." She said "You still have to eat and live a normal life."

Nothing was normal without Grandma. Normally, we would have gone to school that Friday, but we did not because she died last night, and we were up very late. During breakfast, my parents spoke about notifying all family members and making funeral arrangements. They also spoke of Thanksgiving, which was coming very soon.

Life slowed down to a methodical grind when Grandma's energy left our presence. We went to church that Sunday where her death was announced in service. Relatives and friends wept from shock and loss, because Grandma had not been sick. She had been "under the weather," at times, but she was in church last Sunday. I was so angry, I could not look at Reverend Nelson and did not hear anything he said about God. We also went to school the following Monday because Mother made us go.

Life was a meaningless blur. Grandma's children and other relatives needed ample time to drive down from St. Louis, Chicago, Detroit, Milwaukee, or wherever they were. I don't know what day of the week her funeral was on, but I do recall relatives arriving with lots of food. I think Grandma's passing was celebrated as an early Thanksgiving, but I was not thankful.

St. John Baptist church was packed with mourners on the day of Grandma's funeral. All of her grandchildren were dressed in white, and we sat on the front pew near her casket. Roann and I wore matching white taffeta dresses. They were designed in three-tiers of overlapping skirts, with lace ruffles stitched around each tier. Our black patent leather slippers and white socks also matched. Those were the most beautiful dresses I had ever seen. Ironically, we were wearing them to the most terrible place that we never wanted to see, Grandma Mamie's funeral.

Reverend Nelson preached her funeral, he and used his booming voice to speak above the weeping and crying out of the bereaved. I had already cried out, to say the least. I was too mad and disappointed with God to weep anymore. My heart ached and raced, but I clenched my fists and teeth to endure the unthinkable.

Grandma was still smiling. She appeared amazingly beautiful and peaceful in her white satin lined coffin. She wore her black dress with the white lace collar. She did not wear face powder or lipstick, but the undertakers applied the perfect amount, because she looked marvelous. The array of colorful flowers added to her beauty, and I had never seen that many pretty floral arrangements before.

There appeared to be an endless stream of mourners, weeping and walking slowly past her casket, with some of them leaning over her and crying so hard they almost fell in. After everyone had viewed, kissed, and cried over Grandma, her casket was closed. Her five sons and her husband were pallbearer and rolled her out into the cemetery for burial.

At her grave side, Reverend Nelson was going to "speak a few words," but another eulogistic sermon poured forth from him. Finally, the dreadful end. "Ashes to ashes and dust to dust," and with that, the first shovel of dirt was tossed on top of the wood box containing her casket. When the second shovel of dirt fell on the box, Aunt Effie jumped up from her graveside chair and sobbed, "Don't throw that dirt in my mother's face," which caused a new wave of weeping and crying out, including me and Reverend Nelson.

After Grandma's interment, everyone went to the kitchen fellowship room where plenty of tasty food awaited. What is it about funerals that make mourners extremely hungry? Whatever it is, there was more than enough food to satisfy the most ravenous.

Although my appetite had not returned at home, I managed to eat plenty of homemade chocolate cake and other delectable sweets. There were countless cousins, schoolmates and unfamiliar children, but we immediately bonded, ran around, and played together. All too soon the fun part was over, and it was time to go.

After the funeral, my grandparent's home was full and energized by all of their children, grandchildren, and a great-grandson, Christopher, Loretta's four month old gorgeous son. I had been delighted to finally adore and cuddle him in my arms. Robert and I loved our status as aunt and uncle. Two-year old Kassandra was too young to know or care about being an auntie, but family members were amused over the fact. It was a cycle that repeated. Uncle Rudy is two years older than Loretta.

When Loretta had become married and pregnant, or pregnant and married, she had written and informed Mother of the events. I recall some of Mother's comments, "Loretta was so smart, she got skipped two grades and graduated from Denmark High School when she was 16-years old. Wish she had been smart enough not to have a baby. All children do is tie you down and hold you back. She should have kept her behind in nursing school."

Apparently, Mother found that raising six children and putting up with Daddy extremely irritating. Throughout our childhood she would frequently retort, "I'm sorry that I ever had any of y'all."

Meanwhile, eighteen year old Loretta was happy to have her Army husband, Frank, and her own apartment, which was great compared to living with Aunt Vessye. Everyone knew that fastidious Vessye was impossible to live with, but Uncle Ray had his own space in their lovely home and good coping skills. They did not have any children.

Before long, everyone was gone from my grandparent's home. Loretta and her baby rode back to their home with Aunt Mary and her baby. Mary's husband, Andy, drove them back to St. Louis safely. All of the bereaved would need good coping skills to deal with Grandma's passing, especially those of us who lived in her home.

Grief counseling was unknown within our community which consisted of home, church, and school. Granddad did his best to explain why, "The

Lord giveth and The Lord taketh." Mother lectured me that Grandma was dead and gone, and she was not coming back. "Be thankful that you had her for for as long as you did, and just try to think about the good times."

With the passage of time, I missed her even more, and for that reason I was finished with "Trust in the Lord," but Jesus was my best friend. I could relate to physical assaults, pain and suffering. I talked to Him and cried into my pillow every night. I sobbed when I told Him that I was also mad at God for letting Him hang on the cross. First of all, I wanted to know why God did not stop the angry mob before they beat Him down with whips? I knew what it felt like to be flogged with a whip! Who would want another Father like that? And I cried and cursed God!

Reverend Nelson preached sermons on life, death, heaven, hell, forgiveness and many other topics. Attending church was a must, not an option, but they couldn't make me sit up straight, hold up my head and look at Reverend Nelson. I would slump down in the pew, stare into my lap and twiddle my handkerchief at varying speeds.

One Sunday he preached a message on forgiveness. When he said, "Sometimes you have to forgive God," my head jerked up by itself. I caught my breath, and our eyes saw each other. My heart skipped a beat, and I sat up straight. How did he know? I exhaled a sigh of relief when he slowly turned and looked at somebody else in the congregation. After that, I stopped cursing at God and continued talking to Jesus.

Moreover, I knew that Grandma would wash my mouth with lye soap several times if she knew that I was cursing out God. If He had not taken her, I would not be hurting and angry with Him. The whole thing was painful, frustrating and beyond my understanding. Certainly I was thankful that I had her for as long as I did, but I was only eleven-years old. He could have let her live until I was grown.

I tried to think about the good times, but happy memories of her broke my heart and made me weep, because I knew that they would never come again. In spite of that, one of my happiest memories with her occurred Christmas 1949, a few months after moving in with them. Granddad took me and Robert into the nearby woods so that we could select our own Christmas tree. Excitement drove us from one tree to the next until we found the perfect one. Granddad chopped it down and dragged it home on a light-weight slide that he made for the occasion. We placed the tree on the front porch in front of the parlor. Granddad set the tree in a bucket and made a wood frame that stood on the floor and supported the tree. After Grandma directed Granddad to rearrange some furniture, he placed the tree on a mat in its designated spot. Then he poured an adequate amount of water in the bucket and draped an old white sheet around it. The tree stood waiting for us to decorate it. Robert and I deeply inhaled the sweet fragrance of fresh pine and rejoiced over having a Christmas tree. We told

Grandma that we did not have a Christmas tree in the log cabin because Santa Claus could not find his way to our house. Grandma said, "That's because the roads were washed out, but Santa Claus won't have any trouble getting here."

Time was not moving fast enough towards Christmas. Robert and I performed our chores and did our homework with great zest. We loved school, and all of the students were excitedly cutting out structured Christmas decorations from a wide variety of colorful construction paper. There were plenty of scissors, glue, long colorful ribbons and yarn for each child to create something. However, this fun activity came after we successfully completed our classwork.

Seventh and eighth graders who were "too grown" to cut out Christmas designs were free to help the younger children, after Mrs. DeBerry checked their schoolwork. Cutting our Christmas designs took a few days, and I carefully carried mine home each day and placed them on the white sheet around the tree until it was time to decorate. Robert did more playing around than cutting designs. He and some other little boys were busy folding and tossing paper airplanes, but he did manage to contribute a few colorful Christmas designs.

One evening after supper when all of the chores were finished, including washing dishes, finally it was time to put everything on the tree. Granddad started with a string of electric lights that he bought for the tree. It was my pleasure to stand still and hold the lights while Granddad draped them around the tree, starting from top to bottom. Robert jumped forward for his turn to hold the second string of lights as Granddad draped them around the tree.

Next, he opened a box of beautiful round things that sparkled. They were about the size and shape of large eggs. They were covered in glittering shades of blue, green, red, or white, and there was a round shiny loop on one end. Grandma Mamie told us to be very careful because those were breakable. I practically held my breath as I delicately hung a blue one on a low hanging branch. Robert made me nervous with his less delicate approach.

Granddad opened a box that contained long shreds of shiny stuff. The shreds were slivers of glittering silver. He demonstrated how to dangle the long stringy stuff on the tree branches without knocking off those egg-shaped ornaments. Robert and I dangled silver all around the tree. We stood on our toes and made a game of tossing it up on the high branches and cheering when it stayed. Some shreds slipped to the next branch and decorated it. I found those shreds to be absolutely enchanting wherever they landed.

At last, Robert and I hung our Christmas designs on the tree with Grandma's help. Grandma was a "shortie," but she was still taller than we were. Our parents praised our colorful designs, which included bells, stars, candy canes, and chain-links. Granddad cleared out all of the empty boxes and moved a couple of pieces of small furniture back into place. Audrey had been anxious to help decorate the tree, but she was quite happy playing with the empty boxes that Grandma used to distract her and Jean. Six-month-old Kassandra was happy in her crib, but Mother had to hold on to two-year-old Jean, who went running and looking for trouble.

It was time to see what the tree looked like. Granddad turned off the light in the room and said, "Let's light her up." I ran and brought Kassandra from her crib while Mother held on to Jean, who was screaming and scrambling to get loose. Granddad counted "1-2-3" and plugged in the Christmas tree lights. When the tree lit up, the glow from the lights engulfed me, and Robert. Audrey and I jumped up and down, giggling with joy. I almost floated away from the overwhelming visual impact. Grandma removed the baby from my arms, as I burst into tears.

Surprised and concerned, Grandma asked, "What's the matter Totem?" Pointing towards the tree, I blubbered, "It's soooo pretty!" Grandma said, "Bless your heart Baby, but you don have to cry about it." The bubbling liquid inside the multicolored lights amazed us and created wonderment.

After lighting the tree, I do not know how many days passed by until Santa Claus came. I do know that we went to bed very early on Christmas Eve, because Santa had to make lots of stops. Excitement woke us up at daybreak, and we dashed into the parlor where our grandparents were waiting. Mother was cooking breakfast, but she came to join us. The tree was surrounded with shoes, socks, undershirts, fruit, nuts, candy and toys.

Robert marveled over his little red wagon that was big enough for us to haul each other around the yard. Santa brought the girls a little green wooden table with four matching chairs and some bald head, rubber baby dolls. I received a green china tea set with four little cups and saucers and a huge White doll with blond hair and blue eyes. Her eyes closed when I laid her down and opened when I lifted her up. She also made a monotone crying sound when I laid her down. I was not totally comfortable with her crying, opening and closing her huge blue eyes, and the fact that she did not look like me or anyone who I knew. Nonetheless, as time progressed the two of us and my little sisters enjoyed drinking imaginary tea at my tea parties.

Without knowing anything about the concept, our first Christmas with our grandparents was a transforming culture shock in the best way. We moved from a falling down log cabin to a warm home where we were loved. Christmas 1950 was also magical, but at least I did not cry when Granddad plugged in the tree lights. The joy of Christmas and toys from Santa brought unspeakable pleasure. Every Christmas in the home of my grandparents was wonderful, and nobody had any reason to suspect that

Christmas 1950 would be Grandma's last one.

After Grandma Mamie died, my idyllic world crumbled around me, and nothing was as beautiful as it had been while she lived.

6

RAPED IN ST. LOUIS, MISSOURI

Although Grandma Mamie's death was crushing, I still had to finish elementary school. When I graduated from eighth grade, there were two girls and three boys in my graduating class from Greer Elementary. I was thrilled that Mother allowed me to move to St. Louis and live with Loretta. After the family reunion in July 1954, I rode to St. Louis with Aunt Vessye and Uncle Ray. They lived in St. Louis but always drove back to Denmark for family events. They delivered me safely to my sister. A hug and happy hello to Loretta, then I scooped up my adorable nephews, three year old Chris and one year old Ray. I was proud to be an aunt. My sister was happy to have a free babysitter. I was content to watch my nephews and the black and white television.

Soon, I met my sister's friends. She had spoken highly of them and how much fun they had together. They especially enjoyed the night life, and going over the river to East St. Louis, Illinois was a favorite activity for them. The more I heard, the more I wanted to go.

One Saturday night-Sunday morning around 12:30 a.m., we tiptoed out of the apartment and left the boys sleeping home alone and barely made it back before they woke up for breakfast. The night clubs "over the river" were after hours, and the entertainment was exuberant and embarrassing for a fourteen-year-old, fresh out of St. John Baptist church in Denmark. Therefore, I squirmed, covered my eyes, and gazed through my fingers at the shake-dancer.

Tanya was her name. She wore a bright red, two-piece costume. The scantily cut bottom had three layers of fringe across the gluteus. The top had three loops of fringe around the bra cups, and she danced barefoot.

Her face and eyes were painted like a doll. Long black flowing hair whipped in the wind, as she shook her butt and breasts while leaping around the stage. Her body looked like creamy dark chocolate. She pumped and gyrated to every beat of the drums. The piano, horns, guitar and bass made sounds and evoked emotions within me that were previously unknown. The penetrating sounds of the horns caused me to grab my sister's arm and hold on tightly. Talk about culture shock, I was obviously blown away! It was the first night club I had ever been in, first musicians, first exotic dancer. They were all first things I would never tell Mother. There were other night clubs in East St. Louis, and "jam sessions" were very popular. When Loretta told me that I could go to my first "jam session" with her, I said, "I sure hope they have some blackberry jam." After gaining some control of her laughter, my sister explained that a jam session is when a bunch of musicians get together and out-play each other on their particular instruments.

Every darkly lit night club had its own beckoning attraction, but the one that Tanya danced in was my favorite. The way she rolled her hips around and popped her pelvic area was something to see! And how in the world did she shake one butt cheek at a time, then clap them together? At home, listening to rhythm and blues on the radio, I secretly tried to imitate Tanya's moves. Not even close, it must have been too many years of listening to The Grand Ole Opry when I lived with Grandma Mamie and Grandpa Walker. I could still hear "Cousin Minnie Pearl say "E-l-m-e-r, don't fergit the American Ace c-o-f-f-e-e." But that did not stop me from shaking my body without rhythm and jumping around my sister's apartment. When I told Loretta that I wanted to be a pretty lady like Tanya, she laughed and said, "I don't think so. Tanya is a man."

Of course, I did not believe my sister. She had teased and played jokes on me all of my life. She tried to explain that Tanya was a "sissy," and a "sissy" was a man who wanted to be a woman. She further explained that a "sissy" was also a "punk," and a "punk" and a "sissy" were the same thing. That was very confusing to me, but I didn't care. I admired Tanya and wished that I could shake it like she did. Remembering the words of Grandma Lizzy, I said, "If you see anything God didn't give him, throw your hat at it." Loretta laughed. She had heard Grandma say that long before I was born.

Loretta knew that I was puzzled over Tanya. She reminded me that I was "just a little country girl," and there were all kinds of people and things in the world that I did not know about, and Tanya had a right to do her thing. She enjoyed my wide-eyed reactions to city life.

I flinched from the noise, and I was afraid of the speeding traffic. Since Loretta was deprived of her childhood by taking care of me and Robert, working the cotton fields, and surviving severe beatings by Daddy, she was making up for lost time by going out to various events. She did not consume any alcohol, but she smoked cigarettes and ate crunchy pieces of Argo starch straight from the box. She always carried some in her bag, which she crunched wherever she went, even in nightclubs.

Loretta carried starch to a wonderful cultural event on Labor Day, 1954. There was so much food, I do not recall Loretta crunching any starch during the event. With friends, and without taking food or anything, we took the kids to a free concert and picnic in a park-like setting with green grass and plenty of shade trees. It was somewhere in East St. Louis. A stage had been built for the performers, and several musicians and singers entertained the huge field of people.

There were no chairs set up in concert style, some brought their own chairs or crates to sit on. People sat in cars and trucks, and some sat on top of them. Others sat on the ground, while young men and big boys climbed up in trees for a better view of the stage. I did not know there were so many Negroes in the world! I'm guessing that at least two hundred fifty to three hundred people or more were at the event from start to finish, and people came and left from around noon until the concert ended at dusk. I was amused and amazed to be among my first huge group of people and did not know any of them. What a shock! Short ones, tall ones, skinny, fat and bald ones. Every shade was present at that event, from "Mighty near White," to "You need a flashlight to see him in daylight." Without knowing it, that was my first feeling of "empowerment" and racial pride.

Who knew there were so many "Colored" people who could do countless, wondrous things? And cooking mouthwatering, tasty food was one of them. Men brought barbecue grills and equipment to the park in their pickup trucks, and the grill competition was ongoing with their individual and original homemade barbecue sauce: ribs, steaks, chicken, hot links, hot dogs, and hamburgers. There was golden, crispy fried chicken, and the women had baked pies, cakes, cookies, cobblers, and every soul food dish known at the time.

All of the people with food supplies were friendly, and they invited and insisted that whoever passed by should try some of their food, and they all claimed: "We got the best barbecue out here," as they handed a plate full of whatever you wanted. It felt like a big family reunion without knowing any of those long, lost relatives. There were no problems, just music, entertainment, fun, and delicious food. What an amazing and embracing event that was! After the event was over, Loretta told me, "Hope you had fun before you start high school."

On May 17, 1954, the United State Supreme Court issued its historic decision declaring state supported segregated schools unconstitutional, but the schools were not really integrated. Loretta had been trying to get me enrolled, but none of the notable Negro high schools would accept me, because I had never attended school in St. Louis. Just before my sister gave up and put me on a Greyhound bus back to Denmark, a friend told her to try and enroll me in Washington Tech. My sister said, "That's the worst high school in St. Louis; that's where all of the hoodlums go."

Hoodlums or not, George Washington Carver High School on 19th and Franklin was the beginning of my urban education. The school was reportedly named after the century's greatest scientist. Born a slave, he rose from slavery and became one of the world's most respected and honored men. George Washington Carver is best known for developing crop-rotation methods that kept nutrients in the soil. He discovered hundreds of new uses for the peanut and countless other discoveries.

During the enrollment process, my sister took me to school on the trolley trains so that I would know how to travel from home to school and back. The trolley cars were like something from outer space to me. They ran on railroad type tracks, but they had long cords on top of the trains that were attached and slid along overhead electric cable wires. Frequently, electrically charged sparks flew from the overhead cables, which made me dread riding them.

To say that my beginning at "Tech" was lonely and scary would be a serious understatement. It was a nightmare during daylight hours. I did not know one soul. Many of the students were loud, rude, and disrespectful. I heard that some thuggish boys had thrown a "sissy" music teacher out of a fourth floor window, just because he was a "sissy." I was constantly teased about my slow, southern speech patterns and addressed as, "Hey Country."

One day for no apparent reason, a girl jumped in my face, called me "Country" and said, "Yo mama is a hoe." Without backing up, I shouted back at her, "So what! Yo mama is a rake and a plow." The two girls with her laughed long and loudly as they flounced off down the school hallway.

All of the students were not hoodlums by far. Soon, I was befriended by Ellis, a trumpet player in the school band and his sister Zenobia, a cheerleader. Suddenly, my school experience changed from nightmares to sweet dreams. I had two friends and more friends from their friends. Ellis took me to my very first football game where he marched and played his trumpet with the school band, and I beamed at him in his handsome uniform.

Zenobia and the cheerleaders twirled batons, marched in high steps and performed learned routines that I could only daydream about. I longed to be a cheerleader, and Zenobia did her best to teach me baton twirling and cheerleader routines, but I was beyond hope with no sense of timing, and self confidence was unknown at the time. Even so, I was tickled to hang out with them at football games, although I did not have a clue about the game of football. Ellis explained what the players were doing, but I only recognized a touchdown.

Ellis, Zenobia, and her boyfriend also took me to my first house party. There were party decorations and red light bulbs that made people look like something I had never seen before. I was amused and intrigued by people moving around and dancing in the red light. When Ellis attempted to dance with me, I panicked. He kept saying relax, and follow me, but I stepped on his feet and almost made both of us fall down. The party host repetitiously played a popular song called, "Work With Me Annie," which I hated, because some knuckle-headed boys would see me in the school hallway, make a hissing sound and say, "Hey, don't you want to work with me Annie?" At the time, my name was Ann Williamson.

Besides meeting Ellis and Zenobia, another good thing about George Washington High was the little store on the corner that sold hot, salted, roasted peanuts with jelly beans, a brand new combination for my taste buds. The little brown paper bags containing the jelly beans and peanuts quickly turned greasy and were easily recognized by fellow students who wanted some. Looking back, that was a huge and yummy snack for 25 cents, but the warm sweet and salty taste required a cold bottle of soda pop, another 25 cents.

Another sweet thing about Washington Tech was its close location to something else that I had never seen before, a doughnut shop. There, I met for the first time and fell head- over-heels in love with glazed doughnuts. How could anything taste so flakey sweet and greasy delicious?

However, my love affair with them quickly diminished after I bought and gobbled down almost a dozen of those delicious delights, fresh out of hot grease. They held me close through the night and kept me running to the bathroom, purging from both ends. That caused an abrupt breakup between us. We eventually made up, but I have remained very cautious, because too much sweet, greasy goodness cannot be trusted.

A wonderful thing about Washington Tech High School was that most of the teachers were there to help us learn, and I was very interested in learning. I loved to read. I had won several spelling contests in Greer Elementary School when I lived in Denmark with my maternal grandparents. I especially enjoyed writing, geography, and history. Attending high school in St. Louis held much more appeal than working the cotton fields.

When we lived in the log cabin, usually all of the cotton had not been picked when school started in the early fall. If the sun was shining, we had to pick cotton while our cousins and friends went to school. Daddy only allowed us to attend school on rainy days, until all of the cotton had been picked. My cotton picking background endowed me with a deep appreciation for high school.

Since I was well-behaved and a polite church girl, I did well in Washington Tech, which turned out to be a last stop for under-achievers and misguided teenagers who had been expelled from the more reputable Negro high schools in St. Louis.

Although polite and well-behaved, field and farm work did not make me academically prepared for high school, not even at Washington Tech, especially in math. With my basic reading, writing, and language skills, Ellis helped me with all of my homework. He and Zenobia were "A" students, and Ellis loved math. He made sure that all of our homework was completed before we attended any football games or social activities. Ellis was my first love, and he remained one of the nicest young men I have ever known. He did not make any sexual advances towards me, especially after I told him about the neighborhood boy named Donald, who had raped me a few weeks after I arrived in St. Louis.

I avoided verbalizing any details to Ellis, but my memory painfully recalled the city slick, good-looking, fast-talking Donald, who would invite himself to walk with me and my little nephews to the store when I took them to get ice cream cones and snacks. Knowing that I was fresh from the country, eighteen year-old Donald told me that I was cute, and he wanted to be my boyfriend. Blushing and smiling, I told him, "I don't need no boyfriend," but my words did not deter Donald.

One day when my sister was not home, Donald came to the house and "took it." The experience was horrifying, painful, and bloody, but at least I did not end up pregnant. My nephews were down for a nap. Donald sat beside me on the sofa and groped my breasts. I rejected his advances and attempted to get up from the sofa. He grabbed me around my waist and pulled me into a horizontal position on the sofa.

He put his right arm across my chest and held me down. He used his thighs and knees to anchor me on the sofa. Sharp cutting pain shot through my abdominal area. I started to scream, but he put a hand over my mouth, and muffled my scream into a whimper. Like a nightmare, it was over, and he was gone. Trying not to wake up the boys, I cried silently, took a bath, and changed clothes.   I thought he liked me as a friend. Why would he do something like that to somebody if he liked them? I hated Donald for hurting me and wished that I could knock him to the ground on his back. I wanted to stab him up and down with the same pitchfork that I had visually used to stab Daddy to death! Then I cried myself to sleep, and my little nephews had slept through my unimaginable ordeal.

When my sister came home around 3:00 p.m., I did not tell her what had occurred, but she knew that something was drastically wrong, because I was sorrowful. She did not give up, and the following day I told her that Donald "took it." She went to his house, but he was not there, and he was not ever seen in the neighborhood afterwards.

A few weeks after I was raped, Loretta and her sister-in-law, Olive, moved all of us to a huge, old stately home on Washington Street. Olive and her husband had two boys, and she was pregnant with the third child. My sister was also pregnant with her third child, and her husband, Frank, was in the Army. Loretta and Olive were excited about the very low rent on such a huge home, which would provide ample space with lots of room for the kids to run around and play.

The three story home had several huge bedrooms, convenient bathrooms and endless nooks, alcoves, and crawl spaces. There was also a huge basement and attic, but I had no desire to investigate them. The structure of the house resembled an old plantation mansion. Two huge, round white pillars supported the front of the house, and the thick, heavy front door resembled a moat to a castle.

The living room was massive, and the fireplace was tall enough for me to walk in, but it was inoperative. Loretta's and Olive's furniture combined was not enough to furnish that huge living room. There was no furniture in the living room; it was just a walk through to the rest of the house. With hardwood floors, no rugs and no furniture, the living room echoed when we walked and spoke while passing through.

Very wide hardwood steps circled around and up to the second floor landing, and continued to the third floor landing, but nobody lived on the third floor. The kids loved running up the steps and sliding down the bannisters, and so did I. Those wide hardwood steps squeaked, and I did not like walking on them, because they made a creaking, crying sound with every step.

I told Loretta that the creaking steps and the huge house was too scary for us to live there. She said, "Scary or not, the rent is good, and we are not moving again." My sister, the boys and I lived in three of the four bedrooms on the first floor, and we had our own kitchen- dining area and bathroom. The other bedroom was empty and locked off.

Olive and her family lived on the second floor, and they also had three or four bedrooms, their own kitchen and bathroom. For me, it was comforting that Olive always knocked on our door to say "Hello" or "Goodnight," whenever they left or returned home.

We had been living in our spacious home for almost one month. Early one evening, around 6:00 p.m., I was sitting at the kitchen table doing homework. I heard the heavy front door swing open and shut. The door's hinges were long overdue for oil, and they seemed to moan in pain every time they opened and closed. I smiled to myself when I heard the familiar creaky sound of feet walking through the living room and up the steps. I heard muffled voices without clarity of their words. Cheerfully, I continued preparing my homework but wondered why they did not stop by, as usual. I suspected that Olive and family were in a hurry. Perhaps the kids had to use the bathroom.

A couple of hours later, I heard the front door hinges moan and creak again. I heard foot steps and muffled voices. Olive knocked on the door. Her husband and kids stood beside her with pleasant expressions on their faces. My face showed fear. Olive's eyes grew bigger when she asked, "Ann, what's wrong with you?" I told Olive and her husband that I heard them come in the house and walk up the steps about two hours ago, and I was wondering why they did not stop as usual.

Olive and her family walked inside of our living quarters and closed the door. They seriously swore that this was the first time they had entered the house that evening. Furthermore, I did not hear them come back down the steps and walk out through the crying front door. So, whoever went up the steps a couple hours ago should still be up there. Right?

The kids were unaware of the unknown visitors and played uninterrupted. Olive, her husband and I flinched in fear when we heard the front door swing open. Fortunately, it was my sister returning home. The second she walked in, she knew that something was disturbing. I quickly provided a detailed account of what I had heard. Olive and her husband both stated that they had heard us entering or leaving the house when we had not, and they had wondered why we did not holler up at them, which we always did. I blurted out, "See, Loretta, I told you that this house was too big and scary." Our collective epiphany was that we all understood why the rent was low and why the house had been vacant for such a long time. We were living in a haunted house!

Additionally, the unoccupied house had become home to several stray cats. They were living and rapidly multiplying around the house and in the basement. Like street gangs, the cats hung out on the back stoop and on the ledge in front of the huge kitchen window, above the sink.

Behaving like rival gang members, the cats fought, growled, and clawed each other through the night. Their eerie cries and high-pitched growls in the dark of night made me hide under my blanket and cover my head with pillows. There was one particular cat who appeared to be angry; he was especially scary. He was huge, black, and had piercing green eyes. For unprovoked reasons, he would hiss at me and scratch the window glass while I washed dishes in the kitchen sink. He frequently raised his leg and sprayed yellow urine on the windowpane, which made me jump back. Even when I closed the window shade, I could hear him clawing his sharp nails on the window glass. That screeching sound gave me chills and hurt my teeth.

Loretta called Animal Control. They finally came out with food in traps and hauled away countless cats, including the angry one. But that night, the big black cat was back scratching on the kitchen window. My sister called Animal Control again regarding the menacing black cat. The person who answered the phone at Animal Control assured Loretta that all of the cats had been put to sleep. My sister said, "The angry black cat is still here." The worker at Animal Control said "It has to be another black cat." My sister and I certainly knew that somehow, the big black cat was still there, and it was mysterious how he could just disappear from the window without jumping down and running away. It took a couple of weeks before my sister could find an affordable apartment. Olive and her family made arrangements to move in with relatives temporarily, but they waited so that we could all move out together. In those remaining days while my sister searched for another place to live, Olive and her family moved in with us, but that did not stop the muffled voices and creaking steps. Unknown things continued thumping and moving around upstairs. Even when Olive's husband searched the house, called out "Who's there," and threatened to shoot them, no one ever responded.

My dear friends Ellis and Zenobia were very supportive through the haunted house ordeal and others, including recounts of Daddy's vicious physical abuse upon us. They picked me up from wherever I lived, and I rode to school with them. Ellis was thrilled to have worked and bought himself a car at age sixteen. When he had band practice and work after school, I had to take public transportation home. Truly, Ellis and Zenobia made my transition from Denmark to St. Louis much better than it ever would have been without them, and we had fun along the way.

Even so, it had been difficult for me and Loretta, regarding school clothes, shoes, and supplies. My little country girl dresses would have brought more teasing and insults from my schoolmates. So my sister bought me some shoes and dressed me in her fashionable outfits. I could not avoid staining or snagging her clothes, no matter how careful I was. With every snag or spot that I put on her clothes, Loretta spouted angry words against our parents for not sending her "a dime" for my school clothes and supplies. She felt that they could help a little since Daddy was gainfully employed at LinkBelt.

When Loretta made an early request for school support for the next year, our parents told her that I had to move to Indianapolis and live with them: Mother, Daddy, Audrey, El' Nora Jean and Kassandra. The minute school was out, Mother mailed a money order for a one-way Greyhound bus ticket to Indianapolis, and I took Chris and Ray with me to spend a few summer days with their grandmother and young aunts.

7

DOOMED IN
INDIANAPOLIS, INDIANA

Except for Donald, I had been happy living in St. Louis with Loretta, and moving to Indianapolis to live with my parents was not my desire. Fortunately, I had some fun and adventure while living in St. Louis, before my doomed life sentence began in Indianapolis. Nonetheless, an option was not available, because my parents needed a free babysitter, cook and housekeeper for themselves and my three younger sisters.

My two little nephews and I arrived in Indianapolis on a Saturday afternoon in June 1955. Before I finished unpacking, I was writing letters to Ellis, telling him how much I missed him and could not wait for his visit to Indianapolis. Nevertheless, we had to wait until Ellis drove Loretta to Indianapolis to pick up Chris and Ray in a couple of weeks. The boys and I had been there for a couple of hours before Daddy staggered home. He greeted me smelling like whiskey. Immediately, I felt uncomfortable and did not like the way his eyebrows raised when he took a close look at my developed body, which he had not seen for six years. His first words to me were, "Gal you sho is done growed up ain't ya."

Hugs were unknown in my family, but as Daddy passed by me, he deliberately brushed one of his shoulders against my breasts, pretending like it was an accident. I had been a little nine-year old girl the last time I had lived with him. At age fifteen, I had big body measurements. It was embarrassing. My breasts were heavy, and the straps from my bra cut into my shoulders and left marks.

Daddy was drunk but still standing. He was wearing his steel toed boots that he wore at work to protect his feet from the hot smelting steel that he poured at LinkBelt. He also wore his red plaid shirt, unbuttoned in the collar and cuffs. One suspender from his blue, bibbed overalls always hung loose from one shoulder. That was his "uniform," and he wore it most of the time.

Daddy was wearing his uniform when Ellis drove Loretta to Indianapolis to pick up Chris and Ray two weeks after we had arrived. They also arrived on a Saturday afternoon while Daddy was out drinking. Daddy stumbled home soon enough to prevent me from going to the movies with Ellis. I could not even leave the house with him and Loretta. Ellis stayed at the YMCA during his two night stay in Indianapolis. When he came to the house to visit me the next day, Daddy made sure that he had his whiskey stinking self on the porch, in the living room or wherever Ellis and I sat. Talk about embarrassing--Daddy's behavior was totally disgusting. He was still big and tall, but not fat. His behavior towards me was disturbing. He acted like a junk yard dog, guarding his territory, unlike a caring father.

The junkyard dog instantly made my life miserable. I could not believe that Daddy would not allow me to go anywhere with Ellis. It was Ellis who befriended me, tutored, and helped me earn A's and B's in Washington Tech. He took care of me. He did not take advantage of me in anyway. Ellis was wonderful, and Daddy caused emotional turmoil and injury to me and Ellis. Ellis and I stared at each other in disbelief! He was obviously crushed by my Dad's ignorant behavior.

My heart sank as I watched the tail lights on Ellis's car disappear into the distance. I felt a huge lump pulsating in my throat. I swallowed hard. My throat was totally dry. Like a drum, my heart pounded in rage against Daddy. I hated him for not allowing me and Ellis to go anywhere, and all of the hatred came rushing back from my early childhood in the log cabin. Without concentrated effort, I realized there had not been a lump in my throat like that since the last time I lived with Daddy. I felt sick to my stomach and sensed impending doom.

There was nothing for me to like about my hopeless and miserable situation. I did not like the uninviting house. It was too big and uncomfortable. The basement had three rooms, and the coal burning furnace and coal bin were in the middle room. The first floor consisted of a living room, dining room, kitchen, my parents' bedroom, and a back porch led to a big backyard with a built-in barbecue pit. On the first floor, there were double steps. Coming down stairs, from the landing, the steps on the right led into the dining room, and the steps on the left went into the living room. Three bedrooms and the only bathroom were on the second floor. Two bedrooms were in the attic, and they were not insulated to prevent sweltering heat or freezing cold.

Although I did not like the circumstances, I did love my three little sisters and was happy to see them. They appeared extremely happy and somewhat relieved that I had come to live with and look out for them.

My three little sisters lived in the attic bedrooms, and so did I. The first room at the top of the narrow steps was assigned to me. There was a wooden door to the attic, but the top half of the door had a windowpane. Anyone passing by could look up the steps that led to our bedrooms. There was no way to lock the door. The narrow, steep steps made me feel like I was climbing a ladder to the attic. Walking up the steps, the first thing I saw was the dusty floor and every item stored under the bed. There were no closets. A dresser stood on the north wall and a chair was at the foot of the bed. There was no ceiling. The room was shaped like a tee-pee with uncovered rafters. One front window allowed sun and heat to fill the room, but it had a roller shade.

Turning left at the top of the steps led to the sleeping area for my sisters. A short wall separated the two areas, but there were no doors. Their room was huge. It contained a double bed, two smaller beds, two chests of drawers, a dresser, and there were two large wardrobes.

Mother's Singer sewing machine, sewing equipment and fabrics occupied the front area of my sister's bedroom. Mom allowed me to select the fabric and make a curtain to cover the windowpane on the attic door. I was concerned about the uncovered window because the three bedrooms on the second floor were rented out to single men. The rented out rooms were the reason why my sisters and I had to live in the attic, and our only brother was relegated to live in the basement, after Delores and I brought him from Denmark on the Greyhound bus in August.

Thoughts of attic dwelling and Daddy's behavior presented dismal images, but thinking of going places with my first cousin Delores made me smile. She was there when we arrived, and she warmly welcomed me to Indianapolis and was excited about helping me learn my way around. She had a pretty face, long legs, and curved hips. Her nick name was "Long Tall Sally." At five feet, eleven inches and 155 pounds, she towered over me, but I was still one year older.

When Delores and her mother came to visit one Saturday morning, our happy thoughts were crushed when Daddy said, "Delores is too got-dammed fass, and Ann ain't goin no got-dammed whar with hur. She gonna be pregnant foe you kno it." That caused Delores's mother, who is Daddy's older sister, to curse him out for making such remarks about her youngest child. Daddy always had a speech impediment, and he stuttered, "Uh-uh-uh sh-sh-sh-it" repeatedly, while Aunt El' Nora beat him down with curse words. Then she gave us some spending money, and we walked with my three sisters to get some snacks, while our parents argued, yelled and cursed at each other. My mother worked on Saturday mornings.

We lived at 2006 Highland Place. I did like the street, because it had a large island, covered with vibrant green grass that separated the street, so that traffic flowed one way up and one way down Highland Place. The grassy island was a great place for kids to run up and down and play. The homes on Highland Place looked neat, and some of them were outstanding with beautiful flowers growing in the yards.

Happy to escape the yelling and cursing, my sisters and I walked with Delores down Highland Place, a right turn onto 21st Street and a couple of blocks to Boulevard Place, about four long blocks from the house. There was a store or shop on every corner and along the streets. There were two grocery stores, a clothing and shoe store, a beauty shop, barber shop, dry cleaners, and a doctor's office. A very nice drugstore was situated on the corner of 21st and Boulevard, but a group of sub-standard apartment buildings stood behind the drugstore.

There was a row of four, three story buildings. From some of the apartments, dingy beige curtains flapped in the wind, outside of unscreened windows. Little snotty-nosed Negro children ran around barefoot and poorly groomed, but they happily played in the building's courtyard. Loud music blared through open windows as some of the children's parents drank, yelled foul language, and physically fought each other.

A sleazy bar and pool hall stood on 21st Street, several feet away from the drug- store. Delores said, "That place is called The Bucket of Blood, because somebody is always getting cut or shot in there, and that's where your daddy goes to get drunk."

However, around the corner from the chaos of the sleazy bar and apartments, there was a clean and comfortable eatery, fondly referred to as "The Greasy Spoon." They served tasty, deep-fried shrimp and catfish, burgers, fries, chili dogs, malts, sodas, and everything that teenagers loved to eat. This was an acceptable place for me, Delores, and my three little sisters, and we thoroughly enjoyed our deep-fried shrimp, cole slaw, French fries and soda.

Moreover, there was a huge and brightly colored jukebox, which exceeded my height. However, the money slot was within reach of my little sisters. The jukebox stood on the floor in an easily accessible corner. It featured the latest rhythm and blues hits that cost twenty-five cents per song, or five songs for a dollar.

In the neighborhood, 21st Street and Boulevard was known as "The Corner." Delores pointed out that different groups of neighborhood fellows had their own corner to hangout on, and they stood around on their same corner every weekend. Since Delores and her family lived on a satisfactory street, a few blocks on the other side of "The Corner," she knew the area well and looked forward to showing me around as time progressed. While we crunched our shrimp and slurped our soda in "The Greasy Spoon," Delores continued providing information in her fast-talking, "Hoosier" accent.

She indicated that people had to catch the bus on "The Corner" to get downtown, to the movies, to school or wherever they were trying to get to, and sometimes they had to transfer from one bus to another. She said that's where our mothers, and other female workers, caught the bus that took them to their maid jobs in wealthy homes, way out in the White neighborhoods. Delores said our mothers were not maids because they do "day work," in different homes, and the more days they worked, the more money they made.

Delores warned me and my sisters to be careful and read the signs on the front of each bus, because different buses took you to different places, and she did not want us to get lost riding the bus or walking home. Our dollars in the Jukebox had played out, and our fried shrimp and treats were all gone. Reluctantly, we left the "Greasy Spoon," and Delores walked us down Boulevard for a couple of blocks, a right turn, and another right, delivered us back to Highland Place, across the street from where we lived, which means we walked home in the opposite direction so that my sisters and I could see the difference.

It was mid-afternoon by the time we walked back home. Daddy was gone, and Mother had returned home from her job, where she worked as a seamstress. Delores's mother was named Eleanor. She and Mother were having a discussion about Daddy's drinking. Mother said, "I know he's up on 'The Corner' drinking, but the kids and I still need to get some groceries." My sisters, Delores and I were happy to get a second walk to "The Corner" on the same day.

We fondly called Delores's mother, "Aunt Nodee," and all of us walked back down Highland Place, but we crossed over and walked up 21st Street on the opposite side from "The Bucket of Blood" and proceeded until we reached the market where my parents had an open account. Mom said the other market across the street charged more money for the same products, but that was Aunt Nodee's market of choice, and she had an open account there, which allowed them to "buy now, pay later." When I asked Mom why they shopped at different markets, she said, "So we don't have to walk across busy Boulevard carrying a lot of stuff." We waved good-bye to Delores and her mom as they crossed the street to do their shopping.

My parents' market of choice had a butcher shop in the meat department, and the butcher chopped and sliced whatever customers ordered. My senses automatically cringed from the sharp knives on the bloody butcher's block. It reminded me of hog killing time.

"Mr. Butcher" smiled broadly at my breasts when I gave him the meat order. A couple of weeks later, Daddy told Mother that "Mr. Butcher" said to him, "Why don't you put me nex to dat new young gal you got renting a room in yo house?" Daddy told the man, "You put me nex to yo fifteen year old daughter, and I'll put you nex to mines." He said the man's mouth flew open and his eyes got big as he mumbled his apologies. After that, whenever I ordered meat, "Mr. Butcher" did not smile broadly at my breasts, but I could feel his eyeball energy on them when I was not looking in his direction.

Nonetheless, for that shopping event, my sisters and I were happy with all of the food Mother had allowed us to select, including peanut butter, jelly, and cornflakes. As we happily grabbed up items, Mother reminded us that we had to carry them home. We left the market carrying heavy bags and wearing happy smiles. It was not long before our hands and arms were tired from the heavy load we were carrying. We sat our bags on the ground, shook and rubbed our hands and arms, picked up our load and walked as far as we could before we had to stop again and again.

By the time we made it home, our enthusiasm had waned. I put the groceries away and cooked dinner. There was always laundry, ironing, house cleaning, child care, and endless chores for me to do with Mother, who spent a lot of time cutting out patterns and making clothes for my sisters. She also made her own suits and dresses. Mother told me that I would have to make my own clothes in the future.

Between chores and when Daddy was not home, I ran across the street to drink iced tea, eat snacks, and listen to music with my first new friend in Indianapolis, Odeana. She and her family were long-time friends to Delores and family. Odeana was a left-handed cutie with pretty brown eyes, doll like eyelashes and dimples in her cheeks. Her black hair grew long, thick and beautiful, but she kept it cut short. She lived in a very nice single story home with her parents and older brother Earl, a recent high school graduate.

Amazingly, Odeana had her very own "lavishly" furnished bedroom, which contained a three-piece cherry wood bedroom set, a love seat and a table with two chairs for preparing homework. Moreover, the focal point in her room was the four-foot long, matching cherry wood stereo that stood on four legs, approximately two feet tall. The top opened like a cedar chest or trunk. The unit contained a radio and a turntable that played 78 rpm records and albums. There was also an attachable device that played the latest hit singles on 45 rpm records. She had all of the latest music, but she dearly loved Johnny Mathis and bought all of his recordings. Odeana's room was my favorite place to hang out, and I was not the only one. On weekends, her room was like a social club for several of her teenaged girlfriends and schoolmates.

Subsequently, Odeana's brother held a similar position with his older teenaged buddies, and some of them were in their early twenties. The fellows also hung out in Earl's room and on the spacious front porch where they played music, harmonized, told jokes, talked about girls and bragged about their cars. Still caught up in "basketball fever," everyone who came to Odeana's house boasted that Crispus Attucks High had won the state championship for 1955.

Unconcerned about the championship and ongoing celebrations, Daddy did not allow boys in cars to take me anyplace, but I was happy to hang out at Odeana's, especially when Delores came over. Delores, Odeana, and all of their friends made me feel like a welcomed member to the group. The few visits that I was able to sneak in with them made the time go faster, and then August was upon us.

8

BEATINGS, MAYHEM
AND MURDER

August came quickly, and it was time for me and Delores to ride the Greyhound Bus to Jackson and move Robert from Grandaddy Walker's farm to live with our family in Indianapolis. Robert was very attached to Grandaddy, and he did not want to move to Indianapolis and live with Daddy. Nobody wanted to live with Daddy! Robert was concerned that the farm work and animals would not do well without him, but our parents wanted all of us together, and Robert did not have a choice.

The day we left to get Robert, Mother and Aunt Nodee packed a shoe box full of home cooked fried chicken, potato salad, buttered dinner rolls, sweet potato pie and chocolate cake. After a few miles of riding on the bus, which seemed like forever, Delores and I gobbled down the pie and cake. We happily ran to buy hotdogs and sodas along the way. Then, we could not wait to use the bathroom at the next stop as the bus discharged and picked up other passengers. Things were going smoothly until we stopped in Kentucky and Tennessee, where there were "Colored and White only" bathrooms signs, which Delores promptly ignored. After the first one, I reluctantly went along with her, and we used the same stall together. Interestingly, as we darted in and out of the "White only" bathrooms, there was only one complaint. By the time some White person came looking for us, we had peed and gone.

Fortunately, we arrived safely, and Uncle Eddie and Robert were waiting in the Greyhound bus station when we finally arrived in Jackson. Robert, Delores, and I squealed with joy as we ran towards each other. We hugged and jumped up and down! Giggling, I ran towards my uncle. With a big grin, he said, "If y'all don't call me Uncle Eddie, I will drive off and make you walk home." Thirteen miles later, we were driving up the private dirt road to the house where I had lived the happiest five years of my young life. Upon arrival, Granddad's appearance was shocking to me. It had only been thirteen months since the last time I had seen him, but he looked a lot older, and his shoulders were hunched. Obviously, he was sad and still grief-stricken over the death of his beloved Mamie.

Even so, he smiled and seemed uplifted by our visit. After giving him a big hug, I slowly walked through every room in the house and reminisced over my cherished memories there. Soon, I was in the kitchen cooking and cleaning up for my grandfather and the rest of us. There were several relatives and friends to see, and some of them came to the house to visit. Jimmy Lee, Moo-Moo, and everyone else seems to have known that Delores and I were coming to take Robert away from all of them.

Our stay in Denmark was most enjoyable due to activities with relatives and St. John Baptist Church. All too soon our week-long visit was ending, and Uncle Eddie would drive us back to the Greyhound bus station.

Uncle Eddie drove us to the bus station in a timely manner. We were responsible teenagers with bus tickets in hand. There was no need for him to wait around for our bus to leave. A hug, a kiss on the cheek, a "Y'all be good," and we waved good-bye to Uncle Eddie.

He was pleased that a sixteen-year old male cousin, nicknamed Moo-Moo, and a lifelong sixteen-year old friend, Jimmy Lee, were waiting at the bus station to see us off. When we went to board our bus, we realized that our watches had Indianapolis time, and the buses were running on Jackson time. We were disappointed and grumbled for a few minutes. To avoid boredom, Delores, the guys, and I decided to walk around and look in the store windows nearby. Robert stayed in the bus station reading a comic book, eating chips, and drinking soda.

We had walked less than one block. Jimmy Lee and I were walking ahead of Delores and Moo-Moo. I had stopped to gaze through the window of a jewelry store and pointed towards a sparkling diamond that I would receive from my "Prince Charming" someday. Jimmy Lee chuckled. There were a few people on the street and cars passing by.

Suddenly, two screeching carloads of troublemaking White boys were upon us. As the two speeding cars screeched their tires and slammed the brakes, we recognized trouble and headed back to the bus station quickly. I could smell whiskey oozing from them. I knew that smell all too well. In their late teens, they were red-eyed and crazed over the senseless murder of Emmett Till. He was murdered on August 28, 1955, the day we were traveling back to Indianapolis. Word of mouth news circulated that fourteen-year-old Emmett had been lynched, castrated, and had his tongue cut out, because he reportedly "whistled at a White woman."

Three of the White boys had jumped out of the moving car to chase after Moo-Moo and Jimmy Lee, but both of the had sensed evil and sprinted away like the wind. Delores and I immediately headed back to the bus station. She was a few hundred feet in front of me, which placed her closer to the station. The remaining five troublemakers had stumbled out of the cars, calling us names and rendering threats.

By then, the three chasing bullies came staggering back, huffing and puffing, "We couldn' ketch them niggas." They only staggered a few feet, because they were too drunk to run anywhere. One of the boys yelled at me, "Hey lil' nigga what you doin out here?" I shot back, "Yo mama is a gotdammed nigga. Look at you, blacker than I will ever be," and his friends started laughing because the boy had a very dark tan. I said to another one, "And what are you laughing at? Look like a mule kicked all of your teeth down your throat, you snaggled tooth bastard." I went onto the next one, "And look at you, your head look like sheep shit in shallow water," and his friends laughed out loud at his uncombed curly hair. "And you, your face looks like five miles of gravel road," which described his acute case of acne. "Dumbo ears your ass ought to be in the jungle somewhere, and all of you smell like a herd of billy goats, living in a pig pen. You ought to go somewhere and wash your funky asses. And look at your little bony ass. A strong fart would blow you to hell. And you and your fat ass, I saw your manna walking down the street with a mattress on her back yelling curb service."

With every retort, I was swiftly walking towards the bus station. We had to pass by the police station, which was just a hop away from Greyhound. As we approached the station, an officer came out and asked, "You boys all right?"

Suddenly, the eight of them had other things to do. The officer disregarded me and walked back inside the station. Delores was waiting for me by the police station. We walked back inside the bus terminal and told Robert what happened. Delores said, "I can't believe how you were strolling along and steady running your mouth with those hoodlums." I said, "I can't believe it either. That wasn't me. That was Grandma Lizzy," and the three of us laughed and laughed, but our hearts cried over what we heard about Emmett Till.

When Robert, Delores, and I arrived back in Indianapolis and told our friends and family what happened, they thanked and praised God for our safe delivery. Since Emmett was only fourteen years old, his death brought cries of outrage and exposed wounds of injustice that minority people, and Negro men in particular, suffered on a continuous basis. In spite of our sorrow for Emmett and his family, especially his mother, the process of life moved forward.

School would be starting soon, and I looked forward to attending

Crispus Attucks. Years later, I learned that Attucks was built in 1927 because White residents did not want their children attending an integrated high school. Negro students who were enrolled in Arsenal Technical, Shortridge, or other schools, were removed from those high schools and forced to enroll in Crispus Attucks. The staff of Black educators had at least a Master's Degree, and many of them had earned a Ph.D. Teachers were recognized as high caliber educators, and the students were known as academic achievers who went on to colleges and universities and became successful professionals: educators, doctors, dentists, lawyers and entrepreneurs.

Moreover, Attucks had a basketball team that could not be defeated, and Delores's brother Willie Floyd was a star teammate with Oscar Robertson, "The Big O." Although I was a newcomer and did not see them play, I was elated that they had won the 1955 Indiana State championship and became the first Black school in the nation to win a state title. Hanging out at Odeana's and hearing Earl and the guys boisterously replay the championship peaked my anticipation for attending Attucks. Additionally, I had inherited status from being the first cousin of star forward, Willie Floyd Merriweather.

Imagine the crushing blow when Delores and I were not allowed to attend Crispus Attucks! Robert was enrolled in eighth grade at School 32 with our three younger sisters, but Delores and I had to attend Shortridge because "the district required us to do so," even though we lived closer to Attucks.

Odeana had been attending Shortridge for two years. No historical or integration mandate was found that would have required us to attend Shortridge, which initially opened in 1864 as the state's first free school. In 1955 it was located at 34th Street and Meridian Street. Minority students had attended Shortridge from the beginning, but the student population was predominately White. In 1927 the Indiana State Legislature passed the first desegregation laws. Reportedly, during that period of time in Indianapolis, the effects of the Ku Klux Klan were present in the city. Therefore, the construction of Crispus Attucks in 1927 created segregation by rule, or separate but equal, when all of the Negro students were removed from the other high schools and redirected to Attucks.

Delores and her family had moved in with us after the three renters had been given ample time to relocate. The house that we lived in had belonged to Daddy's older brother, Walter Lee, who was Uncle Walt to us. Unmarried and without children, Uncle Walt had died a few years earlier. It is unknown if Uncle Walt left a will or not, but his live-in girlfriend was determined to keep the house, and she told lies and falsified documents that did not hold up in court.

When the renters moved out, Aunt Nodee and her family occupied those rooms. Delores and her mom occupied the first floor bedroom. Mom and Dad moved into a second floor bedroom. Willie Floyd and his older sister Ruth occupied the other two bedrooms on the second floor, and my siblings and I remained sleeping in the attic and basement.

Even though disappointed about Attucks, I was very excited about going to school anywhere. For my first day at Shortridge, I dressed in one of my three new school outfits, aknee length, straight, black skirt with flared pleats at the bottom, a long sleeved white blouse with black polka dots, and black and white oxfords with white socks. The oxfords were a "must," and the white socks had to be rolled down over a piece of round, thick foam, that made our legs look like they were in the middle of a giant glazed doughnut. Delores had given me the foam and "how-to" practice sessions: put on socks, stick your feet through the foam, slide the foam up to the top of socks, roll down socks and foam below the ankles, then put on your oxfords. Capezio shoes and penny loafers were also popular footwear, but I was lucky to get oxfords.

When our parents gave us money for school clothes and supplies, Delores, Odeana and I rode the bus downtown together. We dashed into the expensive department stores, L. S. Ayers and W. H. Block. We enjoyed looking at the fashionable clothing, shoes and everything else in the stores. Block's also carried desirable shoes and clothes that were more affordable. I bought my shoes from Block's and so did Odeana and Delores.

For trendy fashions at lower prices, we would go to the Lerner Shop. We loved the bright colors and various styles that we could mix and match. The three of us bought the same styles in different colors. I bought a shrimp colored wool skirt with a matching sweater. Lambswool was popular but very itchy. As we browsed through the store, a long sleeved, formfitting dress caught our attention. The silver, shimmery color in the fabric was a fusion of black, white and gray, similar to the houndstooth pattern. The clingy material moved when we moved. Amused by the hood on the knee length dress and the oddness of the garment, all three of us bought one. We were not the only ones amused by our dresses. Every time we wore them, together or individually, the fellows commented: "Y'all look like the snake sisters."

Their commentary did not discourage us, and we wore our dresses to school and everywhere, knowing that we looked very "cool." Riding the bus to Shortridge with Odeana and Delores was a wonderful experience compared my first days at Washington Tech in St. Louis. Going back and forth to school with them was good, but I felt alone and misplaced in the classrooms, because I was the only Negro in most of my classes, and that was true for all of us attending Shortridge at the time. Odeana was two years ahead of me, and we did not have any classes in common. Delores frequently ditched school and went to hang out with her buddies at Crispus

Attucks. Odeana and I attended classes every day, but as the semester progressed, I was struggling to understand and keep up.

The academic structure and volumes of homework overwhelmed me compared to Washington Tech. Shortridge had a reputation for academic excellence, and most of the students went to college and beyond, including the upper class kids of Negro professionals, and I also hoped and dreamed of going to college, regardless of my family. Honor students studied Latin, French, Spanish and other languages. The curriculum was very comprehensive, and there were various clubs, including the Thespian Society. For several semesters I thought that thespians were a group of quirky, pale White kids who hung out in one particular room on the second floor. One day while having lunch in the cafeteria, I sat with a fellow Negro girl who proudly stated that she belonged to the Thespian Society. Confused, I told her what I thought thespians were. Bursting with giggles, she could hardly speak as she laughed, "Thespians study drama and the theater so that we can become actors." I also laughed, "Then they should call it the Actors Society."

Shortridge was also known as the "rich kids school," because many of their parents were indeed affluent. As time progressed, I met Wendy Block. We bought our shoes in her family's department store. I also met Elliot Lerner, whose family owned the Lerner Shops. Since Wendy and Elliot were rich and White, I was shocked that they were friendly and greeted me with a smile.

Odeana already knew them. She told me that they were nice because they were Jews, and Hitler had tried to kill off all of the Jewish people during the 'hollycost.' I had heard about the Jews during church services in St. John Baptist Church in Denmark. Reverend Nelson had preached many sermons about Moses and the children of Israel and that Jesus was a Jew, but I did not relate that to my schoolmates. I said, "Jews? What's the difference? All White people are White, and what's a "hollycost?" She explained that it's not "hollycost," it was the Holocaust. Later, she took me to the amazing school library and located books and articles for me to read on the subject before and during World War II. I could not believe the Nazi horrors that Hitler and his insane regime inflicted upon the Jewish and other people for several years: freezing cold concentration camps, starvation, torture, death ovens, and unbearable accounts of other atrocities. As I read, hot tears streamed down my face and dripped on the pages faster than I could wipe them away. I thought that White people hated us because we are strong and Black. Why would White people do something like that to other White people? I wept, "That's worse than slavery." None of that made any sense to me! Why couldn't people just be nice to one another?

Without knowing the word empathetic, reading about the Holocaust filled my consciousness with empathy for other ethnic groups and disdain for evil deeds. It also indicated that all White people are definitely not the same!

Shortridge was my first induction to integration and the caste system, although I did not know there was a caste system at the time. But I did become aware that there were the rich Jewish kids, upper class "snooty" Negro kids, upper class White kids and lower income Negroes and Whites. If there were any Latino or Asian students enrolled, I never did see or hear about them.

I learned some heartbreaking information about the viciousness and mental illness of war, the Jewish people, and other ethnic groups, but such learning did not translate to my first midterm grades, which were all D's and F's. Disappointment and discouragement became a part of my existence. I realized that while I had been chopping and picking cotton, most of my Shortridge schoolmates had been engaged in structured and progressive learning since birth. Even when we went to our rural elementary schools, there was no comparison to the academic structure and available teaching materials that they received. My A's and B's from Washington Tech reflected a disparity in academic excellence.

After the midterm grades, I tried even harder. I loved the school's library, and most of the bifocal-wearing, spinster-looking librarians were friendly and genuinely helpful. The library appeared very large to me with many study tables and chairs. Just going into the library made me feel smart. But I was not privileged to spend much time in the library, and it was not due to racism, even though all of the librarians were White. My library and study privileges were circumvented by Daddy and my family obligations.

After school, I had to take the first bus home so that I could look after my little sisters, do chores, and have dinner ready before Daddy came home from work, around 5:00 p.m. His work shift started at 6:00 a.m.

If Daddy came home and caught me sitting at the dining room table doing homework, he threatened to "whup my ass" if dinner was not on the table when he walked in. Usually, I was working in the kitchen by the time he was due home. Wherever I was within the kitchen, near the sink, refrigerator or stove, Daddy had to walk through that space and bump against my breasts. His covert actions made my blood boil and forced me to restrain my hands from throwing hot chicken frying grease in his face.

On most Fridays, Daddy came home from work, then he went drinking in "The Bucket of Blood" on 21st Street. But late one Friday evening in October, he came home smelling like whiskey. I had cooked dinner. The kids had eaten, and they were playing on the front porch and in the front yard. There was plenty of warm food on the stove for Daddy. The weather was pleasant, and I ran across the street to Odeana's for a few minutes.

Earl and the guys were on the front porch talking and laughing. Delores and a couple of other girls were in Odeana's room. The late evening sun was setting as I darted past the guys and their flirtatious comments, down the front porch steps and across the grassy island. As I ran towards home, I looked to my left and saw Daddy walking home. I did not look directly at him, but I felt his angry glare, knowing that he had seen the guys on Odeana's front porch. A huge lump stuck in my throat. I ran in the kitchen to fix his plate.

Daddy came huffing into the kitchen, clamped his big right hand on the back of my neck, pushed me ahead of him out the kitchen door to the back porch, grabbed the razor strap from a hook on the screened-in back porch. Still clinching the back of my neck, he steered me down the basement steps into the furnace room. Terror griped every cell in my body when he ripped off all my clothing and stared at my nakedness with bulging eyes. Every object in the area swirled around when he snatched me up off the floor and turned me upside down. He grabbed me and put his left arm under my stomach. My head dangled above the concrete floor, and my behind was slightly under his chin, and I could feel him breathing on my backside. He locked my head between his knees. Then he rubbed his hand all over my behind for what seemed like an eternity. My bare breasts felt smashed against his stomach, and my feet desperately kicked the air. As he rubbed my behind, I could hear and feel his heavy breathing and felt his erect penis pressing against the right side of my jaw and ear area.

After an infinite amount of rubbing my behind, the razor strap sent shock waves through my body as it cut the skin on my backside. I could not scream because I was suffocating between his funky thighs. He beat me until he ran out of breath.

By then my three sisters were jumping up and down and screaming at the top of the basement steps. Daddy dropped me, and I crashed in a puddle of water on the cold floor. Still breathing heavy, he cursed and yelled at my sisters as he went up the steps, and they came running and crying to check on me. Scrambling to put my clothes on, I realized that the puddle of water on the floor came from me. Embarrassment washed over me when my younger siblings noticed the wetness and helped me get dressed.

Daddy's razor strap left bloody slash marks on my behind and the back of my thighs. My breasts ached. I had a thundering headache, and my disheveled hair looked like I had been shocked with powerful electrodes.

The trauma of the beating caused my monthly cycle to start. In general, that time of the month was unusually painful and required doctor visits and medication. I was hoping that the physical assault had been a nightmare that I would wake up from, but it was not. I don't know who called the police, but by the time they arrived, Daddy was long gone. Mother had made it home from work. Her seamstress job had required her to work a few hours over her regular shift, because they had to complete an order of commercial uniforms.

Two White police officers responded and asked what happened. I was reluctant to say much, because there was a noticeable smell of liquor on them, but I told them what happened nonetheless. Mother could not provide any information because she was not there at the time. My three sisters told what they had seen. Before the officers left, Delores and Odeana were standing beside me. Robert had made it home from wherever he had been. Earl and the fellows were standing in their yard looking at our house and so were most of the other neighbors, but Daddy was gone to "The Bucket of Blood."

Barely a few months in Indianapolis and my life was an inescapable living hell. My greatest offense was having been born my Daddy's daughter. When Aunt Nodee came home and heard that Daddy had beaten me bloody, she responded angrily. Daddy knew that she would fight him if necessary. He knew that she would hit him on his head with the brother, but that did not stop him from attacking us when she was not present.

Emotionally upset and fearful, my sisters and I were in bed but not sleeping when Daddy came home. Several hours had passed when Daddy came home sloppy drunk from "The Bucket of Blood." Aunt Nodee yelled and cursed at him for jumping on me for no good reason. She yelled, "Othelder you bout the biggest gotdammed fool I have ever seen. You crazy out of yo drunk-assed mind," but Daddy was too intoxicated to understand or care what she said.

Painfully, time and life dragged on. It was a longtime before I went to hang out at Odeana's. After the beating I felt humiliated and unwilling to face my peers. I was ashamed of my Dad, and I feared and hated him. My angry thoughts focused on how many different ways I could kill him.

On one occasion, a Saturday afternoon as he began drinking, he told me to fix his plate. I loaded his food with rat poison. Before he gobbled down the poison, mentally I heard a clinking sound and saw myself locked behind steel bars. Knowing that he was not worth jail time, I snatched the plate away from him as he cursed and yelled at me for taking his food.

I resorted to my mental survival tool from the log cabin. I knocked Daddy to the ground, on his back, and stabbed him with my pitchfork from his head to his toes, with blood spurting through the holes in his body like an oil gusher.

With my injured body and broken spirit, cramps from my menstrual cycle made me even more miserable. Excessive cramping, nausea and vomiting came with every cycle. The smell of food made me feel sick to my stomach and caused gagging. Intense pain streamed through my abdominal area. My head felt like someone was hammering three inch nails into my temples, which caused excruciating pain. My eyeballs ached from bright lights, and loud sounds sent more pain waves rushing through my head. For the first three days of the cycle, all I could do was crawl into bed, curl into the fetal position, rock, moan and cry while holding my stomach. Frequently, I clinched my fists, closed my eyes, and prayed to die. Welcome death and set me free from Daddy and the cramps!

As time dragged into the future, Mother took me to see Doctor Brown. The Negro doctor's office was on Boulevard, next door to "The Greasy Spoon." The doctor gave me a shot in my right hip. It stopped the menstrual pain but caused stinging needle pain. I preferred the needle. He also prescribed some dark green, jumbo pills about the size of the first joint on my index finger. One time I had a near-death choking experience trying to swallow the huge pills, and that made me avoid taking them as prescribed.

Mother and I wanted to know why my periods were so extreme. We did not know anybody who suffered so greatly from a monthly period. The doctor explained that my symptoms fit the description of an unusual condition called "dysmenorrhea." Mother sighed, " Dis-mina-what? Lord have mercy, I hope it don't kill her."

Mother made an appointment for me to have a complete medical exam when my period was over. After the exam, Dr. Brown explained to me and Mother that my uterus was twisted, and the tip of it slightly protruded into my vaginal track, which prevented me from wearing tampons. It also added another layer of agony when I was raped.

Gathering family history and information, Dr. Brown asked if I had ever lifted heavy objects that caused pain, strain, or discomfort? Heavy objects! I told him that my Dad had made us do all kinds of hard work when we lived on a farm in Tennessee.

Recalling a painful incident, I told the doctor that when I was approximately eight years old, I was injured by a sack of falling fertilizer.

Every fall season, after Daddy sold the cotton, he bought cotton seeds and fertilizer for planting the next crop. He had bought and stored several twenty-five pound bags of fertilizer in the barn's hay loft. He stored the bags by putting a sack on one shoulder, then he climbed up the ladder just high enough to roll the sacks from his shoulder on to the hay loft floor, where they remained dry until the spring season.

When it was spring time, Daddy started preparing the soil for planting, and he had to get the fertilizer sacks down from the hay loft. Instead of bringing down the sacks the same way he took them up, he used me. He opened the door at the front of the hay loft and told me to catch the sacks so that they would not break open from hitting the ground when he dropped them.

I stood on the ground looking up at Daddy with outstretched arms in front of me, palms up, elbows back, ready to catch. He dropped the first sack. I caught it, but the impact caused ripping sensations, and hot burning pain shot through my stomach, back, arms and legs. Screams erupted from my throat, caused by shock and pain. My body crumbled on the ground. Paralyzed by pain, I wiggled around on the ground, clutched my stomach and tried to breathe. I remember desperately trying to stand up before Daddy beat me with the bull whip for falling down. But I could not move, even when Daddy came rushing towards me. He said, "Git up gal. Whut's da matter wid yu. Git up and take yo ass to da house."

After a few minutes on the ground and fear of the bull whip, Robert helped me up off of the ground, but I could not stand up straight. Bending forward like a very, very old lady with back problems, Robert helped me hobble to the house, an estimated distance equivalent to a couple of long city blocks. With every step my abdominal area throbbed with excruciating pain.

When Mother saw my tears and condition, she asked what did Daddy beat me for? I explained that he had not beaten me, and I told her what happened. She moaned, mumbled some words under her breath and shook her head in disgust over Daddy's stupidity. The only thing I could do was barely get myself into bed and cry myself to sleep. The next morning I could not get out of bed. My body felt broken and sore. Before I went to sleep, Mother gave me a hot tea home remedy, made from the bark of a sassafras tree. She also heated up a brick on the wood-burning stove, wrapped it in clean, white cloth and told me to rub it where I hurt.

My low back and stomach continued to burn. It was so bad, Mother insisted that I should be taken to see Dr. Meachum in Jackson, and Daddy had to take me, but I had to get well enough to go. I don't remember what day it was, but I do recall the long walk, about two miles or more, through the fields and woods to the main road, to catch a ride to Jackson. Cousin Joe Bond lived on the main road, and he drove me and Daddy to and from Jackson in his black pick-up truck. He claimed that he was "jest gittin ready to run to Jackson."

Walking to the main road, I could not keep up with Daddy's long steps, and I was in no condition to be walking that distance to begin with. By the time we arrived in Jackson and walked up the steps to the doctor's office on the second floor, I was in extreme discomfort and tried not to show it, but the doctor knew. When he asked Daddy if I had lifted anything heavy or straining, Daddy's eyes shot me a look that said, "Gal keep yo gotdammed mouth shet." Daddy lied, " Naw-suh" to all of the doctor's questions that pointed to the truth of my injuries. Dr. Meachum's caring eyes gave me a look that said, "Don't worry. I know that you are scared, and he is lying." On the exam table, everywhere the doctor touched my body, I flinched from pain. The doctor gave me an injection in my upper right hip and told me I was brave for not fearing the needle.

Perhaps he sensed that nothing was more fearful to me than my own dad. The doctor told Daddy to make sure that I did not strain myself doing heavy farm work. "Yas Suh," Daddy lied again. After the doctor visit, we went down the hall and down the steps to the Colored drug store where Daddy picked up the medications for my injuries. He also bought a few sundry items that Mother had written on a little piece of paper that Daddy handed to the drug store clerk. My most healing medication was a strawberry ice cream cone, and I selected a big bag of candy to take home to my brother and sisters. Now flash forward, back to Indianapolis and my visit with Doctor Brown, after Daddy physically assaulted me.

9

SHORTRIDGE HIGH SCHOOL AND "UNEDUCABLE"

After explaining my abdominal injury caused by Daddy, Dr. Brown was seemingly spellbound over my outpouring of family history. When I stopped to catch my breath, Dr. Brown further stated that dysmenorrhea is a menstrual medical condition that many women suffer from, and catching a twenty five pound sack of fertilizer would not necessarily cause the condition, but the impact probably caused the dislocation of my uterus.

Following my visit to Dr, Brown, a few days of recovery and medication, I was riding the bus to school with Odeana and Delores. Relating to schoolwork was difficult with all of the drama taking place at home. In spite of that, I loved school and all of the activities and excitement that went on, even though I could not be a part of it. Just being in the "rich" Shortridge environment allowed me a few hours of freedom to daydream and escape from my living prison.

Soon it was time for final exams. Delores and I were in the same History class. Except for illness and injuries from beatings, I went to all of my classes while Delores hung out at Crispus Attucks. On the final exam, Delores got a "C," and I received a "F," which stunned and dismayed me. I cried over it in the girls' bathroom. Final grades for all of my classes were "D's" and "F's."

When Aunt Nodee heard that Delores got a "C" in History and I got a "F," she laughed as she told me, "Ann you bout dummer than cat shit, sittin up in class every day. Delores didn't even take her dumb ass to school, and she passed and you didn't. Ha-ha-ha-ha!"

Without any tutorial help, study groups, or counseling from school, and no time, place or privilege to study at home, my grades and I suffered through Shortridge. For my second semester I was placed in all "R" classes. Fellow students who recognized the class rooms taunted us that "R" stood for retarded. Several years later I learned that "R" meant remedial, but none of my teachers intended to find a remedy or cure for my learning difficulties.

Nonetheless, I enjoyed learning what I learned, and my bird-watching class provided an interesting learning experience. The teacher walked us to a wooded area near the school's campus. Students were required to bring a stack of 3x5 index cards and pens or pencils. We numbered our cards to identify the various birds. The teacher cautioned us to be quiet as we tiptoed through the leaves and twigs on the ground to watch birds. Invariably, some fun-loving, mischievous, boys would fake a loud cough and make the birds scatter, after the class had sat quietly for several minutes, waiting for them to appear. Birdwatching was fun, and I passed the class with a "C."

Music Appreciation was a required class and initially hated by most students, and I was one of them. The boom-boom-boom and slow eerie sounds were irritating. We wanted to hear Chuck Berry play "Roll Over Beethoven."

One day our teacher played Handel's Messiah, and the soft tears running down my cheeks caught me totally off guard. I did not understand why the music evoked tears, but it did. By the end of the semester, I had fallen in love with Handel, Bach, Mozart, Beethoven, Mendelssohn, Chopin and Wagner, but especially Beethoven. During the semester, the teacher, Mr. Wise, played the 78rpm records on his little turntable. He also provided historical data on each artist.

For the final exam, Mr. Wise played various musical selections as he had done during the semester. We listened, identified the artist, and title, and wrote answers on our test papers. We also had to fill in the blanks with historical information.

There was one other component of Music Appreciation. A Stradivarius violin was mounted high on gold satin material and locked inside of an elegant glass case. The beautiful case was in the hallway, next door to the Music Appreciation classroom, and students had to bow down and salute Stradivarius before entering class. Not really, but the teacher treasured it, and we also had to learn the history of the Stradivarius violin and fill in the blanks on the final exam.

Music Appreciation was one of the few classes where I made a "B," and classical music has calmed my nerves and uplifted my spirit through the years. However, my love of country music from The Grand Ole Opry, earned me the title of "Hillbilly Annie" from my neighborhood peer, who also called me "The Tennessee Ridge Runner." Music has always provided some joy in my life and so has the fun of cooking.

Home Economics was fun, even though we had to follow recipes instead of "a pinch of this and a dab of that." Mouthwatering aromas floated through the hallways and brought the guys running for samples. My final grade was a "B," which brought a big smile to my face.

Sewing was also fun, and whatever we chose to sew, we had to model in our final exam fashion show. Since Mother was a seamstress, I knew how to sew, but altering patterns and designing my own fashions was creative, stimulating and more fun. Sewing was familiar but meeting a blind typewriter in my typing class was interesting and intriguing. Lack of the alphabet, numbers and symbols on the typewriter keys rendered it "blind." It was a manual machine, and our fingers were the driving force. At the end of every sentence, we had to reach up, push the lever on the left hand side of the typewriter and "throw the carriage" to begin typing the next line. The brightly colored typing chart hung on the blackboard and showed the alphabet, numbers and symbols as they would have appeared on the keyboard. We learned to type by touch, and I earned a "B." Upon completing Typewriting III, I was typing 70 words per minute. Otherwise, I flunked most of my classes each semester and passed them with a "D" the second time around.

Odeana did well in Shortridge and most of her grades were "B's" and "C's." When she graduated in 1957, I felt abandoned, but Robert was also attending Shortridge, and we would still be riding the bus together.

I did have a few school buddies, and one of them was an attractive blond girl. Her hair was cut in a short pixie style, with wispy strands combed forward on her forehead. We empathized with each other due to physical circumstances. Her breasts were much larger than mine, and insensitive boys nicknamed her "Jugs."

My nickname was "Chesty," which was also the name of everyone's favorite potato chips. Whenever I snapped back at the boys, "My name is not Chesty," they laughed loudly and claimed that they were just talking about potato chips. Actually, I preferred "Chesty," because my other nickname was "Tits."

"Jugs" and I were in the same Biology class. When we walked together in the hallways, the boys taunted, "Here come Tits and Jugs." After Biology, we went to lunch and frequently sat together in the cafeteria. Empathy caused us to became "breast friends." "Jugs" had a strong personality, and a sense of humor.

We did some gross things in Biology, but "Jugs" always made jokes about it. One time we had to dissect a pig fetus. It made me sick to my stomach and reminded me of hog killing time.

I remember one assignment required us to examine a live frog's foot under the microscope. Our student worksheet contained a list of things to identify in the frog's foot. The assignment required us to work in pairs, and "Jugs" was my partner. Studying Biology was the first time I had ever looked at something through a microscope, and I was awe-stricken and excited.

After class we went to lunch, as usual. We finished eating, and "Jugs" opened her bag to show me that she "rescued" our frog. Apparently, the frog heard her and leaped up out of the bag. I screeched when the frog leaped. "Jugs" giggled and screamed as she jumped up to catch it. The frog leaped over to the next table and landed in a bowl of chili that some boy was eating, and he jumped up hollering.

Kids jumping around, laughing, and yelling created temporary pandemonium and brought school staff running onto the scene. "Jugs" chased after the frog, which left a chili trail as it leaped around the cafeteria. Confusion and exhaustion probably brought the frog to a halt. With glazed eyes, it sat on the cafeteria floor in a corner, huffing and puffing. "Jugs" picked it up. The frog was returned to Biology, and "Jugs" had to serve several days in study hall.

My home life did not provide study time, as revealed by my grades. At the age of eighteen and beginning my senior year, the principal summoned me from class to report to his office. Usually students were summoned to the principal's office for getting in trouble. I had never cut school nor violated any rules. What could it be?

I squirmed in the outer office chair for a few minutes before the secretary told me to go into the principal's office. My heart felt like it was pounding inside of my ears. The principal, Mr. Hadley, motioned for me to sit down. His eyes peered at me above his black horn-rimmed bifocals. While shuffling papers inside of a folder, he said "I have your school records here. You are performing below standards. You should be a graduating senior, but you barely have junior credits due to failed grades. Perhaps you should drop out and get a job at Western Electric. You don't need a high school diploma to work there. You are uneducable and non-college material." Everyone of his negative words stung me like a swarm of disrupted bees, and angry tears flowed.

"Uneducable!" I sprang from my chair and told him, "You old four-eyed, flat-assed pecker wood! I have you know that I learned everything I know. Yo mama is uneducable or she never would have had your dumb ass." The secretary stared at me wide-eyed and open-mouthed as I ran from the office, down the hall, around the corner, into the girls' bathroom, locked myself in a stall and cried my eyes dry. I had daydreamed about going away to college and becoming an elementary school teacher. Damned at school! Doomed at home! What was I supposed to do? I thought, "They might flunk me out, but I'm not dropping out."

At home my dysfunctional family continued without the "fun." The principal's discouragement made me determined to keep going until I graduated. When I told Mother about the incident, she said "I thought they were supposed to be teaching you something."

Midterm exams approached, and I told Mother that I wanted to study with my friend Jackie and some other students and make passing grades. Jackie and I were in the same general math class, and we became good friends in the cooking class. She was a cute and friendly Negro girl with a shapely figure. We were in the same age and size division. She wore pretty clothes, and her hair always looked great. She pressed, curled, and styled her own hair, as well as everyone's hair in her family. On weekends she earned spending money by doing hair for others. A few years after graduation, she opened her own beauty shop.

Meanwhile, Mother knew Jackie's family and agreed to the anticipated study session in their home, a few miles from where we lived. On the day of the study session I went home with Jackie after school. She lived in a well furnished and comfortable home with her parents and three younger teenaged siblings - a sister and two brothers. Jackie's siblings and mother were home when we arrived. Her mother was doing chores and preparing dinner. Tempting aromas of chicken and dumplings floated from the kitchen and made me wish that I was staying for dinner.

Jackie cleared everything from their spacious dining room table so that we could use the space to read and write. For the study session Jackie had made Kool-Aid and lots of sugar cookies, which distracted the study group from the chicken and dumplings. The cookie recipe was from our cooking class.

There were eight of us for the study session, five girls and three boys. I had seen them at school but did not know everyone's name. I was happy to meet some new friends. We started with general math. I never did make it to algebra. We worked through several problems, and my confidence increased with every problem that I solved correctly. Fellow student, Charles, reminded us that we could not spend all of our study time on math, and we moved on to English, American History, and Social Studies.

I temporarily froze in fear when I looked up and saw Jackie's big, stocky father quietly standing in the archway to the dining room, observing us at his dining room table. Jackie smiled and said "Hi Daddy." He answered "Hi Baby." She introduced me. He knew all of the other kids. He said "I don't mean to disturb y'all. Keep studying and make good grades," as he smiled and left the room. Relieved and amazed, I wondered why Daddy couldn't be like that.

Approximately four hours later, our study session was over, and I felt assured that I would pass my midterm exams. Charles offered me a ride home and saved me from waiting for the bus and riding home alone.

Charles and I wished each other good luck on our midterms. I thanked him and got out of his car in front of our home. Feeling better than ever about school, I bounced up the steps into our front yard.

Daddy pounced up from behind the shrubs, swinging the razor strap like a madman. The tip of the razor strap delivered a blinding blow to my right eye! Stars flickered! Sharp pains swirled around inside my eye and circulated through every nerve fiber in my body. My head and inner ears throbbed in agony and induced nausea. I covered both of my eyes and face with my hands. Screams from fear and pain rushed from my throat. I could not see, but heard Daddy yelling, "Dis don't look lak no homework ta me," as he repeatedly pounded me on my head, back, shoulders and arms. I heard my book bag fall on the ground and papers scattered in the wind. I heard the tires burn rubber as Charles sped away.

Having a harmless thing spring from behind the bushes was startling within itself, but an unwarranted assault by a crazy monster surpassed any horror movies that I would see in the future.

As I cringed and screamed from every blow, my family came running out the front door into the yard. Neighbors gathered in their yards and stared at our house. My siblings cried. Mother fussed at Daddy, "Othelder I told her that she could go." I cried, "All the boy did was give me a ride home from Jackie's so that I wouldn't have to ride the bus." Aunt Nodee yelled and cursed at Daddy.

By the time police arrived, Daddy was gone. It was a weekday around the second week of November when Daddy ambushed me, and he was not even drunk, but he had a few drinks while he was up on "The Corner."

The following morning was a work day, and Daddy never missed, no matter how drunk he had been. I was unable to attend school the following morning because my black-and-blue right eye was swollen shut and throbbed in pain. I had not realized that the razor strap struck the back of my right hand. When I woke up, it was stiff, and I could not open and close my fingers without pain. Attending school would have been futile. I could not see or use my right hand to grip a pen for my midterm exams.

Before Mother went to work she told me to go see Dr. Brown. Around 10:00 a.m., I managed to get out of bed and gathered the strength to walk to the doctor's office. My right eye was closed and throbbing with every step, and the sun's glare also caused my left eye to ache. Terror gripped my imagination, because I thought for sure that I was totally blind in my right eye.

When I walked into the doctor's office, the nurse's eyes showed concern when she observed the condition of my eye. After a few minutes, she ushered me into the exam room, and I sat on a chair. Without delay, the doctor entered the room and asked several questions as he examined and documented my injuries. He used a hand-held cylinder light to examine my eyes and face. He irrigated my eyes with a soothing solution, and he applied some cream to the area. Then he placed a comfortable piece of gauze over my right eye and covered it with white tape. He bandaged it to my nose and the right side of my face, which made me feel unbalanced.

He advised me not to touch the eye dressing and to be careful. Only Dr. Brown's professionalism prevented him from spewing angry words about Daddy as I explained that he had beaten me with a razor strap and why. I saw smoldering rage in Dr. Brown's eyes when he clinched his teeth and his temples pulsated over the details and insanity of my abuse. He assured me that I was not blind and that my eye would heal. After making an appointment for a follow-up visit, he gave me a few pills to prevent pain and nausea.

Feeling better from the empathy shown by the doctor and nurse, I walked back home, took two pills, got into bed and covered up my head, but I could not sleep. Wishing that I could have gone to school, silent tears leaked into the right eye patch and some trickled down my left cheek. I pitied myself and wished that I was dead.

Moreover, I wished that Daddy was dead and that he had died long before I was ever born! He had to be totally insane for a lifetime of unwarranted abuse upon me and my siblings. Even as young children living in the backwoods, we knew that Daddy was crazy, but we were powerless to do anything about his behavior or our condition.

My siblings and I, especially Loretta, wondered what was wrong with Mother for staying with him and allowing him to terrify and abuse us? Loretta had explained that since Daddy did not beat up on Mother, she did not feel our pain when he brutalized us. Loretta frequently stated that if a man ever beat her kids the way Daddy beat us, she would "kill him, spit on him, step over his dead ass and never look back." Loretta was an equal opportunity hater of both parents, but hatred did not bring about a positive change.

Even so, I hated Daddy to the core and wanted to kill him for hitting me in my eye for studying. The only thing that prevented me from killing him was my clear understanding that I would go to jail, no matter what he had already done to us, and he was not worth my life in prison, but I would be better off dead.

One day when I was home alone with my damaged eye and feeling sorrowful, I thought of killing myself, but I did not know exactly how to do it. Perhaps if I plunged head first from my third floor attic window, I would crash on my head and die. I kneeled on my knees, staring down at the ground with my left eye, weeping for my siblings when they discovered my lifeless, cold body lying crumpled on the ground.

I rationalized that Mother did not care, because she did not protect nor defend us from Daddy's abuse. Furthermore, all of my life she had fussed and complained about how much better off she would have been if she never had us. As far as she was concerned, having babies was the worst thing that could ever happen to a woman.

I felt the childhood pain of her yanking my short hair and burning my scalp with melted hot grease from the pressing comb, because my hair was too short to straighten without touching my scalp. She never hugged us or told us that she loved us, never baked a birthday cake. So I felt like she didn't care, but my siblings would have been devastated by their grief over my death.

Contemplating my demise drained me. Kneeling on my knees in front of the attic window, I dozed off and dreamed a nightmare. In the dream, I dove head first out of the window, crashed on the ground, broke my back, and both legs below my knees. I was confined to a wheelchair, and Daddy was beating me on my head, face, arms and chest with the razor strap. He was cursing and yelling at me with every strike for breaking my back and legs. He cursed at me for not being able to cook, take care of the kids and do chores.

I screamed and covered my face with my hands, which snapped me out of the nightmare. My head ached, and my knees were stiff. Blood rushed through my veins like a flooding river, and my heart pounded loudly in my ears. I felt truly happy that my legs and back were not broken, and I was able to get up from the floor. Somehow that nightmare provided the determination for me to stand up, look forward to turning eighteen and escaping my parents. That was my last suicidal ideation.

Upon my return visit to Dr. Brown, he removed the eye dressing, and I could see clearly, but my eye was sensitive to light. Again, he irrigated both of my eyes and applied cream around my eye and cheek. He sent me home with a supply of eye solution, eye cream, sunglasses and a pirate's patch.

I returned to school with a doctor's note and took the midterm makeup exams. Surprise and disappointment did not overwhelm me from the failing grades. After failing the midterm, my miserable bookkeeping teacher, Ms. Gripenstroph, called me up to her desk and said "You will never pass bookkeeping." She was built like a six-foot fingernail file. Her teeth protruded like she had sucked her thumb since birth. She wore thick eyeglasses, and she presented a caustic disposition towards me.

Bookkeeping was important to me. I figured that if I could not go to college, I could type and do office work. Therefore, I took it the following semester. On the first day of class, Ms. Gripenstroph walked up, stood beside my desk and hissed, "You will never pass bookkeeping." When I failed the class for the third time, I knew that I would never pass bookkeeping, because she was the only one teaching the class.

Passing classes was a double challenge and far beyond my control. I felt like Dad hated everything except drinking alcohol and physically abusing his children. Seemingly, my teachers hated me for being Negro and attending Shortridge. Even when my class assignments were well done, I did not believe that I received the corresponding grade. That painful truth revealed itself in my social studies-current events class at the beginning of senior year. The captain of the football team always sat next to me in social studies. We had a secret crush on each other. It was very secret. He was a husky, handsome White boy with ocean blue eyes and light brown hair, which he wore in a short, spiked cut. He and some of the other White boys and girls were pledging for something that required each pledgee to carry a cigar box filled with suckers and many other popular candies. I had free access to all of the candy in the captain's cigar box, and we also used it to exchange notes to each other.

During the semester, the captain missed several days of class. One time while he was absent, the class had written and handed in a current events assignment. To complete the assignment, I went to the library where a friendly librarian helped. Upon completion, she read my paper and said, "Very good, your assignment is well written." The teacher gave me a "C."

The captain came to class a few minutes late on the same day the teacher returned our graded assignment. When he asked about the assignment, I showed him my paper. He asked if he could copy what I had written. I asked, "What if you get caught?" He flashed a big smile and those pleading blue eyes as he emphasized, "The teacher will never know the difference." He passed me the cigar box, and I passed him my two page hand-written assignment. Rapidly, he copied it verbatim, including my name.

Observing my name on his paper, I pointed it out and covered my mouth with both hands to stifle the giggles. He chuckled as he quickly erased my name and wrote his. Then he rushed to the teacher's desk, said some flattering things to her and handed her his assignment. Class was dismissed, but he remained at the teacher's desk, and I waited by the lockers in the hall, holding his cigar box. In a couple of minutes, he dashed out of the classroom with a big smile and his graded paper.

When I noticed the huge red "A" on my work, I gasped and hot tears flooded my face. Disturbed and upset by what he had witnessed, the football captain cursed and pounded a locker with the palm of his hand. His pounding and my tears immediately

brought unwanted attention. I made a fast dash to the nearest girl's bathroom, locked myself in a stall, covered my face with both hands and cried. Finally, there was no more body shaking sobbing. Rubbing the last tears away with my hands revealed that I had run off with the cigar box. In spite of the circumstances, the cigar box made me smile. I went to the sink, washed my face in cold water, left the bathroom and ate candy.

That big red "A" did me more good than harm. The teacher confirmed that I was smart and capable and that she, the bookkeeping teacher, the principal, and most of the teaching staff were racists.

The captain did not come to class the following day, but I was there with his cigar box, which contained fewer candies. The next day he came to class with a new cigar box full of candy. Perplexed, he apologized for the teacher's injustice, but we did not know what to do about it. Therefore, school and life continued the status quo.

After Odeana graduated in 1957, Al offered me and Robert a ride to school. Al was a young man who lived with his parents, directly across the street from us. He taught math and music in an elementary school near Shortridge.

I was six years younger than Al, but he appeared very youthful and chuckled over the fact that he had to show identification when attempting to buy liquor. Al told me that on Friday and Saturday nights, he played tenor saxophone with a jazz band in an upscale Negro-owned nightclub, where the men wore suits and ties, and the ladies wore fashionable suits and fancy dresses.

As time progressed, my dream of wearing a fancy dress and high-heeled shoes came true when Ruth took me, Delores and Odeana to the nightclub to hear Al and the band play. I wore a tan, short-sleeved, form-fitting dress. It criss-crossed my chest and had a long zipper down the back. The dress also had four criss-cross loops around the waist, which held the black elasticized belt in place and made my waist appear smaller than it was. The black high-heeled pumps pinched my toes, but the added height and excitement of being there was well worth the pinch.

Al's big smile and beaming eyes transmitted his joy of seeing me all dressed up. He gently hugged me and introduced all of us to his fellow musicians, and I could feel their eyes rapidly dart over my chest. Al fit the stereotypical description of a "preppy" or a "nerd," with his black horn-rimmed glasses and scalp-short hair cut. He dressed fashionably in creased slacks and shined shoes. He wore colorful V-neck sweaters over a white shirt with a black or colorful bow-tie and a variety of blazers. Al's kindness and concern about my academic performance reminded me of Ellis. Al was comforting, and he empathized with me regarding my abusive, alcoholic father and our chaotic home environment.

Everyone in the neighborhood knew that the police frequently responded to our home, and we knew that the neighbors called them. Calling the police on Daddy never occurred to me or anyone in our family. It was impossible for me to call during an assault, and afterwards Daddy always rushed to "The Corner," and we rushed to treat our injuries.

For those reasons and more, Al was especially compassionate towards me. He had a dear friend who had a beautiful wife, a five-year-old son, and a three-year-old daughter. With Mother's permission, on Sunday afternoons when Dad was in deep hang-over sleep, Al took me and my school work to his friend's home. The couple made their kitchen table available for homework. Consequently my grades improved from "F" to "D."

Certainly, I looked forward to these sessions, because Al always took me to a very nice restaurant afterwards where we could talk and fall in love. Even though he never spoke of it or made any moves, I could feel his tender emotions for me, and I was daydreaming of becoming his bride. In my mind, my daydreams were validated on my eighteenth birthday when Al gave me a pearl necklace on a gold chain with matching pearl earrings that clamped on, because my ears were not pierced. I was anxious to graduate, because I knew that a teacher and accomplished musician would not marry a high school dropout.

Meanwhile, Odeana was enjoying the benefits of her Shortridge diploma and making good money as a key punch operator. Delores had quit school, fell in love with Tobie, and they got married. She gave birth to a beautiful baby girl in 1957 and named her Sherri. She was a bright baby who functioned in fast forward. At eight-months-old, she could say little words like "no," "go," "mama," and "eat." From fast crawling, she stood up and walked on her own when she was approximately nine-months-old. We nicknamed her "Sputnik," because we thought that she was just as bright and fast as the Sputnik rocket that Russia launched on October 4, 1957.

When the Soviet Union launched Sputnik into outer space, it was big news, and Nikita Khrushchev, a communist party leader, promised to "bury" the United States, but the United States and life continued until school was out for summer. It was June 1958, the year I should have graduated.

With school out, Al did not have a justifiable reason for seeing me every Sunday afternoon to help with homework. But he found many reasons to keep seeing me. He provided magazines and books to read, and he would ask content questions, which I answered comprehensively. He also gave me little writing assignments, which he checked and praised. He told me that I was a good writer.

During that summer, I did some "daywork" to earn my own money. Since Mother worked as a seamstress, she no longer did day-work. To avoid Daddy's weekend, drunken drama, Mother also worked on Friday and Saturday nights. She was the clerk and housekeeper in a Negro-owned motel, approximately three miles from home. However, Aunt Nodee's employer had a friend who occasionally needed her house cleaned, and my Aunt referred me, and I was willing to earn some money.

10

GIRL SHOT AND
A MAN MURDERED

One Thursday afternoon I returned from daywork and got off of the bus on "The Corner," where I had planned to pick up some sundry items from the drug store and walk home as usual. The instant my feet touched the pavement from getting off the bus, several familiar faces with sad eyes and worried expressions rushed towards me. I sensed that something was seriously wrong, and my heart started beating faster.

The familiar faces spoke in unison, "Delores got shot." I screamed "Oh no!" and dashed towards home with burning tears running faster than I was. The bearers of the bad news ran along beside me. Everyone talked at once, each anxious to tell what they had heard. Someone said, "Tobie lost his mind and shot her three or four times." Another voice consoled, "He didn't kill her though." Someone else said, "The ambulance took her to General Hospital." Another voice trailed, "The police are looking for Tobie's ass right now." Someone else shouted "He's already in jail."

I was so filled with fear, anger and worry over Delores, I did not remember running home, but suddenly I was there. In disbelief and shock, I cried and stared at the bullet holes in the living room wall, bullet holes and blood on the stuffed chair and pillows where Delores sat when Tobie shot her.

Ruth heard me, and came running as she cried, "I can't believe he shot my baby sister." Ruth and Aunt Nodee were home when Tobie came to the house shortly after I left for work around 8:00 a.m. He begged Delores to take him back just one more time. Delores and "Sputnik" had moved back home with us about two weeks prior. Delores told Tobie that she had enough of his physical and emotional abuse, and that she was not going back for more. Ruth and Aunt Nodee were upstairs in Ruth's bedroom with baby "Sputnik," and they were talking and amusing the baby.

Delores had walked downstairs when Tobie came calling. When the first shot resounded, Delores screamed! Ruth dashed out of her room, down the steps to the landing. She yelled, "Tobie, don't kill my sister" as she leaped over the landing rail and pounced on top of Tobie. The gun flew out of his hand as he and Ruth bounced on the living room floor by the fireplace. By then, Tobie had fired four shots, and three of them hit Delores. Amazingly, one bullet passed through her left arm, just below her elbow. Another bullet went through her upper abdominals, below her breasts and above her belly button. The third bullet lodged in her lower abdominals.

Delores was holding sofa pillows in her lap which she hid behind when Tobie opened fire upon her. I don't know what kind of pistol he shot her with, but remarkably Delores did not sustain any lasting damage to any internal organs, and there was no bone damage.

When Odeana and I went to the hospital to see Delores, she gave her account of the shooting, which she described as burning and stinging sensations. She said it happened so fast she did not have time to get scared. In the ambulance ride to the hospital with her mother, Delores kept singing "Rockin' Robin," by Bobby Day. She told us that she had no idea why she kept singing that particular song, except it kept her from losing consciousness, and she was afraid to close her eyes. The song ends with an upbeat "Tweet-tweet." Delores said, "When they put me under for surgery, I was slowly mumbling "Tweet-tweet-tweet.""

The most amazing, remarkable and miraculous survival segment of the shooting was that unknowingly, Delores was six weeks pregnant. Her womb and the fetus were not injured. We worried that the surgical scars would split open as her stomach expanded in pregnancy. The surgical scars appeared dangerously thin and scary looking, but they did not pop open. She did not have problems during the pregnancy, and about seven and a half months later, the miracle baby boy, Tony, was born. As time progressed into the future, Delores divorced Tobie, eventually married a nice young man, gave birth to six more children, and she became a nurse. Trauma, sorrow, and activities surrounding Delores caused summer of 1958 to rapidly fade into the past.

With Tobie in jail and Delores recovering, Odeana and the rest of us were looking forward to an end of summer "hop" at the YWCA, around the third Friday in August. Odeana and several friends who hung out at her house planned to go, and so did I.

Mother still worked her second job as a hotel clerk on Friday and Saturday nights, which was her escape and avoidance from Daddy's weekend drama. Nonetheless, she told me that I could go to the dance with them. Aunt Nodee volunteered to look after my sisters, but they claimed that they could take care of themselves. Kassandra was nine, El' Nora eleven, and Audrey would become a teenager in December. In retrospect, when I was nine years old, I was taking care of all three of them. By age eleven, I was taking care of them and cooking for the field hands. Surely my three sisters could collectively take care of themselves while I went to the dance at the "Y," even though I did not know how to dance.

Odeana told all of us to wear a full skirt, which was an unspoken requirement for fast whirls when dancing the jitterbug. Full skirts required support to make them puff up like an open umbrella. Every teenaged girl owned at least one hoop crinoline and a couple of bouffant net petticoats to hold up their skirts.

Using a 'Vogue' pattern, I had cut out and sewn my own puffy pink skirt with matching short sleeve blouse and wrap-around sash. The tight waist and voluminous skirts suggested a tiny waistline for any size girl who wore one, not to mention the tight girdles that squeezed and compressed us from under our breasts to the top of our knees.

Brown penny loafers, and white sponge-rolled bobby socks completed my ensemble. Like a ground-level parachute, I floated across the street to Odeana's house. There were four of us, and we had not considered the logistics of getting four voluminous skirts into one car. Fortunately, Betty wore a fitted dress.

Odeana, the shortest and smallest among us, leaned forward to step into the car and sit in the back seat. When she leaned forward, her skirt ballooned out as we giggled and pointed. When she sat down the bottom of her skirt puffed up behind the front seat, and we laughed even harder. Betty slid into the middle seat beside Odeana. Then it was my turn to amuse everyone when my skirt hoop swished up behind the driver's seat. Wanda's hoop crinoline filled up the front seat and dashboard. There were no seat belts to mashdown our skirts or protect us, since we grew up before child safety became an issue.

Odeana's brother and the fellows laughed and offered their social commentary on our fashionable attire. Eddie, one of the nicest young men in our group, drove us to the "Y" around 8:45 p.m. and agreed to pick us up at 11:30.

Although I did not know how to dance or follow a rhythmic beat, I watched and wished that I could step and spin around like Odeana and the other girls when they rocked out to the popular up-beat song titled, "Tequila," by The Champs. Initially, a couple of boys asked me to fast dance, but after I nervously crashed into them and stepped on their feet, I became a "wallflower" until a slow song played. Then the boys came running with their sweaty faces so that they could squeeze me and press against my breasts, which made me a voluntary "wallflower."

Eddie and some of the other guys arrived around 11:00 p.m. to show off their smooth dance moves. All too soon, it was 11:30, the dance was over, and the D.J. played the last song of the evening, "Good Night Sweetheart" by the Spaniels, a talented "doo-wop" group in the 1950's.

After the dance was over everyone was hungry, and all of us wanted something from Jones Barbecue Pit. Mouthwatering aromas of hickory smoked BBQ and delectable spices permeated the air when we neared the location. It was the favorite eatery and hang-out spot for the youth. We ordered at the window and ate in the car. It was not a sit-down restaurant.

There were three or four teenagers in the Jones family, boys and girls, and all of them worked with their parents in the family business. Even though the Jones teenagers were physically attractive, drove nice cars, and lived well, they were friendly and down-to- earth, especially Ronald. He had a way of making everyone feel welcome and included.

Therefore, they were never referred to as "seditty," which is a colloquial word, made-up by unknown African-Americans to describe other African-Americans who were affluent and snooty. Moreover, they were friends to Odeana and everyone who hung-out at her house, and I was delighted to be included.

While Eddie was driving us home from the BBQ pit, I daydreamed about the wonderful life my family could have enjoyed if Daddy would have stayed sober long enough to open his own BBQ pit. Instead, he sold $2.00 rib and chicken dinners two times a year, around the 4th of July and Labor Day, and we had to make the side dishes.

With cut-up onions burning our eyes, my sisters and I made large containers of spicy potato salad for the dinners, which included two slices of white bread.

Daddy's claim-to-fame was making the best BBQ in the neighborhood or any place else. He created his own sauce from scratch. Loaded with whole cayenne peppers and a combination of spices and other ingredients, the overpowering smells from the slow simmering sauce made us cough, and it burned our eyes and throat. He made a milder sauce for the faint of heart, but even that one was spicy enough to make your nose run. Tantalizing aromas penetrated the air and caused people to stop by and place their orders for ribs, chicken or both.

Those happy thoughts of what our family life could have been floated through my mind while Eddie drove us back to Odeana's house. On the way, Wanda, Betty, Odeana and I offered our commentary about the attire worn by other girls at the "Y," who they were with, and how they danced. My friends also laughed at my inability to dance, and they offered to remove one of my two left feet. Upon safe arrival at Odeana's, we maneuvered our Cinderella-styled hoop skirts out of the car and spent a few minutes chitchatting with each other on the sidewalk in front of Odeana's house. Then I dashed across the street.

Like Cinderella, I did not arrive home before midnight, but the front door was unlocked. Otherwise, there was a hidden key, and all of us knew where to find it. I stepped into the living room, but before I reached the steps leading to my attic bedroom, my drunk Daddy sneaked up behind me and landed a blow on my back with the razor strap.

I snapped! Startled and stunned by the the whack on my back, I screamed from the element of surprise and stinging pain. Suddenly, I did not fear Daddy. Pure rage had replaced my fear with the urge to kill him. In a split second, I whirled around to face him. When he drew back to hit me again, I reached out and caught the razor strap with both hands, which threw him off balance, and we engaged in a tug-of-war. I held on and screamed at him, "You burnt-eyed, snaggle-toothed, son-of-a-bitch, hit me one more time, and I will kill your drunk ass! Mother said I could go. I am eighteen-years-old, and I'm sick of you beating up on me, my brother and sisters for nothing!" Daddy stuttered, "You ain't grown long as you livin under my roof. You sposed to be here takin care of these chullens." I yelled in return, "Aunt Nodee was looking after them." Staggering around and trying to pull the razor strap from my death grip, he stuttered, "They ain't her chullens." Outraged by the notion that I was responsible for his children, I hissed back at him, "They are not my children either. You need to beat your own ass!"

By then, Delores and my sisters were standing on the staircase landing. My brother had entered the scene from his basement bedroom. Mother was working the night shift at the hotel. Aunt Nodee was upon Daddy with a black, cast iron skillet in her hand, ready to bash his skull while yelling and cursing at him.

Daddy released the razor strap and backed away before she clobbered him. Suddenly, a cold calmness came upon me. I stared directly into Daddy's eyes. I pointed my right index finger towards him. Slowly and quietly I said, "If you ever hit me again, you will not live to tell about it." After rendering threats of bodily harm and telling Daddy what a stupid fool he was, Aunt Nodee told him to take his dumb, drunk ass to bed, which he did.

I lifted up my hoop skirt and rushed to the bathroom without losing bladder control. I was on my period, and the drama of Daddy hitting me caused a headache and made the blood flow accelerate. I did not know that it had bled through my Kotex pad and girdle, but it did not spot my petticoats because, I had not sat down. In the bathroom, I made repairs and wept over the dismal plight of my life.

Earlier, while getting ready for the dance, I had reflected on my period and was thankful that excruciating monthly cramps had been eliminated from my life. Those results came from Dr. Brown's prescription of "the pill."

Mother had totally disagreed with any suggested surgery to relieve my menstrual suffering. After I turned sixteen, she agreed to the prescription of birth control pills. Those pills were a modern-day miracle for me. They prevented severe cramping, nausea and other unfavorable symptoms.

Life was challenging enough without the burden of dysmenorrhea. I was thrilled about going to the dance, because I was not doubled over with the cramps. After all repairs had been completed in the bathroom, I went to bed. Anger boiled within me and prevented sleep.

Wide awake and frustrated, my thoughts roared loudly, like the propellers of a low hovering helicopter. I had suffered tremendous pain from my period and was now able to function with it. Having endured that, Daddy's assault proved he had alcohol and mental health issues, which were never clinically addressed.

Crazy or not, that was his last attack upon me! I know that I said he was not worth my time in jail, but anger drove me to defend myself. I thought, "It's him or me. If he attacks me one more time, he will die, and I will claim self-defense!"

I was angry with Mother, because she did not divorce Daddy, and she did not threaten to kill him for abusing her children. While he was sleeping, she should have poured boiling hot rice with lye on his behind. I bet he would have thought twice before he beat up on another one of her children, crazy or not!

When we asked Mother why she did not leave Daddy, she said, "He works hard everyday and puts food on the table, and all of you are better off with your own Daddy

than with some other man, and I have too many girls for that." She told us that her parents told all of their children, "The bed you make is the one you have to sleep in."

Hot tears warmed my cheeks, and I wondered why I was ever born. I hated my parents for making my life miserable. I cooked, cleaned the house, took care of the kids, and they never gave me a dime for allowance.

I loved my little sisters and did my best to protect them from Daddy. One time I pushed him down the steps into the dining room to prevent him from wrapping an extension cord around El' Nora's neck to choke her. Screaming from the top of her lungs, she bolted out of the house and ran to the home of two playmates, Theeda and Sandy, who were the same ages as El' Nora and Audrey. They lived five doors away on the same side of the street. El' Nora told their parents that Daddy was trying to kill her, and they called the police. Each thought disgusted me more than the last one.

My mind flashed back to early childhood in the log cabin. I was angry with Daddy for making me massage his stinking feet and clean the toe-jam from between his toes on hot summer days. He made me push blackheads from his face and pick out ingrown hairs, caused by razor bumps. Using my thumbnails, I had to squish the pus out of the bumps, then pull out the hairs with tweezers.

Loretta told me that the lumpy pus was little maggots. Worse yet, I had to push the pores on top and beside his nose and make all of those tiny white worms wiggle out, causing nausea and revulsion within me. When I cried and told Mother, she tried to reassure me, "Those are not worms." I asked, "If they are not worms, why do they wiggle when I push them out?" She could not explain why they wiggled.

There were thousands of reasons for hating Daddy and feeling disappointed with Mother. Even in my misery, I realized that each thought made my headache worse. I prayed that such thoughts would stop whirling through my mind. I also prayed that Jesus would save me from killing Daddy. Mostly, I prayed that Jesus would help me graduate from Shortridge, get a good job like Odeana, and escape from Daddy.

Escaping from Daddy was a pleasant thought, but it also filled me with ambivalence on behalf of my sisters and brother, although Robert referred to himself as my big brother. Nonetheless, I forced myself to think about graduating, marrying Al, and somehow going to college. Thoughts of Al brought a smile through my tears. I was ready for my classes to hurry-up and start so that I could see him everyday when he drove me to school, and before I knew it, sleep had overwhelmed my consciousness.

Interestingly, the following day after the razor strap incident, which was Saturday, I observed Daddy eying me suspiciously and keeping his distance. As time progressed, he did not "accidentally" bump against my breasts or gaze at them. He did not come near me at all.

The following week whizzed by. When Daddy came home from work on Friday, he told us, "Evybody git ready, umma take ya downtown to git some school clothes in da moanin." Then he went up on "The Corner" and "got happy," but he did not come home drunk.

On Saturday morning, he was bathed, shaved, and looked decent with his wavy hair slicked back with fragrant Hair Rep grease to hold it in place. He wore black slacks, shiny black Stacy Adam shoes, a white long-sleeved shirt and sunglasses. Moreover, he was sober. We rode the bus early enough to be among the first customers when the stores opened, and Blocks was our first stop.

Daddy was not a bargain shopper like Mother. After he paid for all of our shoes, he was ready to go home, but he did let us get some treats from G. C. Murphy Dime Store in Fountain Square. From there, we rode the bus home and enjoyed crunching our potato chips and treats.

Our enjoyment abruptly dissipated when we went home, because Daddy told us to hurry up and change clothes so that we could "git ta wirk" in the vegetable garden. There was a vacant lot three doors away, on the same side of the street. I do not know if Daddy received permission or not, but he grew vegetables in that lot every year. He planted a variety of vegetables from one-year-to-the-next, but the basic crops included hot peppers, green beans, corn, collard greens, turnip green with huge turnips, and tomatoes.

Working the garden created extra chores for me and my siblings. Daddy had initiated the planting, but we had to pull the weeds and chop the grass away from the vegetables, just like chopping cotton. The vegetables needed moisture. My siblings and I created the irrigation system. That was accomplished by carrying buckets and buckets of water from our backyard water hose down the alley to water the garden. We also had to pick the vegetables as they ripened.

We were the only children in the community who farmed. Neighborhood kids whizzed by the garden on their bicycles, laughing and having fun at our expense. Working the garden was another source of embarrassment for me. I did not want Al to see me bent over pulling weeds or picking vegetables, but he did. Not only that, word spread whenever we worked the garden, and guys from around the area would drive past very slowly and tease me with remarks like, "Hey Miss Turnip Greens. Sure wish I had some of those tomatoes." They knew that Daddy was up on "The Corner."

Being called "Miss Turnip Greens" by Indianapolis peers was not a compliment, and I hated working the garden. By contrast, when I was a very young child on the farm, I loved gardening and watching the vegetables grow, and seeing green tomatoes turn red was a magical wonder.

In Tennessee, springtime and planting the garden was fun and exciting for me. Daddy used the mules and a plow to prepare the soil. After fertilizing the soil, he made rows where vegetables would be planted. After the seeds were in the ground a few days, I was anxious for them to grow up.

As time slowly passed, frequently I ran to the garden, plopped on the ground on my stomach, placed one ear on the dirt and listened for the sound of growing seeds. Since I never heard any seeds growing, I used my right index fingernail to carefully scratch the dirt off and peeked into the soil to see what they were doing. Only a few days would have passed since they had been planted, but I was disappointed that the seeds were not growing. Finally, after the correct amount of time had passed, I ran into the garden and scratched away the dirt. There were tiny, pale, green sprouts, doubled over under the soil. Thrilled and filled with wonderment, I quickly covered the little sprouts so that they could grow up through the dirt. I was only four or five years old, and watching things grow was very exciting.

Perhaps the lack of toys, coloring books, crayons or children's books made the growth process from seed to ripe vegetables totally fascinating for me. For unknown reasons, the growth of corn captured my curiosity. I asked Mother how could one itty-bitty grain of corn grow into a tall stalk with so many big ears of corn, and how could each corn cob have countless kernels? She said "Because God created it to do just that."

During my early childhood in Denmark, watching vegetables grow was fun and fascinating, but as a young lady in Indianapolis, it was disgusting, frustrating and embarrassing.

Loathe it or love it, we did not have a choice. Working the garden was bad enough, but being teased by kids on bicycles and young men in cars was painful for me and my siblings. All the more reasons to hurry-up and graduate so that I could get away.

I could not wait for school to start, because I was totally looking forward to riding with Al again. Although he only called a couple of times over summer, I secretly day- dreamed about our wedding. During Labor Day weekend, Al finally called. Ecstatic best described my response to his phone call. His soothing voice tickled my heart until he said, "I will be teaching in a different school, and it's not near Shortridge. So, I can't drive you to school or see you anymore. I'm very sorry." His words caused a huge lump in my throat, and I caught my breath. My heart broke like the shattered water jug in the cotton field, and it felt like slithers of hot glass shot through my heart and entire body.

My stomach churned, and my head throbbed. Hot tears met under my chin as I dashed upstairs to the bathroom. Why had I even dared to daydream about Al? I very well knew that his mother did not approve of his affection towards me. With a father like mine, I was nowhere near good enough for her only son, a college graduate who was getting his Master's Degree in music.

School started, and regardless of my sorrow and disappointment, I was determined to graduate. With Al living across the street, we could not avoid seeing each other in passing, and I knew that he was also broken-hearted and obviously miserable. There was nothing I could do about our situation, and Al would do nothing to displease his mother.

That was fall semester of 1958, and it flew by like a blur. The librarians remained a helpful resource. The typing and office machines classes were progressive, like Typing I, II, etc. I made passing grades because using office machines was mechanical and not subjective. After we completed classroom-timed assignments, we had to circle our own errors with a red pen and do the math to determine our accurate speed for typing or machine calculations. If the teacher found overlooked errors, he deducted double points, but my math was very good for determining my accurate typing and machine skills. Home Economics classes were also progressive and mechanical, which enabled me to advance to the next level of cooking and sewing.

With my heart bleeding over Al, fall of 1958 was very depressing. My distress over him made a sad world even sadder. Added to my personal dramas and traumas there were social issues that could not be ignored. Injustices that drove civil rights leaders to action were upsetting, anger provoking, and frightening. Something horrible had occurred every year since I moved to Indianapolis in 1955, the year that Emmett Till was murdered, and Rosa Parks refused to give up her seat on a segregated bus, which sparked the Montgomery Boycotts.

In 1956 angry White men, acting out their opposition to integration, bombed four Negro churches and the home of Martin Luther King, Jr. and E. D. Nelson. Nonetheless, the University of Alabama admitted their first Negro student but did not allow her to attend classes.

In 1957 Arkansas governor Orval Faubus used the Arkansas National Guard to block the entry of nine Negro students, but President Dwight Eisenhower ordered federal troops to integrate Little Rock High School.

During 1958, in Cooper v. Aaron, the Little Rock School Board had refused to admit the students and claimed that admitting them would cause mob violence by angry White people. The Supreme Court ruled that the potential for mob violence did not justify refusing to desegregate.

Although I did not personally know anyone involved in the movement, tension was high, and we were all involved emotionally. Despite the prevailing circumstances, I still had an alcoholic father to contend with, mostly on behalf of my siblings and our mother who practiced avoidance. I still had household responsibilities and school work to complete for graduation.

Discouragement was pervasive in my life, and there was nothing for me to look forward to since my high school principal had labeled me uneducable, which disqualified me as a college applicant. His judgment hurt my feelings to the core, and made me very angry, but it did not stop me from dreaming about graduating from Indiana University.

Frequently, I heard my fellow students excitedly talking about the college or university that they would be attending. Whenever they asked about my college plans, I smiled and replied, "I'm going to Indiana University and become a teacher."

My Cousin Ruth knew that I was sorrowful that Al's mother had stopped him from seeing me. She said, "Ain't no point in you crying over spilled milk. He's a mama's boy, and she would always be meddling in yo business." Therefore, when school was out for Christmas break, Ruth planned to take me to a Christmas party in a nightclub with some of her friends, and her mother (Aunt Nodee) would be home with my sisters. The lady that Ruth worked for owned a pampered, white poodle that was groomed and treated by a veterinarian. Since Ruth always took the dog to the vet, she knew both of the veterinarians and their wives, who ran the business.

She also knew the vet's assistant, Larry Summers, who helped with the grooming, drove a station wagon with cages, and transported pets for their owners. On a Friday night, three weekends before Christmas, the vets, their wives, Larry and some other friends gathered in an upscale, Negro-owned night club, where the White veterinarians and friends were well-known and welcomed. Ruth proudly introduced me as her first cousin, and I was warmly greeted with favorable comments.

As Ruth introduced me, Larry's face lit up. His big brown eyes and smile widened. He was good-looking, with a pecan-brown complexion with freckles on his nose. Larry was very polite and overly attentive. He secured a seat next to me and never left my side, which prevented anyone else from capturing my attention. He was amusing and fun as we talked, laughed, and barely moved around the dance floor.

My lack of rhythm and dancing ability did not seem to matter, and his dancing was not much better, because he was self-conscious of his bow legs and long narrow feet. Ruth, the vets, their wives and friends were enjoying the event and laughing louder with each drink. Larry drank gin but provided a steady flow of orange juice and soft drinks for me.

By the time the party ended, Larry made sure that I had his address, phone numbers for home and work, and a promise that I would call him the following day. Since he regularly groomed the white poodle for Ruth, he already had access to our phone number, and he knew where we lived. He offered to drive me home, but I told him, "No, I can't do that. I have to go back the same way I came here." I smiled and waved good night to Larry and the vet's party group as Ruth's friend drove us home.

Going home always generated some tension. Even though Daddy had not assaulted me since I threatened to kill him, he could have beaten up any of my four siblings with the razor strap. Fortunately, Daddy was snoring loudly under the influence, and he had not beaten up anyone while we were out. Mother had escaped to her night clerk job at the Colored hotel.

I did not call Larry the following day, but he called me the day after and asked if he had said something to hurt my feelings. He asked if I was sure that I did not have a boyfriend somewhere. He was anxious to know if I liked him. I was flattered and amused by his keen interest in me. The following Saturday he took me to the movies and out to eat. Every weekend following, he wanted to take me somewhere. He took me out to dinner and gave me perfume for Christmas. He took me to a party at his uncle's house for New Year's. Although, I liked having some place to go, I missed the excitement of getting dressed up, going with Al to the night club and hearing him and his band playing upbeat music. Why couldn't Al be the one jumping up and down to take me out on weekends?

Then came my nineteenth birthday in January, and Larry wanted to take me back to that same night club where we had enjoyed the Christmas party.

For my birthday celebration, I wore a red, long sleeved knit dress that fit my body snugly. It had a wide black soft leather belt, and I wore black leather pumps. I also wore a girdle, which fit mid-thigh, and there were hooks inside the girdle legs to hold up my silk stockings (before pantyhose were invented in the 1960s).

Larry looked very sharp in his dark gray wool suit, white shirt, gray and black print tie, and he wore a black hat with a gray band. He made a favorable impression by bringing me flowers and a big box of assorted chocolate candy. I was indeed flattered, because my parents never celebrated our birthdays -- no cakes, no candles, no ice cream, no cards, no good wishes. I did recall a log cabin custom of open palm whacks on the behind. One whack for each year of your life, given by everyone present.

Chocolate candy was a sweeter way to celebrate, and I was thrilled. I had enjoyed celebrating Christmas, New Year's and my birthday with Larry. Time seemed to be moving faster since I met him. Weekends came and went swiftly, especially when school started back from Christmas break.

School was not exactly fun since all of my few friends had graduated. I was downhearted, age nineteen and still in high school. At least Robert was also in school with me, but he was looking forward to escaping from home and school by joining the Army.

Everyday when school was over, Larry was smiling and waiting to drive me (and Robert) home in his like new, 1957 red Chevrolet with sparkling chrome. I especially loved the dazzling bumpers and gleaming grill. Moreover, he let me drive. I already had my driver's license, because Driver Education was mandatory. It was one of the few classes I did not fail. I had enjoyed the class and earned a "B."

Even so, I was not free to go driving around with Larry. Household responsibilities were always waiting for me and so were my three younger sisters. Moreover, I still had school and homework, but we no longer had to hide our books and run for cover when Daddy came home.

After Aunt Nodee moved in and heard about Daddy beating us for doing homework, she cursed him out and threatened to scald his "dumb ass" with a boiling pot of hot rice, laced with lye, a very strong alkaline solution. Daddy ceased referring to homework as "Settin on yo ass doin nothin." Removing the threat of being beaten for studying reduced tension and increased my ability to concentrate. I could see myself graduating, especially after our senior pictures were taken, which was a few months before graduation. Due to anxious anticipation, it seemed like years would drag by before the photo prints were ready. When Larry saw all of my cute pictures, he could not decide which pose he liked better, so he paid for all of them.

Meanwhile, attentive Larry had proposed to me several times, but I always told him that I was planning on becoming an airline stewardess when I graduated in June. Silent panic best described his response. He pleaded that whatever plane I was on would surely crash. I would be killed, and he could not live without me. Six months after we met, Larry's charm and persistence convinced me to marry him, after he assured me that I could still become a stewardess.

For my final sewing project in Home Economics, I selected a 'Vogue' pattern. I chose white-on-white cotton fabric and made my knee length, form-fitted wedding dress, with a full-length zipper in the back. Using the same fabric that the dress was made from, I designed a sash and attached it to make a puffy overskirt. The overskirt was made from white mesh and matched my shoulder length veil, which I also sewed.

After graduation, Larry and I were married on the last Saturday in June. The wedding was performed by Reverend Miller, a local minister whose church we attended infrequently. The ceremony took place in our living room, and Daddy stayed sober long enough to give me away. I was happy and excited about moving into my own one bedroom apartment on Capitol Avenue, but my sisters wept broken heartedly, especially Audrey. Their emotional expressions filled me with ambivalence, and I cried with them as I packed up my belongings.

When I agreed to marry him, Larry and I shopped for and bought a bedroom set, dining table with four chairs and some living room furniture. Not only was I getting away from Daddy, I would have my first brand new bed. On our wedding night Larry could not wait to consummate the marriage, and I could not wait to avoid it. Reflecting on the pain that Donald had caused me, I did not want any part of that. I claimed to be on my period for the next few days. Larry already knew about the trauma of my "monthly," but he cursed it on our wedding night and got drunk.

Periods can only last so long. He was stereotypically endowed. I was physically unprepared due to "female problems," and that caused some early problems in our marriage. I always slept on my stomach for obvious reasons. One time he growled, "You are not asleep. Nobody sleeps holding on to the mattress!"

Even so, my life was better than it had been. I was grown and gone, though not totally on my own. Larry was happy to take me to the movies, out to eat, and to the nightclub to hang out with the veterinarians.

Very soon I realized that Larry was so jealous he could not see straight. Perhaps my breasts clouded his vision. He claimed that every man, everywhere, was staring at my chest, which I must have inherited from both grandmothers, because Mother was an "A cup." His jealousy brought on our first big blowout in August. I was planning to go downtown with Odeana and friends. He accused me of going to meet a boyfriend. An angry argument ensued. We yelled and cursed at each other. He slapped me in the face but caught my hands before I could knock his head off. After some wrestling with each other, he stormed out of the house and sped away in the car like a fool. I grabbed my toothbrush, put a few items in my school bag, and caught the bus to my parents' home where I planned to stay the night. My siblings and I were very happy to see each other.

When Larry finished work, went home, and found me gone, he came speeding to my parents' home. Daddy was home at the time, and Larry was sweeter than honey. I had told Mother that Larry slapped me. She encouraged us to "Work things out." Larry assured her that he would never hit me again, and I went back home with him. Our relationship was good for awhile, and I learned to tolerate him when he stopped behaving like a rapist.

Meanwhile, I had gotten a job with Hooks Drug Stores. I quickly worked my way up from short-order grill cook to stock clerk and alternating cashier. When I worked as stock clerk, I frequently helped the friendly and trusting pharmacist refill prescriptions that patients dropped off. That was easy. I removed the pills from the big containers and put the prescribed amount in each patients' pill bottle.

Sometimes the pharmacist would disappear for thirty minutes or more, but I took care of all the patients. I noticed that the pharmacist took little measuring scoops of fine white powder, wrapped it in a small piece of wax paper and tucked it in a pocket on his white pharmaceutical jacket.

One day, I was working the cash register with four or five people waiting in-line. A man handed me a carton of cigarettes, a pint of liquor and some other items. I looked up into Al's sad eyes and immediately jammed up the register. I was shocked to see him, and past emotions flooded my heart and heated up my work space. After much fumbling with my shaking hands, the cash register functioned properly. Al's hands touched mine when he paid for his items. He looked at me and said, "I'm really, really sorry." He left the store without looking back.

Larry picked me up from work and asked, "How did things go today?" I cheerfully responded, "OK" and hoped that he had not been parked outside and saw Al leaving the store. He did not see Al, and our evening ended without a fight. Arguing and fighting with Larry was a lot better than living with Dad.

Daddy was no longer a physical threat to me, but my siblings were still suffering from physical abuse and mental anguish. Approximately a year after I moved out, my family moved to an unsightly house on 19th Street, about six blocks from Highland Place and "The Corner."

Daddy's irrational behavior was still violent but more menacing. After they moved from Highland Place with his sister, Aunt Nodee, Daddy had waved a loaded revolver around and threatened to shoot Mother and my three sisters. By then, Robert had escaped into the Army. My sisters were afraid of Daddy and consequently experienced great anxiety.

When Audrey was approximately fourteen years old, a stroke twisted the left side of her face and impeded her speech patterns. Fortunately, her face and speech returned to normal in a couple of months, and there were no lingering indications that she had endured a stroke. El' Nora Jean and Kassandra each ran away from home, though not at the same time.

My sisters loathed the tiny decrepit house on 19th Street, and Mother had been looking for a bigger place. She hoped that moving a little farther from "The Corner" would curtail Daddy's drinking. Mother located a huge, three-bedroom apartment on Capital Avenue. It was a second floor walk-up that was situated above a drug store and laundromat.

The negligible distance did not keep Daddy from "The Corner." One Saturday in February 1962, Mother had confirmed a dental appointment for Daddy's decaying teeth. Mother went to work her seamstress job, and Daddy claimed that he forgot to go to the dentist, but he remembered to go drinking.

Larry was still drinking, but he had started-up his own collection agency, and it was doing well financially. He felt empowered that the collection agency made it legal for him to carry a badge and a gun. He started by collecting payments for the vets. He soon had other clients who wanted delinquent debts collected, and his clients and income increased.

He paid the rent on our adorable house on Pruitt Street after we moved from the apartment. My favorite feature was the spacious, screened in front porch. There was one bedroom, one bath, large living room, a dining room, cute kitchen, and lovely hardwood floors in every room, with colorful tiles in the kitchen and bath.

On that particular Saturday in February 1962, I was home alone waxing the dining room floor and smiling at the shine when the phone started ringing. I dashed to answer the phone! Instead of saying "Hello," I asked: "Was he cut or shot?" I asked was he cut or shot, because as the phone rang, I had seen a mental image of Daddy. He was standing with his back against a dingy gray wall. I saw him sliding down, leaving bloody, vertical streaks along the wall, and his body slumped to the floor.

The male caller replied: "He been shot and on de' way ta General Hospital."

The caller hung up without any further information, and I had no clue who he was or how he obtained our home phone number.

Reportedly, it was around noon when the shots rang out. Details were absorbed in a frenzy, as Mother, my sisters and I somehow arrived at the hospital emergency room. Daddy was strapped to a gurney face up. His brown tweed overcoat hung towards the floor on each side of the gurney. Alcohol fumes oozed out of his pores and breath as he hollered, "Lem'me outta hare! Lem'me outta hare!" The length of time that it took for him to be seen by a doctor is unknown, but it was a very long time.

Daddy was not the only emergency victim. The area was chaotic! There was another man who had also been shot. A woman was bleeding to death because her boyfriend had slashed her throat with a sharp razor. There was a lady sobbing over the limp body of her toddler, because the little girl had ingested some poison, and more people were constantly being wheeled into the emergency room. Distraught family members of the other victims screamed, cried, and tried to rush the emergency room staff. I was twenty two years old, but the emergency room was terrifying to me and my sisters.

After an endless amount of time, Daddy's body had swollen so big, he appeared to have been inflated with air. He was finally rolled into the operating room where anesthetics stopped him from hollering "Lem'me outta hare!" A few hours later, the surgeon told us that a single shot pierced through Daddy's chin. The bullet traversed through his chest. It missed his heart by a fraction but extensively damaged his arteries and caused deadly internal bleeding.

In spite of everything Daddy had done to us, my siblings and I felt sad and sorry for him. Mother only fussed, "If he would've took his behind to the dentist like he was supposed to, he wouldn't been shot in the first place. A hard head sure makes a soft behind."

After surgery, Daddy was wheeled into the Intensive Care Unit. He was attached to several tubes and machines. The surgeon had performed a tracheotomy, and a tube had been inserted in the hole in his throat. His decayed front teeth were exposed, because he could not keep his lips closed, and his eyes stared blankly into space. The sight of him was very disconcerting. In the moment, I was totally thankful that I had not done this by stabbing him with a pitchfork. The operating surgeon told us, "Be prepared -- he may not make it through the night." A month flew by and Daddy was transferred to a regular ward, but he had not regained consciousness. Three months passed by, and my sisters and I stopped going to see him. Mother continued to visit occasionally for medical and social worker updates. As time moved on, the medical staff spoke of transferring Daddy to a convalescent home.

Aunt Nodee was his most frequent visitor, and she had the nerve to ask us, "Why don't y'all go see ya daddy?" El' Nora Jean snapped back, "What! After the way he mistreated us and beat us!" Before plans were complete for transferring him to a convalescent home, Daddy died September 14, 1962, a victim of mistaken identity. He was a classic example of being in the wrong place at the wrong time, but he knew that he was hanging out in "The Bucket of Blood." He transcended from drunk to unconscious into the abysmal pit of death. "Lem'me outta hare" were the last words that he uttered.

Robert came from his Army base for the funeral. Loretta and her four children, Christopher, Ray, Sandra, and Phyllis came from St. Louis, but none of us cried. As Reverend Miller was preaching the service, Aunt Nodee boohooed and howled like Daddy had been a saint on earth.

Loretta did not exactly whisper when she said, "Aunt Nodee ought to shut her mouth. She knows how Daddy was." When Reverend Miller eulogized Daddy as a wonderful provider and father, El' Nora Jean was genuinely confused. She innocently whispered to Mother and asked, "Who is the preacher talking about?" Loretta's additional sentiments were, "You are supposed to say something good about the dead. He's dead. That's good."

After Daddy died, I told Larry that is what happens to people when they punch and threaten other people for no good reason. For the remaining years of our marriage, he did not hit me again. Perhaps it was because I had promised to scald his ass with boiling rice, laced with lye. Or maybe it was the sharp butcher knife that unexpectedly fell on the floor from under my side of the mattress when he was helping change the bed sheets one day.

Nonetheless, his Dr. Jekyll and Mr. Hyde personality was a burden that I endured for another two years after Daddy died. It took five long years to finally escape from Larry. I'm sure he would have gone berserk if he had known that I was anywhere near the Playboy Club, not to mention working as a Bunny with men staring at me.

Vikki Richardson

11

HOLLYWOOD PLAYBOY CLUB AND CIVIL UNREST

Certainly, I was thankful to have escaped to the Playboy Club before I was shot or killed, and before I killed Larry. Working the Cincinnati Club was my Cinderella dream come true, but the thought of transferring to the Hollywood Club was beyond any fairy tale imaginable.

Bunny Hope had moved out of the YWCA in Cincinnati and transferred to the Hollywood Playboy Club. She wrote to me describing the Club as twice the size of Cincinnati. She told me there were lots of really gorgeous Bunnies, and they still needed more. She encouraged me to transfer to the Hollywood Club, where we could work together again, rent a big house in Hollywood Hills and be roommates. I went to my Bunny Mother and applied for a transfer to the Hollywood Club. After a couple of weeks and to my utter amazement, another Cinderella wish was granted.

I was tearful, and it was difficult saying goodbye to my sister Bunnies, my Bunny Mother, the wardrobe mistress, bartenders, busboys, and all of the employees who had become part of my Playboy family.

"Mr. High Roller" gave me a going away party in his nightclub. My friends and party people came to wish me well and, some of them called me, "Ms. Hollywood Playboy Bunny." Several hugs and tears later, it was time for the club to close, and I went home to the YWCA to pack. I was fearful of fitting into the Hollywood scene and learning my way around Los Angeles.

Excitement overruled fear when I stepped into the aircraft and sat in my first class seat on Trans World Airlines, my first flight. I wore an expensive tan, suede pantsuit, with matching high-heeled pumps and a beige, high-necked silk blouse.

My Bunny costumes were carefully packed in my brand new, dark brown leather luggage. Three Bunny tails were placed in individual square boxes, and I put them in my carry-on bag with my wire brush.

During the flight, I tediously brushed out each tail, fluffing them up until they looked like cotton candy at the fair. My seat mate, a White business man, and all of the other passengers, wanted to know what was I doing? Explaining the importance of a fluffy Bunny tail made them ask, "Are you a Playboy Bunny?" When I answered in the affirmative, my seat mate wanted the tail fuzz from the wire brush, and so did practically every male and female who heard the conversation. Highly amused, I passed around a little tail fuzz to all of them, until my wire brush was clean. In our open conversation, some of the guys stated that they were already Playboy Club key holders, and others planned to become members the minute the plane landed, and all of them were going to ask for me when they came to the club.

I had barely finished brushing out my Bunny tails and packing them away, when the pilot announced, "Ladies and gentlemen, there is some civil unrest taking place in the South Central area of Los Angeles, at this time." It was August 11, 1965. Gazing from my window seat, I witnessed black billowing smoke towering above red flames from one area, contrasted to an expanse of rolling green land with varying shapes of blue dots, which turned out to be swimming pools in the yards of expensive homes in the wealthy West Los Angeles area. I felt scared and temporarily wished that I had stayed in Cincinnati.

Safely on the ground and luggage retrieved, I took a taxi to my hotel on Sunset Boulevard, several blocks from the Playboy Club. En route, the Negro taxi driver excitedly told me there was a race riot taking place in the city of Watts and surrounding areas, and it was spreading. He said, "The Civil Rights Act didn't mean shit." He further vented, "That's w,hy Malcolm X was militant, and it's a damned shame that his own Muslim peoples blew him away. White folks don't have to kill us. We be killing ourselves." Malcolm X was shot to death February 21, 1965.

Later, I learned that following the Civil Rights Act of 1964, some states, including California, acted to circumvent the new federal law by enacting Proposition 14, which attempted to block the Fair Housing Section Act that was included in the Civil Rights Act.

Uninvited images of past injustices flashed back from my memory of "White only" signs and our mistreatment at Dairy Queen in Jackson.

As a young child, going into the big city of Jackson from the farm in Denmark was indeed a rare occasion, and getting ice cream was an extreme. Although a single dip cone was only five cents, at the time it was a major event for the five of us. My joy of an ice cream cone was diminished, because the "Colored" serving window was in the back on muddy ground, and the "White Only" serving window was in the front on pavement.

My mind also flashed back to the one and only time Loretta ever took me and Robert to the movies in Jackson, where Negroes could only sit in the balcony. Some movie savvy Colored boys told us that we could not laugh at the cartoons until all of the White people had finished laughing. Then they laughed out loud at my wide-eyed, opened-mouthed response.

We saw a 'Lone Ranger' movie. When the first shot was fired, I screamed, jumped out of my seat and hid on the floor. Loretta capped her hand over my mouth and dared me to breathe. She must have felt embarrassed by my frightened scream as she hissed at me through clenched teeth, "Shut up!" That Lone Ranger movie was the first media my eyes had ever seen, and my young mind perceived it as real, especially with the loud sound effects, which were also scary.

My thoughts returned to the situation at hand. Indeed, the leaping flames from Watts and the racial injustices in our nation reminded me that we did not have equal, civil rights. Maybe I should join the civil rights movement. Would it change things if I quit my high profile, sexually charged, controversial job as a Bunny? Yes it would. I would be among the unemployed. Unemployment and missing out on earning a good living held no appeal for me. Would my resignation from Playboy bring about racial equality in America? Regardless of the negative press piled upon Hugh Hefner and Playboy, the chocolate Bunnies hailed him as an equal opportunity employer. He also hired Negro club managers and others in various positions, and we all had equal rights.

Therefore, it behooved me to remain employed. Bunny Hope was delighted that my transfer was granted. She readily invited me to join her and roommate Shelley, who worked as a bookkeeper. After less than a week in the hotel, I moved in with them, and Hope initiated the search for a house to rent in Hollywood Hills.

However, the day after my arrival in Los Angeles, I went to the club to meet the Bunny Mother. Before my scheduled meeting with her, I went into the Bunny room where I met the cutest chocolate Bunny ever. Later on, I learned that she was known as "Bunny Big Butt," and her behind was referred to as "The eighth wonder of the world." That was Bunny Fran. She beamed a big smile and said, "Another chocolate Bunny and a beautiful one at that." It was instant bonding.

The LA Club was adequately staffed with an assortment of chocolate Bunnies, and Bunny Pat was one of them. With a perfectly proportioned body, she was gorgeous with a creamy, caramel complexion. She seemed reserved, but she was very sweet and warmly welcomed me to the LA Club. Pat was the only Bunny I met who was born and raised in Los Angeles,

South Central. In time, I found out that she was a quiet force when we worked together on various Playboy promotions.

In the meantime, Bunny Fran and I had exchanged phone numbers, and she soon invited me to her home in Laurel Canyon. Fran's dear friend Jane and her adorable five- year old son Michael also lived near Fran in Laural Canyon. As time progressed, Jane's home became our home for celebrating Thanksgiving and Christmas dinners. Jane was a very talented animator who made Mickey Mouse and other characters come to life at Disney and Hanna-Barbera Studios.

Like several other Bunnies, Fran also had kids. Leslie was five and Debbie was four years old. Fran introduced me to gorgeous Anna, who was known as "Bunny Lusty Busty." Her oldest daughter, also named Debbie, was five years old, and little sister Jacqueline was four. They lived in Manhattan Beach, a half block from the ocean. As time moved on, work schedules did not allow a lot of time, but all of us enjoyed many quality moments together that endeared us to each other with love and cherished memories.

I also met Fran's friend Bunny Victoria. She had been a recent Playmate of the Month, and her illuminated picture decorated the wall above the cash register in the Playmate Bar where she worked and made above average tips because of her playmate status. She also had a handsome son named Tony. He was a fearless toddler who loved everything and everyone.

Meanwhile, the bubbly, smiling Bunny Mother called me into her office for my appointment. She was fondly known as Mother Alice, a former Bunny and still a young beauty. She looked at me kindly and asked, "What is your name?" " Bunny Ann," I beamed. She looked at her roster and said that she already had thirteen Bunnies named Ann something, "Don't you have another name?" I responded, "My first name is Vessye." She said, "V what? Where in the south are you from?" Then she smiled and said, "We will turn that "V" into "Vikki." She called the key room and ordered my new name badges, and Bunny Vikki was born in August 1965.

Mother Alice thought my Cincinnati costumes were antiquated. She sent me to the wardrobe mistress where I was fitted for three new costumes: hot pink, deep yellow and sky blue. Let's just say that my new costumes were made with much less fabric. Initially, I was a little self-conscious of my new costumes, but busy nights with a heavy tray of drinks to serve did not allow time for modesty. I was pleased with the colors I had chosen for my new costumes, and I loved my new name, but anytime someone said "Ann," I would respond until "Vikki" and I became one.

The first night with my new name, when a customer called "Bunny Vikki," I thought he was talking to someone else, and I did not respond. After that slightly embarrassing incident, I remembered that I was Vikki!

Bunny Vikki adapted well to the more stylish costumes, the new environment and a much faster pace. The club was so huge, it had an elevator to the Penthouse. Thanks to the structure of The Playboy Clubs, the transition was smooth and sweet. The room configurations and service areas were basically the same in all Playboy Clubs, and the call in order for bar service was exactly the same. Based on my Cincinnati work history, my rotation schedule included working The Penthouse, and I continued accumulating merits for announcing shows in The Penthouse and started making more money than I did in Cincinnati.

The Hollywood Club presented more opportunities to work promotions and to work as an extra in movies. Several of the Bunnies were working on an entertainment career of singing, acting, dancing. I could not do any of those, but I did enjoy working as a movie extra as time moved forward. It was exciting but very time consuming. Overall, I made more money working double shifts to cover those Bunnies who heard Hollywood calling them to be the next star. I also worked some daytime lunch hours to help out when a scheduled Bunny called in sick.

I never called in sick. I did not want to spend my savings from Cincinnati. Working kept me busy accumulating more money to buy my first car and to pay rent in the three bedroom, two-bath, fully furnished house that Hope located in ,Hollywood Hills, with Hope, Shelley and Vikki listed on the lease.

Hope told us the landlady was pleased that we were Bunnies, because she knew that we made good money, and she would be paid on time, especially since we initially paid for two months rent in addition to first and last. The landlady was concerned about wild parties and who would clean up. Hope assured her that we worked all of the time and did not have time for wild parties, and a hired housekeeper would keep it clean for us.

The house was literally built in a hill, and the roof was barely visible from the street. We had to walk down several steps to the patio, which led into the living room. The living room revealed an astonishing view, and the city lights were awe inspiring at night.

I do not recall the reason, but one day the landlady stopped by. I was home alone, wearing bright yellow chiffon shortie pajamas and fluffy yellow house slippers. When she walked down the steps, I was sweeping up leaves from the patio and had a scarf tied around my head to prevent dusty hair. She presumed that I was the cleaning lady and addressed me accordingly. When I told her that I was Bunny Vikki, she nearly croaked. She did "A Fred Sanford!" She clutched her right hand to her chest, gasped for air and ran around the patio panting, "I can't have any Negroes living in my house." Red-faced, moaning and mumbling, she flounced her old, wrinkled self up the steps and drove away.

Her racist response added insult and pain to past negative images from my childhood and the civil unrest that was taking place in Watts and Los

Angeles. I forced myself to focus on the words of my maternal grandfather: "All White people are not mean and evil." Working The Playboy Club and living with my White roommates validated our grandfather's words. Those realities caused me to wonder why White people in the entertainment industry, as a rule, treated Negroes better than a lot of churchgoing White people treated us?

When I told Shelley and Hope about the incident, they were hurt and angry. But my reenactment of her behavior made them happy with laughter. Then Hope called and shamed the landlady. The following week she sent us a basket of fresh flowers, and the card was addressed, "To Vikki, Hope, and Shelley."

Life was good at home and work, but Hope and I did not work the exact same shifts. Having moved a greater distance from the club, I really needed a car. So, I bought a brand new 1965 Mustang with a silver body, black vinyl hard top, big white wall tires with wire spoke spinners.

Owning a car enabled me to drive to Hollywood Studios and to work more hours in the club, after trading in my Indiana Driver License for my California License. My entire life revolved around the club because everyone I knew in Los Angeles worked for Playboy. Therefore, I looked forward to going to work where I throughly enjoyed the entertainers, especially the comedians.

Pat Morita and Charlie Callas were my favorites. They were both headliners and never worked the club concurrently. Whenever either of them starred in our club, I was always among the small group of Bunnies that they invited to breakfast after work. Both of them were beyond hilarious in a small setting and caused us to laugh loudly until daybreak and our sides ached.

Tony Bennett was also a Playboy headliner and everyone's favorite crooner. I was also among the Bunnies that he invited to breakfast after work. Unlike the comedians, he was low-key and a concerned father type figure. His favorite topic was his beautiful wife and her great Italian cooking. When he spoke of her, he always flashed a big smile and said, "I can't wait to get back home." Among the Bunnies, Tony was, "Mr. Nice Guy." The entertainers did not know it, but we made up names for all of them.

Overall, most of the entertainers and patrons in the club were polite, respectful, and fun loving. Moreover, my Playboy friends and I looked forward to creating our own fun whenever we found time to do so.

One of our favorite fun places was The Whisky A Go Go on Sunset, a few doors west of Playboy. The Whisky featured some amazing entertainers, including Ike and Tina Turner. Because I was with some people who knew her, I met Tina backstage one time. She was tearful at the time because Ike was mistreating her. When I heard a few details, I cried also, because Ike reminded me of Larry, and I empathized with Tina. I wondered why she had not escaped from him.

Even so, Tina was warm and embracing towards us as we exchanged brief hugs. I marveled over being in her presence for those few minutes. We left her dressing room and took our reserved seats in the club so that she could prepare to perform.

After the MC's high energy introduction with the band playing in the background, Tina Turner hit the stage and exploded in song and dance. I was astonished by her transformation! She appeared to be the most beautiful and happy woman I had ever seen, without a care in the world!

Working for Playboy, hanging out with my friends and learning the Los Angeles area filled me with wonderment. Ron, a Negro busboy, increased my wonderment when I learned that he was a third year student at UCLA. He was one of the most efficient busboys in the club, and we tipped him well. Playboy busboys made great money. Ron was paying his way through UCLA, and he was the first one in his family to attend a university. Amused by my wide-eyed surprise that he was a UCLA student, Ron asked if I would like to see the campus? I nodded yes with my mouth agape, and he laughed at my incredulous reaction.

I thought, if only he knew... Memories flashed back and my heart cracked over "uneducable," and it hurt to think or speak about it. Instead, I said, "Wow! I would love to go to UCLA someday."

We made a plan to meet early one Saturday morning, and Ron drove us to UCLA and around the campus. The acres of sprawling land and the many different buildings were mind-boggling. Before I recovered from the visual impact of UCLA, Ron asked if I had been to the Santa Monica beach? "No I have not." He said, "We are so close, we may as well go."

He drove west on Wilshire Boulevard and turned onto some other streets until he wound his way into a parking space close to the ocean. I could see the rolling waves from the car, and I squealed with excitement! The ocean breeze was unlike any I had ever breathed before. We removed our shoes and walked across the sand to the water's edge. I was brave enough to let the water roll over my feet before I jumped back, concerned that the waves would suck me in. It was the first time I had ever seen an ocean, and I found it majestically beautiful, powerful, and uplifting. Experiencing the Pacific Ocean and UCLA on the same day remains one of the most imprinted days in my life.

In spite of turbulent times and civil unrest in our nation, my personal life was fabulous, but my first Christmas in Los Angeles did not seem real. It was entertaining and fun, but it did not feel connected to the birth of Jesus, according to my programmed perception of the event. Furthermore, Christmas always came with cold weather and snow. I laughed out loud when Hope, Shelley, and I decorated our fresh cut tree. The trees' fragrance flashed back to joyful memories of my first Christmas with Grandma Mamie. As Hope, Shelley and I decorated our tree, I could not stop giggling, because the three of us were wearing shorts and sandals. They laughed also, happy to be out of Ohio, where they were born and raised in the ice and snow of many winters. I was surprised to learn that California had winter snow so close in Big Bear, wherever that was.

Shorts and sandals were worn year-round in Southern California, and the continuous warm weather made it difficult for me to distinguish one month from another and keep track of time. Consequently, my first year blew by faster than anticipated. I wished for more time to enjoy the unlimited California universe. Over the past year, I had worked hard and saved money.

Like most of the Bunnies, I was also frugal. We frequently joked about our short-term positions as a Bunny. We laughed that there were no "Bunny Maternity" costumes, and no "Bunny Granny" costumes either. We frequently spoke of things we would like to do after working for Playboy. Some of us wanted to become a movie star, marry a rich handsome guy, have some children, go to college or law school, start a business, travel around the world. Our minds were fertile with bright ideas. We were well aware of the time constraints and thankful that we hadbeen given a glamorous opportunity for a short span of time.

Meanwhile, I was working promotions and as an extra in movies, and the concept of modeling and acting translated as a possibility for me. After all, since I had been hired as a Bunny, maybe I could.

One day I was talking with Hope and Shelley about the possibilities. Both of them agreed that if I wanted to become a really good actress, I should perform in theater first, but before that I must take lots and lots of acting classes. Hope and Shelley were college graduates with some background in theater. The more they talked, the more I thought, "Oh well, maybe some day, but no time for all of that now."

By summer 1966, my life was like a happy movie. My self-confidence had been increased for possibilities when my picture was featured in the centerfold of 'Jet Magazine' dated July 28, 1966. I wore a white bikini and stood leaning against a tree, by the little lake in MacArthur Park, close to downtown Los Angeles. The caption reads in part: "...Vikki Summers, aspirant actress, 37-23-37..." Stokely Carmichael, a "Black Power" advocate was on the front cover. In spite of my happy fairy-tale life, I was painfully aware of the civil rights struggles as reminded by Stokley on the front cover of 'Jet' and wished that everybody else could work together like we did in The Playboy Clubs.

As mentioned, the chocolate Bunnies considered Playboy an equal opportunity employer because they hired us. Playboy was interested in hiring reliable employees regardless of ethnicity, and Mr. Dudley just happened to be a tall, intelligent Negro man and a top manager in Hollywood. He was fondly known as "Mr. Dudley-Do-Right," because everything went right on his shifts.

The clubs hired women and men from wherever they came from, and the Hollywood Club was like the United Nations with Bunnies from France, Germany, Italy, China and Mexico.

I did not know of any Latino people in Tennessee, Missouri, Indiana or Ohio, but I met my first Mexican friends in The Hollywood Club. I had heard German and French spoken while working The Cincinnati Club, but not Spanish. When the Mexicans talked to each other in Spanish, I wondered why they had to say it so fast? Perhaps it was because Hollywood was fast. There was always an element of excitement and festivity.

In October, one festive night during the week, Bunny Fran and I were working the Playmate Bar. The jazz trio was playing lively music, and our patrons were eating, drinking, laughing, and enjoying themselves. The crowd flow was comfortably busy compared to crazy busy.

There was a "celebrity booth" near the life-sized, dazzling photographs of several playmates, who made the room very popular. There were a couple of steps leading up to the booth, which appeared elevated in the room. Purple velvet covered the cushy, gold-trimmed sofa and chairs. A super-sized golden colored rope with royal tassels cordoned off that section.

Various celebrities had been seated there. If there were no big name celebrities at the time, Hef's executives were also seated in the booth. They were known as "C-1" key holders, and Bunnies were privileged to date them. Otherwise, we could not date our customers. Some of the executives were attractive and desirable but unavailable. Others were not so desirable, and one in particular was obnoxious. The end of his last name was "burg," but among the Bunnies he was known as "Mr. Leesleezburg," and none of us had a burning desire to hang with him. However, our charming and attentive service led him to believe the contrary.

On that October night, "Mr. Leesleezburg" was seated in the booth, and his arrogant attitude indicated that he was trying to make a big impression on the people in his party. Fran was their serving Bunny. With all of my customers over-serviced and satisfied, I perched on the arm of an empty sofa, where all of my customers could see and signal me. Bunnies could not sit down in the club. We were trained to perch on furniture like pretty birds. As the evening progressed and more alcohol was consumed, I noticed Fran walking towards me with a bursting smile on her gorgeous face. Her shoulders were shaking from silent laughter. She perched her fluffy tail next to mine. She giggled, "Mr. Leesleezeburg" sent me to tell you that he would love to take you out tonight when you finish work.

I covered my mouth with my right hand, but laughter bubbled through me, which upset my balanced tray, and it crashed on the floor from my left hand. My tray was not loaded, and there was no mess to clean up, just a few napkins and a couple of ashtrays and matches. I picked up my tray in a flash, and Fran returned to her prized customer. "Mr. Leesleezburg" asked Fran, "What did Bunny Vikki say?" Fran duplicated my reactions by covering her mouth and bursting with giggles, and "Mr. Leesleezburg's" pack of wolves howled with laughter.

The following night when I went to work, the manager told me that my services were no longer needed by The Playboy Club. My brain could not process that information. "What! Why?" He said that a customer made a complaint about me, and that's why my services were no longer needed. The manager instructed me to clear my locker and leave my Bunny tails, ears and costumes with the wardrobe mistress.

Stunned and numbed by the shocking information, I was only able to move from muscle memory. This had to be a bad dream that I would soon wake up from. It was not a bad dream. My Cinderella coach had crashed and turned into a pumpkin. Mother Alice, Fran, Hope, Shelley and and all of my friends were equally shocked. How could that be? One of my nicknames at work was "Bunny Goodie Two Shoes." I did not smoke or drink. I never missed work. I was always willing to cover a shift. I always earned merits instead of demerits. I was among the top five Bunnies for the highest sales for drink averages, and there were approximately seventy Bunnies in the club.

If I had known anything about fragile, inflated egos and bullshit politics, I would have known to send "Mr. Leesleezburg" a bullshit reply that would have satisfied his ego. If I had known, I would have told Fran to tell him that, "I would love to go out with you, but my boyfriend is extremely jealous. He keeps track of every move I make, and he would beat me badly. You would not want him to hurt me like that would you?"

I experienced the flip side of joy when I was fired from Playboy, but the agony of being fired did not alter the ecstasy of having been hired. For the next couple of weeks I cried in my pillow when necessary. I felt displaced, because my Los Angeles world totally revolved around The Playboy Club.

12

TOPLESS GO GO GIRL

I was no longer a Playboy employee, but I still had my Bunny status and continued working as an extra in movies, but those infrequent jobs were not enough to support my lifestyle, and I did not want to deplete my savings. Hanging out with my friends from Playboy did not change. One night we were partying at the Whiskey with some guys who owned a topless club, and they were looking for attractive, shapely women to work there.

When they discovered that I was no longer a Bunny, they asked if I would come in for an interview? I said, "Topless! I don't know if I can do that." They convinced me that it would not hurt to come and take a look at the girls working there. I took their phone number with a promise to call. A couple of days later I called and agreed to go in and talk to Mark in their topless club, which was also located on Sunset in the vicinity of Playboy and The Whiskey. As requested, I wore a two-piece bikini under my clothes and spike-heeled pumps. The topless club was a restaurant that served bloody-rare roast beef with a complete lunch menu.

When I arrived around 2:00 p.m., lunch was officially over, but there were three stunning White girls working at the time. One girl was bartending. The floor behind the bar appeared to have been designed so that the bartender's nipples swayed slightly above the noses of customers sitting on the bar stools, wishing for more than drinks.

Another girl was wearing a tall white chef's hat. She had a red linen napkin tied across the front of her bikini which made a tiny apron. Her bare breasts bobbled above the roast beef as she gently sliced it paper thin with her razor sharp butcher's knife.

The third girl was serving the few remaining customers seated at tables.

Wearing a big smile, she came to take my drink order, but my eyes were fixated on her huge two-toned breasts with bright pink nipples. She was proud of her tanned lines, which made her white breasts appear even bigger. I ordered a Coke. As requested, I had removed my bikini top, and I had to follow her and select my own lunch from the buffet serving area. I felt embarrassed but tried not to show it.

As I picked over my salad, Mark explained the the job was "Hands off" by the customers, but "If you want to go out with them afterwards, that's your business." We pay $10.00 an hour for a four hour shift, plus whatever you make in tips. He told me to walk around and talk to all of the girls and ask them any questions that I had in mind. All three of the ladies were very friendly and encouraging. Upon leaving the club, I told Mark that I would call him the following day.

Topless! I realized how well-dressed I had been working as a Bunny. I did not tell anyone about the topless job interview. I felt like I was sliding downhill. During my restless sleep, I had a nightmare about my grandparents' and Reverend Nelson's disapproval. Their voices overlapped, "You got saved! You are sinking in sin from bad to worse! What happened to your Salvation?"

The next day I called Mark and said, "I can't do that." He said, "Listen, I'll pay you $12.00 an hour, but keep your mouth shut. I'm counting on you because it's difficult to find really cute and qualified Negro girls to work topless." I asked myself if my grandparents or Reverend Nelson would financially support me? Thereby, I put my nightmares to sleep, and went to work as a topless hostess the next day.

I kept my mouth shut regarding my hourly wage of $12.00 and agreed with everyone who said that earning $10.00 an hour is a lot of money. It was 1966 and the basic minimum wage in California was around $1.30 per hour. So $10.00 an hour was "big money."

My shift was 10:00 a.m. - 2:00 p.m, Tuesday - Friday. Fortunately, I had worked some lunch hours at Playboy, which prepared me to work days, but I was definitely a nightbird. It was painful passing by Playboy on my way to work. At least my new work location also had an upscale appearance. The topless club occupied the second floor of a two story building, and patrons had to walk up a flight of steps.

My spike-heeled shoes, round chocolate breasts and a nervous smile greeted everyone who entered the club. "Welcome to lunch. How many are in your party?" Raising my hands, I held up the appropriate number of fingers towards the male host. As I walked patrons to him for seating, their unrestricted eyeball energy burned my behind when I turned around to greet other incoming guests. Fast reflexes enabled me to intercept their tips with a gracious "Thank you," before they could stuff money into my bikini. Since we could not stuff money in our bosoms, we folded the bills length

144

wise and wore them draped around our fingers.

All of us were making fistfuls of dollars, and we liked how Mark rotated the schedule. One day I was working the tables and serving a party of two sharply dressed business men. They ordered drinks and two packs of cigarettes. I returned from the bar and automatically did the "Bunny dip" when I served their drinks. They lifted a cigarette to their lips, and flames from my lighter lit it for them.

While blowing smoke through his nose, one of the men said, "I bet you do a good blow job." Without pondering, I said, "Oh no sir, I never learned how to smoke." They pounded the table with red-faced laughter, and they each gave me a $20.00 tip. Wasn't that crazy! I instantly realized how strenuous working Playboy had been. As a topless server, we did not have to work hard for the money, men just gave it to us. When customers asked me, "Why is a nice girl like you working topless?" My standard answer was, "My father died, and I have to pay my own way through UCLA."

"Working my way through UCLA or USC" became a standard line for most of the topless servers, and it provided content for conversations as customers stared at our breasts.

A funny thing happened at work one day when Laura got the biggest tuition tip ever. As usual, customers were rapidly occupying all of the tables and chairs that were available. Topless servers were an added bonus to the tasty food served for lunch. Laura, a beautiful, busty brunette, had been recently hired on her twenty-first birthday. She had moved from Phoenix, Arizona a short time ago to become an actress. All of us had "swallowed our pride" and removed our tops for the remarkable pay scale. Laura told us that she went topless to replace her old unreliable, "hand-me-down" car with a new one. She said, "My dad can easily afford to help me get one, but he's such a jerk and told me to earn it myself."

Laura and I were working tables near each other, serving drinks and food to those who did not want to walk to the buffet. Suddenly Laura gasped and gawked at a handsome man who was smooching on his sexy blond eye candy. Her top was designed so that the men could gaze at her breasts instead of ours.

Laura stared at the couple in a state of disbelief and said, "Oh my God! That's my dad!" She panicked and ran to hide in the kitchen. I ran behind her and so did another server who heard her say, "My dad." We developed an instant plan. We told Laura that she had the upper hand in this situation and to go and serve her dad like she served all of her customers. With new found confidence, Laura strutted to her dad's table and said, "Good afternoon Sir, may I get a drink for you and your lady?"

Laura's dad looked up at her naked breasts, and they rendered him speechless! He recoiled from the blond like she was a viper. His body shifted in his seat, but he could not find a comfortable spot, as he loosened his necktie. His face flushed beet red. Beads of sweat formed on his forehead. Then the beet red color drained from his face, and he literally appeared "ghost white."

The words, "Laura's dad" had spread like wild fire among everyone who was working at the time. We hid our faces behind menus to conceal exploding giggles, but we could not prevent our boobs from bouncing while our bodies shook with laughter. Laura was in control of the situation and loved every minute. She smiled at him and said, "If you don't tell my mom about me, I won't tell her about you."

Her dad appeared to have lost his appetite. Shortly thereafter, he paid his tab and gave Laura the biggest tip ever, a new car and more help with rent if she would find "a decent job." Later on, Laura flashed a big smile and said, "This job is very decent," and she continued her topless career in different clubs. Like the other busty girls, Laura and I quickly became aware of countless, topless clubs where men were waiting to hand us cash.

The girl with deep tan lines across her breasts told us about the topless circuit that included most of the topless clubs in the Los Angeles area. Her name was Mary, and she became my best topless friend. She also danced as a topless "Go Go Girl" at night. She said, "I told the manager about you, and he can't wait to hire you." I gulped, "Go Go! I don't know how to dance at all, not to mention dancing practically naked!" She laughed and said, "Don't worry, the men won't notice anything except your gorgeous body. All you have to do is pretend that you are an actress playing the part of a topless Go Go dancer."

One day after we finished our lunch hour shift, Mary took me to a shop that supplied glittering G-string bottoms and accessories for topless dancers. Each costume that I examined seemed to have less material than the other one. I bought a white satin bottom with lots of rhinestones and a red bottom with removable suspenders that criss-crossed my chest. Mary said, "You will also need some pasties." I asked, "What are pasties?" She giggled and pointed towards two little glittering cones in a small box and said, "You will have to glue these over your nipples."

Already feeling naked and foolish, knowing that I could not dance, why did I let Mary talk me into this? Because I was working two or three days a week instead of five. It was customary for managers to reduce the number of days that we worked, so that they could keep hiring fresh breasts for old customers.

Mary had arranged for me to meet with Scott, the manager of the upscale Go Go club in North Hollywood. She told me, "He has already hired you." I agreed to meet them at the club a couple of hours prior to show time. The show consisted of five dancers. Scott and I sat at a table in the audience so that I could observe the dancers and get some ideas. Five different sets of various sized breasts bounced around the stage, as each girl wiggled through her routine. The manager told me that it was important to move around the entire stage so that every man would think that I was dancing just for him. Scott knew that I was embarrassed and filled with fear and self-doubt. He said, "Don't worry. You will be up on the stage, and they are down here. There is no contact between you and the customers."

At the beginning of each routine, I noticed that every dancer placed a glass beer pitcher center stage. It was conveniently located for drooling customers to drop in money, while the dancer did bumps and grinds around and over the pitcher.

When the fifth girl finished dancing to her second song, she blew kisses, accepted applause and whistles, blew more kisses, picked up her pitcher full of cash and disappeared backstage. The girls changed costumes wigs and makeup for their next routine. When the last dancer finished, it was time for the first girl's next routine. All too soon my turn was coming up, and I would be the third dancer on stage.

Mary showed me some pelvic gyrations, told me to just keep smiling and moving around the stage. My thoughts returned to Tanya, the shake-dancer, and I wished that I could do everything that she had done. Mary encouraged me, "Remember you're just an actress pretending to be a topless Go Go dancer, and don't forget to shake it up over your pitcher." Scott scheduled me to go on after Mary. She was relaxed, happy, and very comfortable on stage. She made the guys roar and stuff money in her pitcher.

Then it was my turn. I was wearing glittering spike heels and my red criss-cross G-string. Music played, and the stage lights came on. Men whistled and applauded and so did the women. I tried to remember everything Mary had told me.

My non-existent routine was beyond my control. I was on stage for an eternity, but I only recalled shaking from fear, running around the stage, and some guy yelling, "Hey, slow down." Each girl had to dance through two songs, and that included me. Near the end of my second song, I was bouncing around and the pastie popped off my left breast and glittered across the stage. The audience howled and cheered. Some man hollered, "Yeah, hot chocolate," and money poured into my pitcher. When my pastie fell off, I threw up my hands like, "What can I say," and I blew kisses to the audience, grabbed my pitcher and ran backstage, a few steps ahead of my tears.

Mary was waiting for me near the stage steps. I blubbered, "I can't do this. I feel so ridiculous." She gave me a reassuring hug, which almost smothered me between her breasts, where dark tan lines made them look like four instead of two. She said, "Oh, don't cry. You did good. Don't worry. Would you like some coke?" I sobbed, "Yes please, with lots of ice and cherries." Mary was shaking from laughter as she leaned back from the hug and looked at me. I burst into giggles when I saw my right eyelash stuck on her left breast. Mary stared at me and said, "You don't smoke, drink, or nothing. You will make a fortune."

Go Go dancers used several different names to earn their fortunes, and I was "Bambi, Cookie, Candy or Hot Chocolate," depending upon which club I worked, but my fellow dancers called me "Mustang Sally." Each of my personas required glitter. As time moved forward, I met the seamstress who designed individual costumes for us, and I chose some fabrics that matched my high-heeled pumps from my Bunny costumes.

However, one of my favorite things to dance in was a pair of high-heeled, white pleather boots that covered most of my upper thighs, and I wore long white gloves. I would slide the top of my boots slightly down my thigh like a stripper, and the men would go crazy. Their reactions to boot stripping and removing my gloves made me laugh out loud. Since I was already practically naked, why did they hoot and holler over lowered boot tops and gloves?

I had learned the basics of stripping while working as a non-topless waitress in "The Pink Pussycat," a strip club on Santa Monica Boulevard in Hollywood. This occurred between Playboy and working topless. During my few weeks of working there, a friendly stripper known as Brandy used a few minutes of her time to show me and two other girls some moves. After the club closed at 2:00 a.m., we went up on stage and attempted to duplicate Brandy's examples. I did not become a stripper because it was technical, and there were more work opportunities for free-form Go Go Girls.

Boot stripping was amusing, but the guys also groveled when I slid my arms out of shoulder length gloves. As I became more comfortable on stage, my most intriguing props were feather boas, which I bought in every available color. I would slowly dance near the edge of the stage, twirl the boa all around my bare body, pull it through my thighs and wave it from side-to-side like a device for hypnosis. As I gyrated and waved my boa over the stage's edge, the customers appeared transfixed, and their heads automatically swayed from side to side with each move of the boa.

After a couple of weeks of pretending to be an actress, working topless was just another job, which was made easier from the wisdom of Grandma Lizzy, "If ya see anythang God didn't gimme, tho yo hat at it." No one ever threw a hat at me, but they did throw lots of dollars with my approval.

Actually, I did not approve of some beer bars where I worked in the San Fernando Valley, but they were part of the circuit. All of those bars had tap beer, a pool, table and jukeboxes where customers played our dance music. Favorite tunes for those patrons were songs like, "Woolly Bully" and "Gloria." At least "Woolly Bully" brought back happy memories from Cincinnati. My least favorite was a slow paced country song with a twangy guitar. I do not recall the title, but the male singer drawled, "Hot dammed summer in the city, back of my neck gittin might pretty." Imagine Go Go dancing to that. The beer bars did not have a disc jockey, but there was a light technician.

During the first few weeks of my topless, free-form dancing career, stage lights brought me a brand new experience. One night when I was on stage shaking it up and down to "Gloria," the light technician hit me with strobe lights, and I shrieked from fear. The flickering lights made me feel like I was falling off the stage, which scared me silly. My eyes felt like a million flash bulbs clicked at the same time. When the regular stage lights resumed, my vision was momentarily distorted, but I could hear amused laughter from the audience.

Free-form dancing worked well for all Go Go girls, but some of the clubs also required a group routine for the finale. One of those clubs was located on Century Boulevard near LAX. The club advertised, "A Sizzling Topless Review," which also featured a very fat, topless comedienne. She was White and overly endowed with huge, low-hanging breasts, fat stomach, and a pretty face. Her name was Juicy.

There were six dancers in the review, and I was one of them. Some of the girls had dance backgrounds in ballet and modern, and there was also a tap dancer. Some of them knew how to spin around, leap, and do splits.

Unlike any of the other clubs I had worked, this one had a choreographer named Dennis, who helped with individual routines and structured the group finale. The six of us lined up on stage behind Dennis and watched him demonstrate the finale steps as he verbalized each move. Then he instructed us to duplicate the moves as he spoke each step. Regardless, I felt myself moving in the opposite direction of the other girls.

Very soon, Dennis was in a complete tizzy, because all of my steps were opposite from what he was telling us. Impatiently, he said to me, "Slow down! Don't you know how to count?" I said, "Yes" and began rapidly counting, "1-2-3-4-5-6." Before I got to "7," Dennis threw up both of his hands in the air, spun around, did a dancer's fall, and sprawled out on stage on his stomach, kicking his heels in the air, which made all of us laugh.

Then he got up and asked me, "Do you know what a dance beat is? Where is your natural rhythm? You know that all of us are supposed to know how to sing and dance, and you are the only one of us in the show. Never mind! Just follow me." He snapped his fingers, and repeated, "Boom-boom-boom-boom." I did catch the beat, but Dennis ended up tying a pretty red ribbon above my right knee and a green one above my left knee to help me with the very modified Can-Can finale. Dennis also operated the stage lights and played the records for our dance routines. He introduced Juicy and each one of us as we appeared on stage.

Juicy opened and closed the show. Her body gyrations and jokes made the audience blush and gush with laughter. One of her jokes was: "What do you get if you glue three of those gorgeous topless dancers together?" Pointing towards her breasts, she said: "Me, I'm your three in one." As the laughter subsided, Juicy concluded with: "Not to worry, we are going to bring on the boobs, I mean the dancers, one girl at a time. So sit back, relax and hold on to your jock strap."

Above the whistles and applause, Dennis made some funny comments about Juicy and introduced the first dancer. The show proceeded with each of us dancing to one song, but we did five shows per night. After the last dancer finished, the lights faded. Music blasted, Dennis further pumped up the audience, and stage lights flashed on all of us for the finale, which we danced at the end of each show.

I was shocked that Juicy could dance, and she executed the steps and turns with ease and fun. For the finale, Juicy was positioned in the middle, with three of us on each side, and I was always next to her for comedic reasons. She held a microphone in her left hand and held her right hand above my head. She indicated, "No way," by turning her head from side-to-side and blasting, "Ladies and gentlemen I don't care what you have heard, all of them can't sing and dance. I have more rhythm in one tit than this one has in her entire sexy body. Here we go, red ribbon, green ribbon..." The audience laughed, cheered and whistled, and all of us made considerably more money than office or factory workers, nurses, teachers, and dental assistants.

Although my salary was $12 an hour, most of my income came from tips that customers stuffed into my beer pitcher on stage. Most of the cash was $1 and $5 dollar bills with a few $10s and $20s sprinkled in. The greater number of bills were singles, but one customer could drop in $20 or more throughout the night.

One night I was working an upscale club in North Hollywood. Reportedly, some Hollywood producers and directors were frequent patrons, but I never knew who was in the audience. One Saturday night the club was still packed when I closed out the show with my last routine for the evening. I blew "Thank you" kisses, scooped up my money and dashed off stage to the dressing room. When I started unfolding and counting money from my pitcher, a $100 bill caused me to gasp! I had been given over $200 for my last routine of dancing through two records, not to mention tips I had already made on three previous routines.

Excitement and underlying fear came upon me. I had so much money it was scary, almost $500, plus $60 salary. An astonishing amount for wiggling around the stage topless for five hours. That night remains the highest pay I ever received for one night, or day, of work. Comparing that to some prior incomes caused flashbacks from Denmark, Tennessee.

I remember it had been an extremely hot day. Too hot for a ten-year-old, or anyone, to be chopping cotton. I had begged to work as a "hired hand" and went with Mother and others to chop cotton for a nice, young White man, who paid $3 a day. But around 11:30 a.m., I passed out from the heat and fell on the ground. And now over $500 for one night of work. Utterly astonishing!

Nonetheless, I nervously wondered who dropped in the $100? Customers frequently dropped in notes and business cards, but they were all mixed in the pitcher, and we could not determine who dropped in what.

Since I was the last dancer, all of the other girls were gone except Mary, and her husband was waiting. After a brief conversation and giggles over audience reactions, she left with her husband. A few minutes later she came running back to the dressing room and said, "Hey, there's a guy waiting outside, leaning against a yellow and black '66 El Dorado, just so you know." We had to stand on a stool to see out of the tall window. We looked out, and Mary pointed towards the waiting man. She said, "Get the bartender or one of the stock guys to walk you to your car." Mary walked out and fear rushed in! My heart pounded rapidly, and I suspected that he must be the man who dropped in the $100. Now what?

Maybe I should run out there and hand it back. But what if he was not the one? Maybe he was one of those men who dropped in a note or business card with "call me" written on? Maybe not... I thought, "Never mind, I'll just wait for him to leave." I gave him ample time before looking out of the window again.

After reading a magazine article, I climbed up, peeked out, and there he stood, resolute, arms folded across his chest, one foot crossed over the other. He was dressed in black, wearing dark sunglasses and leaning against the car. I hopped off the stool and recoiled behind the dressing room door. I tried to read more of the magazine and waited a long time before looking out again. Certain that he was long gone, I looked out, and he was still standing in the same position. My panic meter escalated! "What should I do?"

All of the guys were busy working, getting the club ready for the next day, and none of them were within view from our dressing room. Furthermore, having the bartender or one of the stock guys walk me to my car was not a good idea, because the man could follow me, see that I was driving a silver and black 1965 Mustang and memorize my license plate information for future reference. The club closed at 2:00 a.m. It was 2:30, and the guy was rooted like a tree.

Fear overrode panic, and tears flooded my glued on eyelashes. There was a small sofa and footstool, a little table, a couple of stuffed chairs, and a mirrored makeup vanity with a bench. Anxiety prevented me from sitting down. I paced around our small dressing room crying and condemning myself for working topless, as daunting images of Grandma Mamie and

Reverend Nelson flashed in my mind.

Sniffling and feeling sorry for myself, I turned around and saw Grandma Lizzy sitting on the sofa! Stunned by her apparition, I froze in my tracks, locked in time and space! Her cackling voice broke the silence. "Boohoo yo naked ass Gal. Dat's whut you git fu showing yo ass!" Then she spat snuff and vanished!

Shocked by her totally unexpected appearance, I forgot about everything else in the world! I stood motionless, wide-eyed, both hands covering my open mouth and waited for Grandma Lizzy to come back, but she did not.

Suddenly I remembered my predicament and stood on the stool to look out. To my alarm, the man was still standing in the same position!

I noticed a box of cocoa on the table. We had a coffee pot and a variety of hot drinks to keep us warm. Following Grandma Lizzy's lead, I stuffed a generous amount of cocoa inside my bottom lip and rubbed it over all of my teeth. I peeled off my hanging eyelashes and wiped off my lipstick. I tied a scarf around my head like a cleaning lady and covered my clothing with a long frumpy frock that was hanging on the dressing room door.

Although the shoes were too big, I stuck my feet in somebody's worn out, tennis shoes and clomped out to confront the waiting stranger.

I positioned my tongue inside my bottom lip and kept it there. If you speak with your tongue tucked inside of your bottom lip, it will distort your speech, and your face will look very funny. Armed with a mouth full of cocoa, brown teeth, and a distorted face, I rushed toward the waiting man.

As I approached him, I loudly cleared my throat and spat cocoa on the ground. While wiping cocoa from the corners of my mouth, I said, "Scuse me Mister, is you goin to Hollywood? My ride can't make it to pick me up. Can you drop me off?" More throat clearing sounds loudly emerged, as a big batch of chocolate spit splattered the ground, too close for comfort. I coughed, "Scuse me Suh," and wiped dripping cocoa from my mouth with the back of my right hand and swiped my hand on the front of the frock.

Turning around to open his car door, the man said, "Sorry Ma'am, I don't have time." He slid into the driver's seat and drove off in great haste, leaving the little old cleaning lady to find another way home.

After watching his red tail lights disappear in the darkness, I flew back inside the club to our dressing room, quickly reassembled myself and I dashed to my car.

Car doors locked, feeling triumphant, I pounded my steering wheel, hollered and giggled all the way home. Moreover, I thanked Jesus Christ and believed that He was watching over me. Through all of my childhood pain and suffering in life, I had prayed daily since age ten when "I got saved" in St. John Baptist church. I thanked Jesus for sending Grandma Lizzy to deliver me in a time of need. "Is you goin to Hollywood?" I did not understand how the process of Grandma Lizzy's appearance worked, but the incident exemplified the words of Grandma Mamie, when she frequently claimed that, "The Lawd works in mysterious ways." Mystery surrounded how Grandma Lizzy, Trixie, and Grandma Mamie returned after death. Unable to explain how, I simply accepted them with gratitude, because they solved a problem for me.

The following day, Mary called to find out what happened, and we screeched with laughter as I recounted my experience. Afterwards, I called and told the club manager about the incident and how I resolved it. He asked, "Why didn't you come to the office and get me?" After listening to my explanation, he laughed heartily and rotated me to a different club where I continued praying for safety and protection.

While rotating my way through Playboy and topless clubs, I did not have a significant other or a special person in my life. Building a relationship was not a high priority, because the men I met were basically interested in my assets. I was not the one that they would take home to meet their family.

Although Playboy referred to Bunnies and Playmates as "The girls next door," we were not publicly perceived as a faithful wife or honorable homemaker. Topless women and strippers were generally thought of as hookers or loose women at best. Neither of those professions caused the public to regard us as intelligent and moral women.

We were well aware of negative public opinion but courageous and smart enough to take advantage of the phenomenal earning opportunities, where no man ever touched or insulted me in any manner, which is way more than I could say for my own father. Moreover, I never experienced any racial or financial discrimination and no racial slurs were ever slung towards me. Being called "Hot Chocolate" and "Brown Sugar" were compliments to my profession.

Overall, strippers and topless dancers were less vulnerable to being groped than some women who worked in office buildings or other "decent" occupations. All of us were mindful that we could not remain twenty-something forever. Therefore, we disregarded any other opinions and continued earning more money in one night than a lot of people made in a month.

My bare breasts and G-strings were diametrically opposed to my moral fiber and prayer life, which placed constraints on finding an understanding love connection. Even so, a few months after my arrival in Los Angeles, Fran had introduced me to a young Negro man who was a popular barber in the Crenshaw area.

Bunny Fran was a customer in the barbershop where she kept her hair cut short for wig comfort. I was delighted to go with her to have my hair cut for the same reasons. We partially lived in our variety of wigs, but we kept our hair cut short so that it would remain healthy and cool under any wig.

Leonard was her barber, and he made sure that he was the only one to cut our hair. When Fran and I went to get our hair cut, we did not look like glamor girls. Customers and people in the shop doubted that we were Playboy Bunnies. Our standard response was, "Hey, we are just ordinary women who happen to work in The Playboy Club."

Since we survived on tips, we were overly generous tippers. Fran gave Leonard a $10 tip and so did I. He definitely believed that we were Bunnies! Our visits to the barber shop were infrequent. Leonard had immediately given me his phone number so that I could call for my next appointment, but I had not given him mine. He promised that he and some friends were coming for a night out at The Playboy Club. Knowing that Fran was in love and engaged, he was especially looking forward to seeing me in my Bunny costume. Leonard and friends did eventually come to the club one busy Saturday night. Customers were constantly pouring in. I was working The Playmate Bar, and my station was seated to capacity. Bunny Ginger was their serving Bunny. Initially, Leonard did not recognize me in my shoulder length, black curly wig, makeup, eyelashes, and shocking pink Bunny costume. Upon recognizing my voice and laughter, his facial expression revealed astonishment as he maintained his cool. He groaned and smiled at me with pride and jealousy. While slightly grinding his teeth, he gently scolded, "Why haven't you called me?" As a customer signaled my service, I said, "I've been busy," and dashed off to serve more drinks.

I chuckled as Leonard and his friends engaged in reckless eyeballing. Between the beautiful serving Bunnies and the bigger than life pictures of Playmates decorating the bar, who could blame them? Even so, Leonard had stated that he wanted to be more than my barber and just a friend.

13

AVOIDED HOMICIDE

By January 1967 Leonard and I were more than just friends. Due to my "in demand" work schedule, I did not have a lot of time for Leonard, which greatly annoyed him. Nevertheless, we went to dinner in upscale Hollywood restaurants and to the movies. It did not matter to me that he drove my car, and I paid the tabs frequently. Leonard did take me to meet his mother and some sisters among his many siblings.

Meeting Leonard's mother occurred after he had casually expressed some concerns about her health. Her condition was manageable, but she needed some costly medication. Without asking how much it cost, I immediately gave him $50 for his mother's medication. After that random act of kindness, his mother was anxious to meet me.

Leonard's mother and sisters were embracing and intrigued by the Playboy mystique. I did not tell Leonard that I was no longer a Bunny. They were curious to know how I became a Bunny, and they asked endless questions. One of his jealous sisters said, "It must not be too hard, cause she ain't all that cute." However, his mother was kind and wanted to thank me in person for being, "Such'a God send." She was a beautiful lady with some American Indian in her lineage.

She wanted to know about my background and where I came from. I told her that Grandma Lizzy was part Cherokee Indian and provided her with a brief overview of my family structure, farm life, and St. John Baptist church. Favorably impressed, she said, "Leonard ought to stop fooling around and settle down with you." I was not thinking about settling down, especially not with Leonard. He was too possessive and reminded me of Larry.

Furthermore, Leonard was not focused on settling down. He was busy enjoying himself as a popular barber. His engaging personality made him endearing, especially with the ladies. Though not totally arrogant, Leonard was well aware of his thick, wavy hair and handsome face. His tall frame, sparkling smile, and big light brown eyes were good for business. I could have saved lots of money on eyelashes if mine had grown luxuriously long and thick like his.

In spite of his popularity, Leonard made sure that my limited spare time was spent with him. He thought that I was still working as a Bunny during Christmas 1966. I gave him an expensive jacket of his choice from Wilson's House of Leather and Suede in Hollywood. He gave me an after five, button-down black sweater with a wide black fur collar, but we would not see each other until New Year's.

He told me about a dressy New Year's Eve party that we were going to attend and wear our Christmas gifts. Looking forward to partying instead of working for a change, I had made advanced arrangements for a Saturday night off. Wearing a beautiful black, scoop-neck, short-sleeved, formfitting dress and black spike heels, I arrived at Leonard's house around 10:45 p.m. He welcomed me with a hug and beaming smile. Since neither of us drank, he gave me a soda while he slicked down his hair, applied aftershave and cologne. His phone was ringing with good wishes for the New Year.

Then he answered a call that made him respond with grinding teeth and big eyes. He said to the caller, "Don't worry, I'll be there in a few minutes." Turning towards me he said, "It's my mother. I'll be right back." Looking very sharp from head to toe, wearing expensive black shoes and slacks, white turtleneck sweater, he scooped up his new jacket, kissed me and dashed off in my car before I could respond and grab my own keys, purse, and sweater.

There I sat in disbelief, twiddling my thumbs alone, stranded in Leonard's house on New Year's Eve. It was probably a few minutes after 11:00 p.m. when he left. His phone kept ringing, but some callers hung up when I answered, except his mother. She called to wish us Happy New Year before the party. By midnight, heartbroken tears had washed off my eyelashes and modest makeup. Curled up on the sofa, covered in my fur collar sweater, I cried myself into the 1967 New Year.

Leonard came home around 4:00 a.m. full of lies and lame apologies. He put my keys on the living room table and went to the bathroom. Quickly, I clutched the keys in my right hand. I grabbed my sweater and bolted to my car. He ran after me, "Baby, let me explain..." Just as I opened the car and got my right foot inside, Leonard caught my left arm. He said, "But Baby..." and high-pitched, piercing screams escaped my throat and caused him to jump back. The neighborhood dogs began barking and howling in response to my screams.

That little Mustang burned rubber getting out of his driveway. There were no more tears. They had been replaced with anger and the desire to never see him again. I would have been better off working. At least I would have enjoyed the company and laughter of my topless coworkers and the fun of swinging my feather boas around the stage. Not to mention the cash I would have accumulated. There was plenty of time for my anger to smolder as I drove from the Crenshaw district to my Lankershim Boulevard exit off the 101 Freeway.

I drove home knowing that Shelley had gone to a fun party with friends, because I had also been invited and welcomed to sleep over. As scheduled by the universe, life brings about change. All of us had moved from the house in Hollywood Hills. Hope got married, and that's why Shelley and I were living on Lankershim Boulevard in North Hollywood. We shared a furnished, one bedroom apartment with two beds.

Home alone, I removed my inconspicuous wig. It was made of short black hair with loose curls and was always perceived as my "real hair," compared to my shoulder length wigs. After washing away tear streaks and makeup residue, I went to bed, but sleep did not follow. Early daylight eased in behind the curtains, and I finally drifted into sleep.

Seemingly, the minute I dozed off the phone rang. Actually, it was afternoon, and Leonard was calling to confirm that I had made it home safely, and when could we get together. I said, "I never want to see your lying, cheating ass again." I could hear his teeth grinding as he said, "Baby I'm sorry I got caught up last night, but that wasn't about nothing." I said, "Never mind. Your Mother called while you were out, and I know that you went to the party with another woman," and I hung up my phone.

A few minutes later Shelley came home bubbling with joy from the fun they had at their New Year's Eve party. Being the caring "Jewish Mother" that she was, Shelley was upset over my New Year's disappointment. She did not like Leonard, because she felt that he took advantage of my generosity. Admittedly, there was a spike in "dire" needs after I gave him the $50 for his mother, but I knew how to say, "No." I told Shelley that people can't take advantage unless we allow them. She was annoyed that he had given me the sweater after Christmas. She said he was "Just trying to save face." I said, "But we did not see each other until New Year's Eve.

I did not regret buying the medication for his mother. It was a small amount compared to what I was earning. Nobody had a clue except Mary and other topless dancers who earned equal or greater amounts. None of us, or my fellow Bunnies ever said, "Hey everybody, look how much money I'm making." Among ourselves, it was just normal pay for what we did.

Nonetheless, after further emotional soothing from Shelley, she said, "Boobalah, remember we are invited to the New Year's Day party at John's house, and we can go together." The first time Shelley called me "Boob-a-lah," I thought she was teasing me about my breasts. When she finally stopped laughing, she said, "That's Yiddish for affection and endearment."

Affection and endearment did not describe my feelings towards Leonard. The image of him taking off in my car triggered more angry thoughts. He knew that I normally worked weekends and that taking off was a big deal, and he still blew it! That showed how much he really cared. To hell with him! I was looking forward to the party at John's house.

John and his girlfriend Sallie had been together for a few years but no kids. They were laid-back like hippies, and they lived in Hollywood Hills. Shelley drove us to the party around 5:30 p.m. I was happy to have her and good friends to hang out with. Unlike a dressy New Years Eve party, this one required casual attire, and casual we were! I wore jeans, T-shirt, sandals, and my own shortcut hair, but I did wear my eyelashes and lipstick.

Everyone brought food, dessert, wine, soft drinks, and there was too much of everything. Sallie knew that Shelley and I did not drink, so she made a yummy punch with ginger ale, orange juice, and some other ingredients, which everyone readily guzzled down.

Some kind of instrumental music filled the house with calm energy and good vibrations. The sounds reminded me of my Music Appreciation class in Shortridge High School, with gospel and blues beats mixed in. It also reminded me of some music that Al had played in the nightclub. Glowing candles and burning incense generated intoxicating aromas. It was a happy place. Armed with drinks and food, Sallie, Shelley and I went into the den with others to sit, eat and chit-chat about hopes and dreams for the brand new year of 1967.

As I walked around the right side of the sofa to sit down, I did not see the open shoe box on the floor, partially tucked under the sofa's edge. My left foot mashed down the box a bit. I said, "Oops, sorry I didn't see that." Sallie laughed, "No problem, you just walked on my grass."

While attempting to smooth out the edges, I noticed that the bottom of the box was covered with some kind of lumpy grass. I laughed, "Grass! You don't own a horse. Plus a horse needs way more grass than this." Shelley was cackling with laughter and waving her fork towards me. She said, "Boobalah, don't tell me that you don't know what grass is." I said, "Shelley, you know that I grew up on a farm, and I certainly know what grass is!"

Meanwhile, other people were in and out of the den and everyone was laughing. Suddenly the room was filled with voices and everyone spoke at once explaining grass and the tiny white cigarettes in the shoe box.

Shelley was amazed! She sort of whispered to me, "Boobalah, how could you work as a Bunny and topless Go Go Girl without knowing what grass is?" I said, "That's easy. Nobody ever told me about it. I have never seen any, so how would I know?"

There was a collective decision made by everyone in the den that I should know what grass is and how it works. Simultaneously, every person in the den provided input on the lumpy grass in the shoe box: "It's grass. Weed. Reefer. Hemp. Cannabis. Marijuana. Mary Jane. A herb that soothes your nerves. You can smoke it. Eat it. Wear it. You're supposed to make tea and drink it for health purposes. The little cigarettes are joints. It's in the Bible somewhere in the first chapter of Genesis."

My ears were buzzing with too much information, and I wondered how in the world could one thing be so many different things? If it's in the Bible, why didn't Reverend Nelson or Granddad ever mention it?

After the party was over and much time had elapsed, I read through Genesis, Chapter 1. I had never stopped praying, but it had been years since I looked inside of a Bible, and I did not recall reading anything about grass or all of those other things they called it. However, Genesis 1:11 reads: "And God said, Let the earth bring forth grass, the herb yielding seed, and the fruit tree yielding fruit after his kind, whose seed is in itself, upon the earth, and it was so."

Meanwhile, that was a new experience for New Year's Day! Sallie took one of the little cigarettes from the shoe box and lit it with a lighter. Instead of smoking it the same way she smoked her big cigarettes, she passed it around. I had been living with Shelley and Hope and their big cigarettes, but I had never seen either of them smoke any tiny ones like this. When the little "joint" cigarette reached me, I passed it on to the next person.

Sallie said, "You're supposed to take a hit before you pass it on." I said, "But I don't know how to smoke, and I don't like cigarettes." Laughing out loud, the collective provided a crash course in "Grass Smoking 101." They instructed me to suck in the smoke and hold my breath. I tried, but the smoke wanted out. I puffed, huffed, and coughed as the smoke escaped, which totally amused the collective.

John said, "Let's try this:" He gently held a big, brown paper grocery bag over my head. Sallie slightly lifted up the bag and held the joint to my lips. She said, "Take a big puff and suck it in." I took a huge puff and almost coughed my head off! I was sitting on the sofa as my feet automatically bounced up and down on the floor, and my hands grasped air. John snatched the bag from my head, and I covered my face with both hands and laughed like crazy. There were rolling sounds of laughter and howls from the collective. I could not stop coughing and laughing.

Shelley said, "Boobalah, move your hands from your face and take a sip of water." I took a big gulp, but my coughing made the water spritz towards Shelley. I could hear her laughing "Boobalah," as the collective roared.

I leaned back on the sofa with eyes closed but could feel the room swaying with the rhythmic music, which was my introduction to Jazz, Miles Davis and John Coltrane. It felt like the music magically lifted me from the sofa and made me float on the notes. Those sensations were very amusing, and I could not stop laughing and waving my arms around. Soon I was standing up, swinging my arms, swaying to the music and making happy sounds as I danced around. Sallie, Shelley, and everyone around me appeared brighter and happier than before.

Lights, colors, candles and objects appeared multidimensional. Perhaps that is what made a teddy bear dance on Sallie's rocking chair. For style and fun, Sallie had draped a white T-shirt over the chair. The front of the shirt had a big, brown teddy bear design, and the shirt covered the back and front of the chair. Face-to-face in front of the chair, the teddy bear and I were caught up in John Coltrane's saxophone. I expressed joy and pointed towards the dancing bear on the moving T-shirt. Each note of Coltrane's tenor sax dictated which way I swayed. When Coltrane finished, the teddy bear and I stopped dancing, and I was overcome by thirst and hunger, also known as "the munchies."

I was craving raw, green, and crunchy vegetables. While gobbling down salad and ice water, I asked John about the engulfing music he was playing. He readily reminisced over playing tenor sax in his high school band. He claimed that John Coltrane is the greatest tenor saxophonist ever, and the title of the song that made me and teddy bear dance was "My Favorite Things." With the passage of time, John Coltrane and Jazz music became part of my favorite things, but there was no Coltrane or jazz music in topless Go Go clubs where I worked.

Go Go clubs were on the rise, and there was plenty of work available. I preferred dancing five or six nights a week instead of working as a topless hostess. Working as a lunch hour hostess required getting up early in the morning, which was difficult when I had danced until 2:00 a.m. the prior night.

Furthermore, when I worked as a topless hostess, customers reached to stuff money into my bikini bottom, which I intercepted. While working as a hostess, some of the men were wearing wedding bands when they offered to "keep" me, but I would have to stop working topless and be there for him whenever he could find time to cheat on his wife. I always smiled and said, "But what about your wife," as I darted off to serve other customers.

Some of the men were father figures and cautioned me to be careful. I always cringed when Negro business men came to lunch. They would be staring and smiling at the White girls, but they invariably appeared embarrassed and upset to see my round, brown breasts. Some of them shook an admonishing finger towards me when their White buddies were not looking. I found that to be a very interesting double standard. I did not experience admonishing gestures from the Go Go stage, which eliminated physical contact with the customers. Instead of admonishing gestures, I was greeted with cheers and applause when I danced in a private home in Malibu.

A customer who frequently enjoyed lunch in the topless club on Sunset asked the manager if I would be interested in working a private party. The manager called me and provided some details and phone number. I knew the customer, was comfortable with his demeanor, and called him for additional information. He explained that his dear friend was a reserved Physics professor at UCLA, and he was throwing a surprise party for his fiftieth birthday - "The Big 5-0." I agreed to dance topless for the shy professor on a Sunday afternoon in February 1967.

With handwritten directions, I found my way to the magnificent Malibu home. It was astonishing that their backyard was practically in the Pacific Ocean. No fence, no gates, just walk out the back patio and into the ocean. As requested, I had arrived very early, and the hostess placed me in a luxurious room that connected to the expansive living room where the guests would party.

There was an open door leading into the party room. The host had taped up two crinkly paper curtains that looked like a huge, colorful birthday cake with candles. When the professor and his wife arrived, birthday guests screamed "Surprise!" When they finished singing and clapping "Happy Birthday," that was my clue to enter as rock music blasted.

The professor was indeed surprised when my bare breasts burst through the paper cake curtains that covered the doorway. His mouth flew open, and his face flushed red as he mumbled something to his wife and threw up his hands defensively. His laughing wife and the host couple were the only ones who knew about the topless surprise. Their spacious living room was packed with delightfully shocked guests. They blushed, applauded and giggled as I wiggled my way through two rocking songs. For this I was paid $100 cash, all of the delicious food that I could eat, and a box of delectable sweets to take with me. I also took some requests from female and male guests who wanted to know if I would dance for their future parties.

My life was sweet with one exception, Leonard. I was through with him after he drove off in my car on New Year's Eve. However, that did not stop him from calling me. He insisted that I had a misunderstanding, and he wanted to give us another chance. As time passed, he convinced me to join him for dinner and a movie, which he paid for.

Afterwards he claimed that his mother seriously needed $100. I told him, "I don't have any more money to give you." While grinding his teeth together, he snapped, "You got plenty of money." I snapped back, "No more to give to you." I went home very disappointed but not surprised.

Fortunately, there were no disappointments in my line of work. Topless workers were in great demand. As one of the few chocolate dancers, I had premium opportunities to work all of the time and avoid Leonard.

While avoiding Leonard, I delighted in dancing with my dear friend Lani. She was also a former Bunny from The Phoenix Club, but she did not have time to transfer into The Hollywood Club, because she was escaping an abusive relationship. After securing her three year old son in the care of her parents, Lani packed her car and drove to Hollywood. She did not have time to wait for re-hiring by The Hollywood Playboy Club. Consequently, Lani went to work as a topless dancer, which she preferred instead of carrying a heavy tray loaded with drinks.

Initially when we met, we bonded as former Bunnies and escapees from men who wanted to harm us. We laughed and talked about what to do after our topless days were over. She and Mary were also good friends, but Mary was married and pregnant at the time. Mary was settled, but Lani and I were not. Like most of us, Lani enjoyed the excitement of working as a movie extra, but she longed to become a star. She had a dear friend from The Phoenix Playboy Club who had moved to Manhattan. We joked about moving to New York, becoming top models, and mastering the theater.

Meanwhile, we marveled over the easy money we were earning but did not want our relatives to know that we were working topless. Lani sent her parents at least $100 a week for child care and told them that she loved working The Hollywood Playboy Club. Leonard thought that I was still working The Playboy Club, and I did not provide any additional information. He continued calling even though I declined any further offers for dinner and a movie.

One afternoon, during the third week of March, I was at home sleeping as usual, and Shelley was at work. After dancing through the night, I usually slept late into the day. On that particular day, around 1:00 p.m., I woke up when someone knocked on the front door. I remembered that Shelley had told me the custodian was coming to repair the oven.

I sprang out of bed, threw on my robe, and dashed to the living room. Half asleep and knowing that it was the custodian, I swung open the front door, and Leonard rushed in. Stunned by his appearance, I gasped, "What are you doing here?" He said, "You won't call me, so I came to check up on you." I told him, "I don't need you or anybody else checking up on me, and you can just go on about your business."

We exchanged several words in disagreement. Then he said, "Since you don't have any more money, I know a house where you can make $100 a night." Outraged by his implication, I snapped, "Why don't you take your mama to work there for $100 a night?" Grinding his teeth like crazy, he slapped me on the right side of my face, which caused me to trip over the footstool and fall on the floor at his feet. Pure rage from Daddy and Larry surged through every cell in my body! With both hands, I grabbed Leonard's left foot with a death grip and bit into his ankle like an angry pit bull!

He screamed, "You crazy bitch," as he tried to rescue his ankle from my teeth. In pain and anger, he started slapping my shoulders and back, which drove my primordial bite deeper into his left ankle. My eyes were tightly closed, but I could feel him dragging me across the living room floor as he hollered and called me names. When I heard him open the front door, I unclenched my teeth from his ankle and jumped up off of the floor to do battle. Leonard hobbled out of the living room on his right foot while yelling further insults at me.

I slammed and locked the door. I was absolutely furious and wished him dead! I could feel my blood boiling and the taste of bloody residue was in my mouth. I ran to the bathroom, rinsed my mouth, and spat out pale bloody water. Then I brushed my teeth and used mouthwash. I thought maybe my lip was busted. I rinsed again and again, but there were no more traces of bloody water and no injuries to my mouth.

I realized that the blood came from Leonard's ankle. I was so outraged, I wished that I had bitten his foot off! Maybe that would stop him from coming over here harassing me! Even so, I knew that was not the last of Leonard. His unexpected encounter left me wide awake with several hours to spare before my 9:00 p.m. work schedule.

Unable to sleep, I drove to Hollywood and shopped for some dance supplies. I also remembered to carry two wig cases and picked up two of my wigs from the beauty shop. Loaded down with wig cases and supplies, I stopped in a pawn shop to look at some hand guns. I was going to be prepared for Leonard's next unannounced visit. A 32 caliber with pearl casing caught my attention. The pawn shop clerk removed the gun from the case and placed it in my right hand. I was not about to be slapped in my own apartment while I worked and paid my own rent.

Fortunately, I did not have enough cash to pay for the weapon. The clerk said, "Give me what you have, and I will hold it for you." I said, "Never mind, I have some cash at home, and I will come back and get the gun tomorrow."

Dancing the night away was a great release for all of my frustrations, plus tips. The following day I planned to purchase the weapon. I woke up earlier than usual to go get the pearl handled gun. When I reached in to remove some cash from my lingerie drawer, I saw myself locked behind bars. The image startled me! I had seen myself behind bars when I loaded Daddy's food with rat poison. Escaping to The Playboy Club had saved me from killing Larry. I was not longing to spend the rest of my life in prison. Instead of going to buy the pearly gun, I decided to move to Manhattan, New York.

When I told Shelley about my immediate plans of moving she said, "Boobalah you don't know a soul in New York." I replied, "Shelley, I will have three dear friends in Manhattan: Me, Myself and I, and all of us will live in the YWCA until I learn my way around New York City."

Like Shelley, Mary and Lani rejected my choice when I called and informed them of my decision. Lani made me promise to wait until she called her friend Midge who lived in Manhattan. The daydreams and amusing conversations that Lani and I shared of moving to Manhattan were quickly becoming my reality, but Lani would never move that far away from her son.

Time flew forward, and I continued my work schedule while making plans for the East Coast. Although I was filled with ambivalence, the excitement of a new adventure propelled me forward.

In the interim, Lani spoke with Midge and told her, "I have a totally crazy friend who is moving to Manhattan, please take her in." During my first telephone conversation with Midge, she made me feel like a loved one that she had not seen for a very longtime. She was enthusiastic that I would soon become her roommate.

With great delight she giggled, "Lani told me all about you." Through several phone calls, Midge told me countless things about New York, including, "Don't even think about bringing your car to Manhattan." My heart sank from the thought of selling my stylish Mustang. "Maybe I will keep those dazzling wire spoke spinners as souvenirs? I thought, "Um, maybe not."

Although I did not have an excessive amount of stuff, I picked up a couple of corrugated boxes and began packing. I warned Midge that they would soon be arriving in the mail. She and I had become frequent phone pals, and she fueled my excitement and anticipation of moving to Manhattan with every conversation. Meantime, Leonard had been calling in an effort to convince me that, "We can work this out." I told him that he would be greeted by a bullet if he ever came to my apartment again.

Hope, Fran, Anna, Victoria and all of my friends were informed of my intended move. My topless constituents expressed sorrow about my leaving and joy for my bright future on the East Coast. Within three weeks after the altercation with Leonard, I had sold my car, given away unwanted items, hugged, laughed and cried at my memorable going away party at Jane's. Fran had given me her dad's phone number. She told me, "He works as a subway train operator, and he has some interesting stories." He lived in Brooklyn and was looking forward to taking me to lunch. A couple of days after the party, fear and sadness temporarily crept over me as the taxi driver made his way to LAX.

Traffic near LAX was chaotic, but I had plenty of time to spare before my 9:00 a.m. flight. With two pieces of luggage checked in and a very long wait, it was finally time to board the plane.

I settled into my first class window seat. Without any Bunny tails to brush out, I began reading one of several magazines that I bought for the trip. Reading, eating, and snoozing literally made time fly as the big jet streaked through the sky.

14

MOVED TO
MANHATTAN, NEW YORK

When the pilot announced our approaching arrival to JFK, I stopped reading and stared towards the ground, although fluffy white clouds blocked my view. As the plane descended, the surrounding landscape appeared abruptly different from my descent into LAX from Cincinnati in 1965. There was not an expanse of green land with palm trees and swimming pools. Moreover, there was no fire and floating smoke from civil unrest.

TWA's jet landed safely at JFK on April 11, 1967. While luggage was loading on the carousels, I searched for a phone booth, but I had to wait in line for my turn to use the pay phone. Finally, a businessman emerged from the phone booth. I dashed in, closed the door and called Midge. She was eagerly waiting for my call. After hasty greetings, she said, "You are in Queens." Then she told me the route the taxi driver should travel, and I wrote down the information.

After collecting my luggage, the porter was pleased with his tip for hailing a taxi and loading in my luggage. Speaking with confidence, I gave the taxi driver my preferred travel route for the approximately twelve mile ride to the upper west side of Manhattan. When he asked,"What brings you to New York?" I told him that I was returning home from an extended stay in Los Angeles.

Butterflies fluttered through my stomach every time the taxi whipped in and out of traffic! Suddenly I was in another world that consisted of bricks, stones, concrete, steel and iron. Cars, buses and trucks were all over each other, and the air was filled with honking horns and engine sounds. Monolithic bridges with towering cables, rivers, and the Atlantic Ocean were waiting to greet me. I gazed out of the taxi window as one scene flashed into the next. I did not see any sprawling green lawns with colorful flowers, but I did notice a few trees along the way.

When the taxi arrived at Midge's address in the 300 block of West 76th Street, I was intrigued by the configuration of the buildings. They were all stuck together, side-by-side, all the way down the street and on the other side. They were three-story structures that required address numbers to determine one from the other. There were no front yards, and they all had identical concrete steps and stoops. The taxi driver placed all of my luggage near the steps, accepted his tip with a smiling "Thank you," hopped in his taxi, and rushed on to his next passengers.

I dashed up the steps! Midge swung open the door and greeted me with open arms. There were no elevators, but fortunately she lived on the first floor in a front apartment. We walked a few feet down the hall and stepped inside her apartment. Midge spoke a million words a minute until she interrupted herself with, "Where is your luggage and stuff?" I said, "It's on the sidewalk near the steps." She shrieked, "It's probably gone by now," as she flew out of her apartment and down the steps, with me in close pursuit. She cautioned, "This is New York. You have to be careful. You are very lucky that your things are still out here." Midge grabbed the largest piece of luggage and screamed, "What the hell! Is this thing full of bricks?" We giggled as we carried the heavy bag up the steps and into the hall. After carrying the remaining bag up the steps and into the building, we easily moved them down the hall and filled up Midge's apartment.

During our many phone conversations, Midge had told me that she lived in a "single." I had never seen a one room apartment before. It was a large room, but not spacious enough for two young ladies with lots of stuff.

Nonetheless, Midge was very creative. She had a single bed along one wall that was hidden behind a decorative fold-out room divider. The divider was made from lightweight bamboo that featured three playful kittens in its colorful design. The backside of a dresser served as a headboard and hid the end of the bed. There was a sofa against the opposite wall, and it contained a full-sized pull-out bed. The front wall was circular with two huge windows facing the street. A floor lamp and cushy chair sat in front of the windows, and a little table in the corner was covered with art books and magazines. An expensive, multi-color, round rug covered most of the hardwood floor.

Midge glowed when I admired and complimented her beloved art work. There were two very large oil paintings of fruit on the wall behind the sofa. She claimed that they were originals from a famous artist, and she paid a fortune for them at a New York art gallery. Midge had colorful paintings and pictures covering every wall, including the kitchen and bathroom.

The kitchen was small, but adequate, with a cherry wood, drop-leaf table and four chairs. She even had a chair in the bathroom, made from black wood. It was straight backed and beautiful, like functional art. The huge bathtub stood on four legs, and the wall behind it was covered with paintings of fat, naked baby angels and nude ladies bathing in fountains.

She even had art inside the huge walk-in closet which was situated between the kitchen and bathroom. Affixed to the inner closet door was a full-length poster of Michelangelo's nude sculpture of David. Midge said it gave her something happy to look forward to every day. We giggled as she closed the closet door.

A few minutes later we heard loud scratching sounds coming from inside the closet. Midge yanked open the door, and her cat dashed out. Her name was Pyewacket, and she was Midge's most precious and priceless work of art. She was the most beautiful cat I had ever seen, a bundle of white fluffy fur with bright blue eyes and a loving, comforting, purring personality. Midge and I must have been focused on David's "jewels" when the cat eased herself into the closet, because neither of us saw her.

Midge was thrilled that I adored her cat and ecstatic to have me as a roommate. She could not wait to show me the city. She explained the subway system as "a necessary evil." She rode a taxi most of the time but commented that while they are stuck in traffic, the meter keeps ticking. She went on, "Subways don't get stuck in traffic, but you can get stuck underground, especially during a power failure. Sometimes walking is the fastest way to go, depending on where you're going."

Midge mentioned several places we were going to see and countless things we could do. We talked about various topics and recalled our joyous days and the money we made and saved while working The Playboy Club. She told me that after earning her B.A. Degree in Art History, she became a Bunny because, "It paid a hell of a lot more than teaching." I said, "Wow! No wonder you know so much about art," as a sinking sensation shot through my stomach. I felt like everyone had a college degree except me. "Uneducable!" Every time it surfaced, I felt angry and wished that I could go back and slap some sense through the face of my uninformed principal at Shortridge High School.

Meanwhile, Midge was baking chicken and whipping up a mouthwatering tasty dinner. I had just enough time for a bubble bath, pajamas, and fluffy house slippers, perfectly dressed for my first meal in New York City.

After dinner Midge and I talked and giggled late into the night. Although I had saved enough money to comfortably support myself for a couple of years, I was anxious to start working so that I could keep my savings. I asked her about places of employment as a Go Go Girl or waitress. She said, "Don't worry. My boss will hire you as soon as one of the other girls leave." I thought newspapers ads were a good place to start looking, and she agreed. By then, jet lag set in, and Midge prepared the sofa bed for me. I went to sleep with high hopes of soon becoming a model and actress, the way Lani and I had frequently spoken of while dancing topless.

The following week I responded to a newspaper ad, "Topless Dancers Wanted, Club Mame." I called and was instructed to stop in and ask for the manager anytime from 11:00 a.m. to 10:00 p.m.

On her off day, Midge and I rode a taxi to the club's location, somewhere near 42nd Street. We arrived around 4:00 p.m. A big handsome bouncer lifted the red rope, and we entered the club. Dim lights reflected silhouettes of men, as cigarette smoke and the smell of liquor circled around us. Colorful flickering lights and sultry music embellished seductive gyrations of the topless dancer, and drooling men stuffed greenbacks in the waist band of her G-string, and they were in no hurry to remove their hands.

I gaped at the men stuffing money into her G-string and cringed at the thought of hands-on. How come they were not up on a stage? Midge and I parked ourselves at the bar and ordered a glass of wine. The dancer continued working the audience until the song ended. She danced off stage while the next girl danced on. The stage was almost flat and placed dancers within easy reach of patrons.

We slowly sipped our wine, watched the dancers, and chuckled at audience reactions to their moves. The four dancers were engaging and entertaining. Each of them wiggled and shook through two records. When the first dancer returned for her repeat routine, Midge and I made a graceful exit and so did my topless career.

Several days later I responded to a newspaper ad, "Go Go Dancers Wanted." After calling and getting information on the location, I was looking forward to visiting. On a Tuesday afternoon, Midge and I rode a taxi uptown to a building with a small theater. The theater entry was on the side, like an alley way, and we had to knock hard on the vault-like steel door for entry. A young Puerto Rican man opened the door, and blasting music rushed out. Midge and I introduced ourselves. He said "Hi, my name is Joe Piro, better know as Killer Joe." Motioning towards the stage with one hand, he said, "Come on down." Midge clarified, "I'm not a dancer; I just came with her."

There were several energetic males and females milling around the stage, laughing, talking and bopping to the music. Joe sprang on stage and explained what we were supposed to do. He said, "Form a line. When I say go, first in line run up on stage and do your dance until I yell next." Upbeat Latin rock music with pulsating drums made the room vibrate. We clapped and cheered for each other's half-minute routine until the last person in line cleared the stage. Then Joe danced on stage and called all of us up to remove our shoes and follow him in a grand finale, similar to the topless finale with some extra kicks, turns, and dips.

No problem. I got it. I knew how to count. It was great fun dancing barefoot and wearing clothes, but I had learned to have fun dancing in spike heels and fewer clothes. A few days later, I received a call back. Overjoyed, I accepted the opportunity to dance with the Latin rock group.

The chosen dancers were told when to meet at the theater for rehearsals. Joe told us that we would be dancing for a big convention of union members. Our big production was on a Saturday afternoon. We arrived at the convention location hours early so that we could do a run-through on the huge stage. Ten females and four males filled the stage with rehearsal leaps and moves, led by "Killer Joe," who danced in all of his productions.

As scheduled, the convention's spokesman opened the event and in due time, he welcomed us on stage. Our familiar Latin rock music filled the stage, and we burst forth with high energy, leaps, and shoulder shaking gyrations. Joe and the guys danced in long black tights and no shirts. The ladies wore short black leotards with a colorful sash tied around the waistline, and all of us danced barefoot. We filled the stage with our individual free-form routines.

My thoughts flashed back to the moves of Tanya, the barefoot, shake dancer in the after-hours club in East St. Louis. Confidentially I imagined myself duplicating all of her moves. After several minutes of continuous, individual free-form, we danced our synchronized finale while conventioneers cheered and applauded our high-energy exit from the stage.

For all of my travel time, taxi fares, and rehearsals, I was paid about $100.00 for the performance. At that moment, I recalled the generous amounts of money I had earned as a topless dancer. It seemed like a distant dream, one that would never come again. Realizing that I would not be earning money as a dancer did not make me sad.

After all, my purpose in moving to Manhattan was to become a model and actress, and to avoid killing Leonard. I had escaped Daddy, Larry, Leonard and saved myself from going to prison. I prayed, "Jesus deliver me from meeting any more abusive men who make me want to kill them." I had distant dreams of future love and romance, but becoming an actress was first. Acting schools were listed in the newspaper, and I was making a list so that I could call them.

Meanwhile, I had been going to lunch at Tom Jones Pub during Midge's work shift, which was great fun. Someone always paid for my lunch, and I met the two Jewish guys who owned the pub. They were both named Danny. One was referred to as Danny E., and the other one was Danny S. They also owned The Living Room, a cozy night club on the lower east side. I also met Holly, Midge's friend and fellow waitress. Holly was pursuing an acting career and studying acting at H. B. Studios. She gave me the location information to the studios and said, "Utta is the best instructor. Make sure you get into her basic acting class." By my fourth week in

Manhattan, I was enrolled in Utta's basic acting class and working as a waitress at Tom Jones.

On an unknown date in April or May 1967, 'The New York Daily News' wrote an article about Tom Jones Pub and featured a picture of me at work, wearing a black shoulder length wig, a white low cut peasant's blouse, black minishirt with knee-high black boots. In part the article read:

"Vikki Summers works 6:00 p.m. to 2:00 a.m. as a waitress, and when Freddie Cole's combo (Nat King Cole's brother) gets hot, she frugs (dances) back and forth to the kitchen with the expertise of the professional Go-Go dancer she once was. She is a former Playboy Bunny in Cincinnati and Los Angeles, but now she is determined to make it in New York as a serious dramatic actress."

Utta's acting class was interesting and fun. I could hardly control the giggles when we had to "act like a tree" and "become the wind." Who knew there were so many different exercises involved in studying acting. We uttered strange vocal sounds and laughed out loud at each other. Utta also instructed each student to create a character who was performing an action without dialogue. We had to identify each other's characters and verbalize the actions. As time progressed, we read plays and portrayed various characters.

Our acting class was not the only place with characters. The streets of Manhattan were filled with many different characters: jugglers, singers, dancers, musicians, hotdog vendors, peddlers, beggars. Hippies and cool people were also among the characters seen on the streets of New York. Some of them lived in coveted lofts in Greenwich Village, and Midge loved hanging out in the laid-back atmosphere of The Village. The air was filled with aromas of food and incense. Many interesting shops welcomed tourists and eager buyers to The Village.

Midge's favorite shop was an apothecary where she purchased all of her sundry items and herbal remedies, including tea leaves and cannabis for making tea. Cannabis was openly sold over the counter with its fellow herbs as a natural product. People in The Village were more friendly than any place else I had been in Manhattan. She loved taking me to jazz clubs in The Village, where talented musicians created uplifting music and recorded live albums. Slug's was one of her favorite jazz clubs down there. The club's outward appearance suggested "Grubby's," but Freddie Hubbard, Joe Henderson, Louis Hayes, and many other famous musicians packed the club with jazz enthusiasts until there was "standing room only."

Midge also introduced me to The Village Gate and The Village Vanguard jazz clubs, where a constant flow of jazz music inspired us. As time moved on and our work schedules permitted, we enjoyed the talents of many famous musicians, including Pharoah Sanders and McCoy Tyner and John Coltrane. Recalling the sound of music from John and Sallie's New

Year's party, I could not wait to see Coltrane!

One night we went to The Village Gate to hear John Coltrane and his band, featuring his wife Alice Coltrane on harp. I had never seen anyone play the harp and was amazed that the harpist was a beautiful Negro woman. Interestingly, all of the jazz musicians were Negro, but most of the patrons were White. Alice made the harp sing and whisper, which sent undesired tears spilling down my cheeks.

After the band played their last set, jazz buffs rushed forward to praise the musicians and get autographs. I waited my turn to get autographs and compliment John Coltrane and the band but could not wait to shake hands with Alice and get her autograph. Energy and excitement rushed through my body when she shook my hand. When I explained that her music made me weep, she thanked me with a hug. I almost dropped to the floor! More tears rose up. That was pure exhilaration, which musically bonded me to Alice Coltrane and prompted me to purchase all of their albums. Consequently, I became a jazz buff and bought many other albums by McCoy Tyner and numerous jazz artists.

Hanging out in jazz clubs was our favorite form of entertainment, but work got in the way and prevented me and Midge from going more frequently. We were having fun and time was flying. Why does time fly when you are having a good time and drag when you are miserable? By September, my work location changed from Tom Jones Pub to The Living Room. Danny and Danny thought that I would be an added attraction to The Living Room servers.

Therefore, I became the only female among three male servers. Tommy was Greek, Jakub was Polish and Teddy was Chinese. All of us wore uniforms. I wore my black miniskirt and white blouse from Tom Jones. The guys wore black tuxedo pants, with matching vests, white shirts and black bow ties. Danny E. dressed likewise, and he was the bartender. We served drinks, sandwiches, fish and chips, shrimp and French fries in basket plates, lined with wax paper. The Living Room was a cozy little two-room club, designed to resemble a large living room. The front room had a few small tables with sofa type seats and chairs. There was a mirrored wall behind the bar and stools. The shiny brass bar was the room's focal point and brought favorable comments from patrons.

The show room was a few feet beyond the bar. There was a small stage for performers, but The Living Room did not have a standard band like Tom Jones Pub, where Freddie Cole's band rocked. Nonetheless, every weekend, The Living Room presented a singer or comedian.

Rodney Dangerfield was the club's favorite and most frequently appearing comedian. His one liners were "knee-slapping" funny, and "He got no respect." His routines included lots of jokes about the owners and the club. During a routine Rodney would say, "Can you believe it? The owner told me that I dress like a busboy. I told him if he paid me as much as a busboy makes, I could buy some decent clothes. I tell you, I get no respect."

Sometimes when Rodney saw us serving food he would ask the customer, "Do you see any cockroaches in your food?" The customers would invariably gaze into the food basket. Then Rodney would say, "Don't worry, the food is so bad, all of the cockroaches moved out." Rodney was the funniest comedian, but Bobby Short's singing brought in larger audiences and more generous tippers.

While I was working The Living Room in 1967, Bobby Short packed the house. He was a cabaret singer and pianist, very classy and dignified, yet warm and personable. Bobby loved entertaining, and his fans loved him. In 1968 he went to perform at the Cafe' Carlyle, and I never saw him work The Living Room again.

Things were going well with work. I was enjoying the free entertainment, and my coworkers were delighted that I had joined them. Tommy privately told me that I had increased the tip fund. Initially, I was alarmed when Danny S. told me that all of our tips were put into the lock box during the week. At the close of business on Saturday nights, Danny S. unlocked the tip box in our presence, counted the money, and equally divided it among the four of us and the bartender, Danny E., the club's co-owner, who also put his bar tips in "the kitty." We were taking home approximately $300 - $500 a week, contingent upon the entertainers.

My coworkers became my "big brothers." When the club closed, one of them, usually Tommy, went out and hailed a taxi for me so that I could step out of the club and into the cab without waiting on the street.

Once a month on Saturday nights after the club closed, the four of us would take a taxi to Chinatown to one of Teddy's favorite restaurants. He spoke fluent Chinese, and the servers bowed and treated him like a king, and we were treated like royal members of his court. We knew that we were an eclectic group and made fun of people's surprised reactions to us. We laughed, told jokes, and throughly enjoyed each other's company and diversity. There were a lot of Polish jokes floating around at the time, and Jakub loved telling this one, "How come Polish men wear white socks and ugly brown shoes? Their shoes are brown from kicking the crap out of people for telling Polish jokes."

Teddy was a natural comedian with endless jokes and stories. He did not allow any silverware on our table. He would say, "No chopstick, no food." I immediately learned to eat with chopsticks under Teddy's tutelage.

Although Teddy was very funny, he seriously spoke about Chinese discrimination and segregation in the USA. What! I knew that we were enslaved and that American Indians had been swindled and slaughtered, but I had never heard of the Chinese Exclusion Act of 1882, or Chinese segregation and exploitation. Teddy told us how much the Chinese people benefited from the 1964 Civil Rights Act and the Nationality Act of 1965. Teddy was well-aware and involved. He chuckled that, "Chinese Americans were confined to segregated ghettos. We had to band together to survive, and that's why we have Chinatown."

Tommy was more of the quiet type, and he frequently brought baklava and other Greek treats to work and shared them with us. He introduced me to Greek food and culture, which I loved. Later on, while eating in a Greek restaurant, I participated in the circle dance, which made me laugh out loud, because a lot of them did not know "left foot, right foot." Tommy's friends owned a small Greek restaurant and bakery, and they made a big fuss over me and Midge every time we went there to stuff ourselves on stuffed grape leaves and other "homemade" delicious cuisine.

Due to our work schedules, Midge and I did not have a lot of time for socializing, but we deliberately enjoyed each outing. During many of our conversations, we spoke of traveling abroad. Midge suggested, "We should move to Paris." I laughed, "Don't you think we should at least visit before me move there?" I reminded Midge that our jobs did not provide paid vacations, and if we did not show up to work our shifts, there was no standby, and that was not good for business or our employment.

It was business as usual with Midge at Tom Jones Pub, and The Living Room kept me busy and entertained. As mentioned, some very interesting and noteworthy people frequented The Living Room, and Judy Garland was one of them. Whenever I served her table, she proudly spoke of her beautiful and talented daughter, Liza. Sometimes, Judy came to the club with Tullulah Bankhead, a vintage actress with a deep bass voice. As I ran back and forth from the bar serving several customers, Tullulah would wave her hands in the air and holler out, "Dah-lin, where's my drink?" Both she and Judy were overly generous tippers, and being in their presence was exciting and fun. After initially meeting them, I served two drinks at once, which kept them satisfied.

For a small club, The Living Room presented a variety of interesting artists, including "Big Arthur," a Negro blues singer. His music was upbeat, rocking and seductive. He had been an old school "pretty boy," honey complexion with blue eyes. He brought out the Negro high rollers from Harlem. They and their women came sharply overdressed and dripping in sparkling jewelry.

Arthur had been working The Living Room for years. He was pleased to find me working there and referred to me as, "A rose among the thorns." He joked that he had kids and suits older than I was. Arthur's cousin was his personal limo driver. When they invited me to hang out with them in after-hours night clubs in Harlem, I was happy to go.

On our first outing, there were five of us in the car. As the car rolled towards Harlem, from a little black shaving bag, Arthur removed a shaving mirror and a glass tube full of white powder. He put the powder on the mirror and divided it into lines that resembled tiny rows of white cotton. Next, he made a tube from a crisp $100.00 bill and sniffed some white powder up each nostril.

Intrigued by his actions, I chimed in, "When we were growing up in Denmark, Tennessee, we used baking soda to brush our teeth and as a household remedy, but we never sniffed up any for colds or anything." Silence filled the car as they looked at each other, looked at me, and everyone laughed loudly. When Arthur caught his breath from laughing so hard, he said, "I knew that you fell off a turnip truck," which is a metaphor for "country bumpkin." He explained that the white powder was "coke."

My thoughts flashed back to my topless friend Mary who had asked if I wanted to "do some coke" one time when I was upset and crying from the initial embarrassment of dancing topless. In that moment, I also recalled my teen years of working in Hooks Drug Store and realized that the pharmacist had been doing coke back then.

As we rode to Harlem, I felt somewhat embarrassed for the things I did not know. I remembered my friends in Hollywood laughing like crazy because I thought "grass" was for farm animals. I asked Arthur, "What does coke do?" He said, "Try it and see." In self-defense, I sniffed some white powder up my right nostril. It felt like a thousand barnyard gnats flew up my nose! I started sneezing rapidly. My right eye began twitching and watering, and it felt like ice cubes were floating through my brain.

Meantime, when I started sneezing, Arthur cupped his hands over the white powder and hovered over the mirror like a mother hen protecting her chicks. I could not stop giggling and rubbing my nose. I said, "Noooo thank you," when he offered me a "balancing" sniff for my left nostril. I did not like the feeling of ice cubes and gnats fluttering up my nose and through my brain. Hanging out in Harlem after hours with Arthur and his crew was exciting, fun, and brief. Arthur moved on to his next gig in Chicago, and night life continued at The Living Room.

One Thursday night in November after the club closed, Teddy and Jakub were cleaning up and helping Danny stock the bar. Tommy was scheduled off that night for family reasons. Knowing the guys were busy, I did not wait for one of them to run out and hail a taxi for me.

Winter temperatures were in the air. I put on a long sleeved purple dress and packed my work uniform into my little beige pleather tote bag. Wearing a below-the-knee, black wool coat with a big black fox collar and my black leather work boots, I stepped out on 2nd Avenue to hail my own taxi. Although I was waving my arms and yelling, "Taxi, Taxi," they all sped past me. I noticed that they were picking up passengers, but none of them were Negro. My heart sank from that realization, and my stomach swirled around from the sickness of racial discrimination.

It was already past 2:00 a.m., so I started walking very fast, headed towards home, hoping I could get a taxi to the West Side. I had walked about six or seven blocks when a tall White man approached me. I yelled, "You better get away from me," as I started to run.

The man stuck a gun in my right side and said, "Stop! Hold it right there." Unbridled terror froze my feet! My chest ached from the rapid pounding of my heart. I felt hot and cold at the same time. Fortunately, a NYPD patrol car was rolling up behind us. Desperate screams escaped from my dry throat, "Police! Police!" When the vehicle stopped, I felt somewhat relieved that they had come to rescue me.

A man wearing a police uniform was driving, and there was a man in the back seat not wearing a uniform. With flashing lights, the vehicle rolled to a stop beside us. To my disbelief, the man with the gun motioned me to get in the back seat, and I did. Stunned beyond words, my mind ran wild with horror stories of what was happening to me. My mind screamed, "Obviously, these men are not real police officers. I have been kidnapped and sold into sex slavery." I knew that they were not real police officers, because the police arrest people for committing crimes, and certainly, I had not committed any crimes. The guy with the gun was definitely connected with the men in the patrol car.

As the vehicle pulled away from the curb and merged into the traffic, the perpetrator with the gun said, "So what is your name?" I heard his words reverberate inside the moving patrol car. My dry lips parted, but no words came out. My efforts to speak were mute. Suddenly the loss of my ability to speak was more terrifying than my predicament. I remember convincing myself that this whole thing was just a crazy nightmare that I would soon wake up from.

After riding for I don't know how long, and I did not know where, a wave of relief flooded over me when we arrived at a police precinct and the four of us got out of the car and walked inside the station. I noticed some women working there and concluded that at least I had not been kidnapped and sold into slavery.

Even so, fear hovered over me, because I had no idea why they had picked me up. I sat in a small room alone for quite some time thinking that someone would soon come and tell me that they had made a horrible mistake, and they would take me home. Finally an officer came in, and without effort my words filled the room, "Tell me why I'm here?" Never had I been so happy to hear my own voice! Thankfully, my voice was not permanently lost. The traumatic impact of some big, tall, White guy with a gun drawn had literally scared me speechless.

The officer answered, "You are suspected of prostituting." I hollered, "Prostituting! Oh my God! No way!" I rapidly explained that I had just gotten off work as a waitress at The Living Room night club on 2nd Avenue and was trying to catch a taxi home. I opened my tote bag, showed him my work uniform, an accumulation of pay stubs and bar napkins from my work location. He scribbled down my name, date of birth, home address, work location, and left the room. After a short while, he returned and told me to follow him. I picked up my tote bag and purse, glad to be heading home at last.

Three other young women and I were escorted out of the same door that the officers had brought me in. We were loaded and locked into a police van. A solid block of glass behind iron bars shielded the driver from his passengers. I would have preferred riding home in a police car, but apparently I did not have a choice. As the van rolled on, I asked the girl sitting near me, "Why are they taking us home in this van instead of a police car?" She smirked, "Home my ass, they are taking us to jail." I heard what she said, but I could not comprehend why I was going to jail for nothing.

Her words immobilized me. I did not realize where I was until the van rolled past The Living Room. Rocking back and forth in my seat, I screamed, "That's The Living Room! I just got off from work there. Danny! Danny!" The three women looked at me, rolled their eyeballs upward then silently stared out the windows as street lights and buildings seemingly whizzed past us. Since I did not know my way around Manhattan, I had no idea of the van's direction to our destination.

Soon we arrived at the back door of a huge, dismal looking gray building. The driver unlocked the van's door, and two female officers escorted us into the processing room. Panic seized me! I wondered how long would I remain in jail for something that I had not done?

My body trembled beyond my control, and angry, hot tears met at the bottom of my chin. One of the female officers asked if I was carrying any drugs. I said "No," as she emptied the contents of my purse on a metal table, examined each item, and turned my purse inside out. She did the same with my tote bag. She counted my cash, put it in an envelope, wrote the amount on the envelope with my booking number and sealed it.

My coat and bags were removed from me. Then we were herded into a small room where the unthinkable occurred. We were mandated to remove every stitch of clothing, shoes, socks or pantyhose. There were five or six of us, bare-butt naked, standing in line, waiting to be humiliated.

When the female officer called a name, the arrestee had to walk forward and face the officer. She ordered the arrestee to raise her arms above her head, turn her back and bend over until her head almost touched the floor. Then she ordered the arrestee to spread her legs and use both hands to expose her innermost private parts. The officer looked for hidden objects, but she did not physically touch anyone.

While I was weeping and dying a thousands deaths, some of the women rotated their behinds while they were bending over and taunted the officer with statements like, "Bitch, I know you want some of this." The women who were wearing obvious wigs had to remove them and turn them inside out. Fortunately, my short black wig looked like natural hair. Therefore, I was not asked to remove it. I could not believe what I was experiencing. It felt like a nightmare gone terribly wrong! When the officer called my name, I cried out loud as my body shook involuntarily. I stepped forward, raised my arms above my head, and turned my back to the officer. When she said bend over, I spun around, faced her and said, "I can't do that."

She called the next woman to step forward. The assisting officer returned my clothes, and I put them on faster than ever before, but they did not return my coat or bags. I asked the officer when was I going home? She replied, "I don't know. You have to go to court, and the judge will tell you if you have to serve some time." I stammered, "Serve some time! For something I never did!" I reflected on how I had avoided killing Daddy, Larry, and Leonard at all costs, and now I maybe serving time? How ironic! Her words were devastating, and they made my body and mind feel numb and cold.

There were four women seated on a bench at the opposite end of the small room. An officer unlocked the door near the bench and ordered us to follow her, while a second officer walked behind us. My heart was beating louder and faster than all of our foot steps combined as we walked along the barren concrete corridors, and jailed females peered at us through their cell bars.

All too soon the leading officer said, "Stop." She opened the door of an unoccupied cell. Her sweeping hand motion told us to walk inside where we were greeted by four immovable, steel, bunk beds. When the officer slammed the heavy iron door shut, the clunking sound shouted, "D-o-o-m-e-d!" There I stood, locked behind bars, just like the past visions I had seen from my early youth that prevented me from killing Daddy, Larry, or Leonard. Innocent of any wrong doing, but I was definitely locked behind bars in "The Tombs."

The jail cell and everything within my view started spinning around me. I felt dizzy and held on to the cell bars, but my body sank to the floor. I sat there on my knees with my face in my hands until an officer came to distribute a gray blanket and pillow to each arrestee. The officer told me to get up and sit on my assigned bed. I sat on my bottom bunk bed, buried my face in my hands, and sobbed. My cell mates included a hippie type White girl, a Puerto Rican and an agitated Negro woman. The Puerto Rican and Negro woman appeared to be acquainted. There were no clocks, and our watches and jewelry had been removed.

I had no idea how long I had been sobbing before the agitated Negro woman snapped at me, "Bitch! Shut the fuck up! Your ass been crying all night, and you're gittin on my gotdammed nerves." I blurted out, "I didn't do anything! I don't even know why I'm in here." She said, "You mean you ain't no hoe." I hollered, "No, I'm not a whore." She said, "Well you look like a hoe." I cried, "No! No! No!" -- while stomping my feet, jumping around and flailing my arms in the air. The Puerto Rican said to the Negro, "You know she's not a hoe. Otherwise she would be kicking your ass by now. Just leave the girl alone."

A little while later the Negro woman pulled down her pants, squatted in the corner and stuck her right index finger up her private parts. She made some grunting sounds like a constipated person. Feeling very ill at ease, I wondered why she did not use the toilet. After a few more grunts, she pulled out two capsules from down there. She quickly restored her clothes, opened the capsules and sniffed the contents up each of her nostrils. She mumbled something to herself, laid down on her bunk, and covered her head with her blanket.

I sat on the bunk with my back leaning against the wall. My feet and legs were tucked under the blanket. Consumed by nausea and hopelessness, I silently cried until there were no more tears, then I whimpered into daybreak. Eventually, gray daylight filled our cell, and I could hear people moving around and toilets flushing. After sometime, a female officer came to our cell and told us to get ready for lineup. I screamed within myself, "Get ready!" With what? No toothbrush, toiletries, and fluffy towels for a nice warm shower.

Nevertheless, the officer returned and told us that we were going to be photographed and fingerprinted. She unlocked the cell and marched us down the corridor, around some corners, and into a large room where several women were standing in line waiting their turn for mugshots and fingerprints. My stomach churned and growled as I waited and worried over my fate.

Finally, when there were only two women in front of me, a White man ran to the front of the line. He was wearing a beige trench coat and a brown felt hat. He called out, "Who is Vikki Summers?" Startled by the sound of my name and afraid that he was taking me to another unknown hellhole, I slowly raised my right hand like a scared kid in a classroom and responded, "I am."

The man stepped up to me and said, "I'm so sorry Ms. Summers. Let's get out of here." Sensing my high level of fear and distrust, he said, "Don't worry. You are going home now." I had no idea who the man was and refrained from giving him a spontaneous hug for my happiness. He escorted me to the property department where every penny of my money and all of my items were given back to me.

I asked him why did the police pick me up in the first place? He explained that the police had probably been following a Negro woman, wearing a black coat, who was actually soliciting, but she knew how to drop out of sight, and they mistakenly nabbed me. The man apologized for my misfortune as he escorted me out of the building and onto the streets. Surrounded by tall concrete buildings, I was anxious to escape that bleak environment. Several taxi cabs were waiting to transport newly released arrestees to their destinations. The man in the trench coat walked with me to a waiting taxi and asked if I needed taxi fare. I assured him that I had enough money to pay the driver and thanked him for getting me out of "The Tombs." He opened the taxi door and wished me well. I hopped in, glad to finally be on my way home from an unimaginable incident.

With the meter ticking, the driver asked, "Where to Miss? Leaning forward from the back seat, I gave him my address. I had never seen that area of Manhattan and did not know my way home. The driver happened to be a Negro man named Leon. As the fellow in the trench coat wished me well and closed the taxi door, Leon asked, "What's a nice girl like you doing coming out of a place like that?" Feeling mistreated and angry, I snapped, "I was in there for nothing," and I proceeded to tell him exactly what happened. He said, "Dammit, um sorry they did that to you." Leon started swearing about the injustices that Negro people were constantly subjected to. His animated response lifted my mood. By the time we arrived at my address, Leon had agreed to pick me up from work and keep me safe from future encounters with the NYPD.

When I walked into the apartment it was probably after 10:00 a.m., and Midge was in the bathroom putting on makeup and spraying her hair for work and waiting for me to come home. When she heard me walk in, she dashed into the kitchen wearing undies, bra, and fluffy house slippers. With inquiring eyes and pouting lips, she said, "Well young lady where were you all night, in jail or something and couldn't call your roommate?"

Angry hot tears spilled down my face as I sobbed, "Yes, I was in jail. They locked me away in The Tombs!" Midge rushed to give me a compassionate hug while screaming, "I can't believe those stupid bastards did that to you!" She released me from her bear hug and spun around crying and cursing.

She grabbed a steak knife that happened to be on the kitchen table. With knife in hand, Midge yanked open our apartment door and ran towards the front door of the building crying, "I will kill those bastards!" She had only gone a few feet before I caught her by an arm and steered her back inside.

I said, "Midge you can't go running after the police naked. People will say, "Look at that crazy White girl, and the police will arrest you for indecent exposure." I had to stop crying and laugh at Midge. She said, "I'm so pissed off, I forgot about clothes." She certainly would have stopped traffic. Not only was Midge a compassionate and radical woman, she was

"Bunny Beautiful" and very busty. About five-feet seven inches tall, she wore her light brown hair curled and piled high on her head with wispy bangs, just above her sparkling blue eyes.

Midge snapped back to reality and laughed at herself for flying out of the apartment in a fit of rage. Obviously, both of us were traumatized from my arrest. I went to use the bathroom and recoiled from my mirror image, which looked like a jumbo guppy. My complexion looked dull and gray, and my eyes were two little swollen puffs. I had no idea when tears washed away my eyelashes. There was no trace of makeup or lipstick, just thick, brown, angry lips.

Midge made us some hot tea, then she got dressed and went to work. I soaked in the hottest bubble bath ever and shampooed my hair and wig. Afterwards, I stuffed all of my arrested clothes into a large bag, threw them out and went to bed. Sleep did not come quickly. While tossing and turning, I realized that I needed my winter coat and boots, at least until I found time to go shopping, so I hopped out of bed and retrieved them.

With John Coltrane's soothing music playing softly, sleep eventually engulfed me but not for long. My peaceful space was disrupted by nightmares of the NYPD physically dragging me on the pavement, down some dismal steps, and locking me in a dark manhole, deep underground in an unknown location, and I woke up fighting the covers, hollering and sweating.

Finally, I was sleeping peacefully until Midge's cat purred on my pillow, grabbed a paw full of my hair, and woke me up. She was ready to play in my Afro, but it was time for me to get ready for work. I was anxious to share my "daymare" with my coworkers. I concluded that nightmares scare us out of our sleep, but daymares are frightening, traumatizing experiences that we cannot wake up from.

As usual I called a taxi, but Leon told me to call the company that he worked for, and I did. A courteous young man drove me to work, but Leon and I had agreed that he would pick me up shortly after 2:00 a.m. Anxiety propelled me to work an hour earlier than my regular 6:00 p.m. schedule.

Danny E. was working the bar. When I walked in, his eyebrows went up. He looked at his watch and waved both hands in the air like, "What are you doing here so early?" It was happy hour, but the club was not packed at the time, and I parked myself on a bar stool and gave him the high points while he served the happy hour customers. I told him that I spent the night in "The Tombs." He said, "You must be joking." My facial expression and tone of voice indicated that this was no joke. Danny quietly exploded with angry curse words.

As the evening progressed, Danny S., Teddy, Tommy and Jakub were equally angry and frustrated that I had been arrested for nothing. They expressed regret for not getting a taxi for me, and they offered me the night off. I explained that it was better for me to be at work than home alone brooding over the situation.

They all agreed, and Danny immediately called their friend Levi, who was an attorney. After a brief introduction of my situation, Danny gave me the phone so that I could provide some basic information to Levi. We agreed to meet at the club by 5:00 p.m. the following day. During our meeting I provided time frames and emotional details. As time moved forward, a lawsuit was filed on my behalf against NYPD for false arrest, defamation of character, and psychological damage.

When Levi specifically inquired, I informed him of my background as a Playboy Bunny, auto and boat show model, Go Go dancer and movie extra. He asked, "Why the move from Los Angeles to Manhattan?" I explained my plans of becoming a model and an actress in the theater.

Levi said, "If you want to do theater, you should call my friend, Woodie King, Jr." He explained that Woodie was a young producer and director of theater at Henry Street Settlement, "and he happens to be a smart and talented young Negro guy." Levi gave me the phone number and address to Henry Street. He also called Woodie and told him about me. I called Woodie the following day and established a connection by phone. He told me about some pending theater projects that he and some young Black playwrights were working on. Woodie also suggested a list of reading material by Black authors and poets who were unknown to me. He told me to stay in touch, and I did.

I felt encouraged that Levi had given me the name and phone number of a young Black director and producer for the theater, but my unjustified stay in "The Tombs" had diminished my happy-go-lucky attitude. I was upset and filled with ambivalence about the magic of Manhattan. Suddenly there was a lot going on in my life. I was angry, and things were rapidly changing.

Vikki Richardson

15

FIRST APARTMENT – MODELING AND ACTING

By January 1968, the biggest change was getting my own apartment and living alone for the first time in my life. Midge had fallen in love with a jazz musician, and I was anxious to move so that she could have her space, especially since he was waiting to move in.

Fortunately, money was not an issue. Finding the time to locate an apartment and deciding where to move was the challenge. Meanwhile, I rented a room in a residential hotel, a couple of blocks from the Living Room, and I literally ran home from work. The hotel provided a charming, Irish doorman who looked professional in his uniform. He knew that I got off from work around 2:00 a.m., and it was somewhat comforting that he looked out for me. He made me giggle by opening the doors with a flourish, like I was a prominent person, and my weekly tips to him were endearing and appreciated. I certainly appreciated the weekly tips and salary that I earned from The Living Room, which provided adequate income to pay my weekly hotel rent and continue saving.

My hotel room was adequate, with a bed, table, love seat, chair and lamps, but I shared the bathroom with an unknown person next door. That was a scary thought. Whenever I used the bathroom, I had to lock the door on the neighbor's side, and vice versa. One time I forgot to unlock the neighbor's door, and he could not get in to use the potty. The way he yelled and banged on the bathroom door suggested an emergency! Startled by the sounds, I dashed into the bathroom, unlocked the door, darted into my room, and locked my door unseen. That was the last time I ever forgot to unlock his bathroom door.

Living in the hotel reminded me of my residential days in Cincinnati's YWCA when I was Bunny Ann. During that time my coworkers were my closest associates, and history was repeating itself. Danny S., Danny E., and my coworkers were my closest associates. Midge and I were still friends, but her new love and our jobs did not give us much time. Frequently, my heart longed to be back in sunny Los Angeles with my dear friends that I missed more than I could have imagined. Regardless of discouragement and loneliness, I knew there was no turning back. My arrest and living in a hotel did not stop me from participating in my acting classes. The activity provided some structure, fun, and, I met one very good friend named Nikki.

Nikki was a tall, handsome White guy with a wild sense of humor. He lived with his male partner, and he was comfortable and confident within himself. Thoughts flashed back to Tanya, the pretty girl dancer who was a man. Nikki looked like a handsome man, but he was living with a man. It was confusing. I felt badly that Tanya and men who were different were referred to as a "punk or sissy." That must have been like being called "Nigga, monkey" or some other insulting words Nikki and I were bonded through the coincidental spelling of our names and career paths. As we became friends, Nikki referred to us as "The Oreo Twins." He was into acting, modeling, art, and interior design. We had gotten to know each other by having coffee and dessert after class.

He was informative and assertive. I was thrilled to have him telling me what to do. He took me to the studio of his favorite photographer for a photo shoot. The photographer said I was "very photogenic," and he snapped pictures until my jaws ached from smiling. Nikki and the photographer selected the best five shots for my portfolio. My name and phone number were printed on the bottom of my 8x10 headshot, which would be given to casting agents.

Nikki wrote my resume, had it typed, and printed on high quality paper, which we stapled on the back of my headshot. The phone number and address on the resume and pictures were that of the answering service that we used. The answering service became our "booking agent." With pictures and resumes in a big envelope, Nikki took me to an expensive office store with all kinds of leather bags and cases. A light brown one caught my attention, and I had my initials engraved in gold. With portfolio in hand, I started making rounds with Nikki. We walked countless blocks, in and out of agencies, presenting our pictures and resumes. Along the way, we also looked for an apartment for me, and I was looking forward to working with Nikki in commercials.

I was totally thrilled when we got our first toothpaste commercial together. Both of us were extras and earned $60 an hour, but that did not include travel time and waiting for "Quiet on the set." As time moved on, Nikki and I worked several commercials together. We also worked individually, and I landed a spot as a nurse on a soap opera. In time, I also earned wages as a product print model, which means that pictures of my face were used to advertise makeup and various products. Things were going well. I loved working hard and earning money. In March I moved into my own one bedroom apartment in the 300 block of West 56th Street, near Columbus Circle. My apartment was on the second floor of a four story building. It was a modern building with an elevator and doorman. Nikki became my instant interior designer. He took me to his favorite antique stores. We went to auctions, offbeat shops, estate sales, and going out of business sales, which eventually resulted in my luxuriously furnished apartment at bargain prices, and I paid cash for everything.

Nikki thrived on "good deals," but I wanted a brand new sofa and bought a gold velvet one from Macy's. While there, I also selected a bed, mattress, bedding, and two small antique brass coffee tables imported from Belgium. The removable table tops were made of thick glass, but their heaviness required two people to lift one of them.

Prior to purchasing any furnishings, I got approval to paint the apartment. I ordered wall-to-wall carpeting in the living room and bedroom. The carpet was a champagne shade, like a pale cream or natural straw color. Double rod custom drapes covered the living room windows, which were directly across from the next building, where a male exhibitionist used every opportunity to expose his "small member" and pale behind. The window's under drapes were made from gold satin, and the top ones were beige silk organza. Both were attached by hooks to a traverse rod with individual cords, and I opened and closed the drapes for my own amusement.

The drapes provided a colorful background for the three-leg matching chairs placed in front of them, and they blocked out the naked man. I had never seen three legs on a chair before and was intrigued with the ultra modern design. There was one brown ornate wooden leg in front of the chair and two in the back. The spacious, cushy seats were "U" shaped and upholstered in white velvet with gold designs in the fabric.

Nikki claimed that my Louis the XV flat-top writing desk was my most valuable find. It had one middle drawer and four beautifully curved legs. The color was overlaid shades of beige, gold, and white. I loved touching the intricately carved, decorative gold trimming on the top and bottom of the legs. Before I could use it, Nikki utilized construction paper to trace the desk top. He took it to a friend's shop, and the guy made and delivered a perfectly fitted glass cover for my "valuable find."

The desk light was a Tiffany stained glass hanging lamp that required apartment approval and installation by the maintenance man. The lamp was attached to a long brass chain with the electrical cord threaded through the heavy links and suspended from the ceiling. The colorful stained glass was a work of art on white background with cascading leaves in various shades of blue, green, and purple. Red, blue, purple, and pink flowers bloomed around the lamp's base. The desk and lamp were placed in the living room just beyond my walk-in kitchen, and their beauty greeted everyone who entered.

A round folding card table was covered with an elegant purple tablecloth, a gold candle in the center, surrounded with four brown wooden stools. When entering the apartment, the table was on the right hand side of the living room and hidden behind the door when it was opened. I was happy with the furniture, Louis XV and all, but my heart belonged to my stereo, which closely resembled Odeana's stereo when we were teenagers in Indianapolis. My beautiful mahogany unit had a turntable and FM amplifier that played albums, 78 rpm records, and it had an attachment for 45 rpm records. As time permitted, I bought albums by John Coltrane, Marvin Gaye, and everyone who made music that inspired and moved me.

I was indeed inspired to have my very own first place to live and a brand new bed to sleep in. I had a wall-to-wall mirror attached above the bed, which made the room appear larger than reality. The bedroom was large enough for a full-sized bed, an antique chest of drawers and an Italian provincial, high backed armchair. The chair had short, curved, wooden legs that were carved into a royal design. The carved wood design also outlined the entire chair, including a portion of the armrest. I had the chair reupholstered in crushed red velvet, which made it a functional work of art and a giggly thrill to sit in. I was totally delighted with my first apartment. When my thoughts flashed back images from the decaying log cabin, reflective tears ran down my face, and I pinched myself to see if I was dreaming. Yet, the joy of my most unlikely progress from the log cabin to Manhattan was soon overshadowed.

On April 4, 1968, my joy was abruptly disrupted by the assassination of Dr. Martin Luther King, Jr. I screamed and cried! Felt like I had been kicked in the stomach by an angry mule. My psyche recalled the anguish of President Kennedy's assassination. Outrage surged through my entire being! I called Mother. She, and everyone at home, was weeping beyond words. When she regained her composure, she said, "Remember that we are all born to die, and Reverend King did a lot of good before he died." When there were no more tears to drip down my face, I sat there in my royal red velvet chair, feeling empty, alone, and very angry. Although we had not met, Woodie King was the only Black person in Manhattan that I knew to call and vent over the murder of Dr. King.

At the time I could not imagine how Dr. King's senseless assassination would pour fuel on the fire of The Black Power Movement. The fire began smoldering in the early 1960s. While working with "CORE," the Congress of Racial Equality, Stokley Carmichael fanned the flames and popularized the phrase "Black Power" in 1966. This occurred during a speech Carmichael made after he was released from jail for protesting with Dr. King and many others when James Meredith was shot and wounded during his solitary March Against Fear. Dr. King had marched, faced fear with unconditional non-violence resolve, and for that he was violently slain.

During my childhood in Denmark, Tennessee, Reverend Nelson had preached that "You reap what you sow." Dr. King did not sow violence or hatred. So why was he brutally murdered? Angry thoughts flashed like lightning during a storm. I was angry for having been arrested for nothing! I had not gotten over having been labeled "uneducable" and wished that I could go back and choke my high school principal to death. I was angry with the crazy White people for years of oppression and injustice and mad at God for allowing it to happen. I was frustrated because most of my friends were White. Nonetheless, when I called to bemoan Dr. King's death, Woodie's voice conveyed great distress, but he spoke words of encouragement through his own anger. He also affirmed that the theater productions were still in the works, and I was looking forward to seeing them.

As time moved on, Woodie became my telephonic lifeline. He continued suggesting an endless list of reading material by Black authors. When I told him how much I loved the great poet Langston Hughes, he said, "You will appreciate attending poetry readings by young Black artists. Go see as many as possible." He told me to visit the Negro Ensemble Company and observe their workshop productions. Woodie also told me that his dear friend Barbara Ann Teer was in the process of opening a grassroots theater workshop in Harlem, The National Black Theater. He said, "I think her theater will be great for you."

I knew that I was not going to all of those places alone, and given my work schedule, when would I have time? Inundated with raw emotions and more than enough to do, I made an effort to stay focused and keep working. My acting classes and past performances as a topless hostess and dancer empowered me to "act like" all was well with the world while working a double shift at The Living Room.

Dawn, the daytime bartender, had a family emergency in Arizona for an unknown amount of time, and I covered her shift. It never hurts to earn extra money. Moreover, I was willing to help out Danny and Danny. My coworkers were my only "family" in Manhattan. I became a super bartender and could spin a shot glass down the shiny brass bar without spilling a drop. My customers named me the "Mix Master." Bar tending was like cooking, but easier and more fun.

There was no fun in not being able to attend my acting classes and make rounds with Nikki. Frustration became a part of my existence. I had moved to New York to become a model and actress, but I felt stuck in a bar. Books became my best friends, and I read ravenously. Buying a television never occurred to me, which made more time for reading. Books, music by John Coltrane and other artists, brought comfort during the dreadful loss of Dr. King.

Before I could gain some emotional balance from the death of Dr. King, Senator Robert Kennedy was shot and killed on June 5, 1968, only two months since Dr. King's murder. I was stunned and screamed, "No, not again! President Kennedy, Dr. King and now Bobby!" I cried until there were no more tears streaming down my face.

I was fuming with anger at the crazy White men who had murdered the three men that I believed in for bringing justice and civil rights. No wonder Malcom X was radical! In spite of national turbulence, my anger, pain and apathy, I still had to earn a living. At work nobody knew my frustrations, but I knew that I had to get back to my acting classes and making rounds with Nikki. He and my acting coaches were informed of my work dilemma. After a couple of months or so, I decided to tell Danny S. that I could no longer work days. On that particular day as I was finishing my day shift, Danny S. was stocking the bar. He beamed a big smile and said, "Thanks a million for covering the bar. Dawn will be back in a couple of days."

Knowing that Dawn had returned, a wave of relief washed over me, and the following week, I was participating in my acting classes and making rounds with Nikki. In the right place at the right time, within two weeks I was working as an extra in a kidney pill commercial. A little old lady was the principal character, but I was thrilled with the $240 for my four hours of work. I accepted every work opportunity so that I could continue saving money and avoid starring as "A Starving Actress."

Through it all, I maintained periodic telephonic contact and encouragement from Woodie King. One day in August, he scheduled a meeting and told me how to get to Henry Street on the subway. After verbalizing my fear of the underground and overcrowded herds of pushing people, Woodie assured me that subways were the best way to travel around New York.

On the day of the appointment, my anticipation of finally meeting Woodie overruled all unfavorable aspects of the subway. When the train stopped at my station, I stood up and a wave of seemingly automated people pushed me forward from the train and up the steps to the city streets. I practically ran to Henry Street Settlement. With quickened heartbeats, I dashed into the location and was warmly greeted by a receptionist. She looked at the appointment book on her desk and said "Vikki Summers." I smiled and said, "Yes I am," and she pointed the way to Woodie's office. After all of those phone conversations, I was finally going to meet him.

The office door was open, and I dashed in! He stepped forward and extended his right hand, but I leaped and gave him a bear hug that almost made both of us fall on the floor. Fortunately, he had good balance. He was slightly under six-feet tall with a medium frame. He had a clean-cut image, and his handsome face looked like smooth chocolate. His engaging brown eyes and genuine smile made me feel comfortable and welcomed. Finally meeting him was like greeting a long lost friend. I had never been happier to meet a fellow human being.

Woodie had no idea how much his verbal support had meant to me, especially as a newcomer to New York. He maintained a level of pleasing professionalism and compassion as I enthusiastically described the trauma of having been falsely arrested and locked away in "The Tombs" for nothing. He empathized with me and commented on "The Black Power Movement" for civil and equal rights.

When he asked about my work history in Los Angeles, I did not avoid any details. He listened intently, frequently chuckled, and said "Wow!" After several minutes of my energetic outpouring, Woodie calmly began telling me about the coming production of four one-act plays. He was well-spoken, articulate, and knowledgeable. I just knew that he was a college graduate, and I asked some basic questions about his life. He appeared humble, but I was highly impressed with his knowledge and accomplishments. As he spoke, it was my turn to say, "Wow!" Pictures on his desk revealed a wife and two young children. My soaring imagination halted. Be still my fluttering heart! Hearing him speak triggered a flashback of "uneducable," but I did not yield. Woodie had increased my knowledge, confidence, and Black awareness through books.

He already knew that his dear friend, Barbara Ann Teer, would further increase my knowledge by providing facts, information, and coaching for the development of my acting skills. Woodie did not condemn my acting classes in H. B. Studios, but he told me to participate in Barbara Ann's workshop at The National Black Theater, which opened in 1968. Although I do not know the exact opening date, I was fortunate to be among the first year "Revolutionaries" in The National Black Theater, known as NBT.

NBT was in Harlem on 125th Street and Lennox Avenue. Woodie told me how to get there on the subway. He said, "When you go, you probably should not wear your wig." I felt slightly embarrassed. That was my "real hair" look. Shoulder length hair and bright hair colors looked like a wig on Black women. How did he so readily know that I was wearing a wig? It was made of very short black hair that looked like a press and curl. Woodie was unaware of my inner dialogue regarding my wig, while he verbalized an overview of the social and political dynamics of The National Black Theater.

Looking forward to meeting Barbara Ann, one Saturday morning I fluffed up my short Afro hairstyle, and I rode the subway to Harlem. There were no problems locating the building. When I arrived at the address, I opened the door and stared up a very long flight of steps. I could hear voices and low vibrating sounds from African drums. I would soon learn that the drummers were from West Africa, probably Nigeria. Excitement and anticipation propelled me up the steps to an open door. A young lady was sitting at a table, which was situated in front of the huge room, near the stage. She and her bushy Afro greeted me with a warm smile and she said, "Hi, I'm Fatima." She wrote my name in an attendance notebook, and collected a small fee.

Barbara Ann was informally talking with three or four people, but she came to greet me. Shoulder to shoulder, she and I were in the same approximate height and size division. To her advantage, she was dressed like an African Queen and wore an African gele head wrap, which made her appear taller and stately. She was stunning with smooth brown skin and big, dark, penetrating eyes. When I told her that Woodie King sent me, she flashed a broad smile and said, "I know. Welcome Sista," and she hugged me. Then she introduced me to the people she had been talking with. Everyone warmly greeted me as "Sista." Some of them said, "Asalaam alikum Sista." Later on, I learned that the phrase is Islamic for "Peace and blessings be upon you."

Participants were eagerly entering the room, greeting and embracing each other. To witness Black men greet each other with the Black Power handshake was to witness a rhythmic, ritual unto itself. The volume of the drums increased and the tantalizing fragrance of incense permeated the room. Soon the room was filled with every description of Black women and men, who refused to be Negroes any longer.

A gentle wave of Barbara's right hand and the drumbeats became an echoing distant sound. Standing in front of the stage, she greeted the group, and we cheered. With right fists raised high, all participants started chanting "Right On, Black Power and Power to the people." After much chanting and thunderous applauding, Barbara waved her hands so that she could be heard. She said, "It's nation-building time, and we are Black Nationalist -- Revolutionaries," which brought on another round of cheering, applauding, and louder drum beats.

I was excited to hear that The National Black Theater presented a platform where young artists could dance, write, and present their own poetry and plays. My first experience in The National Black Theater was ethnically grounding, empowering, and spiritually elevating. I eagerly participated in the NBT workshops every Saturday morning and quickly learned that everyone there was upset and angry with "The System" for one reason or another. We, the participants, were 'living theater' according to Barbara Ann. Everyone had a story to tell about life in general and being a

Black American in particular.

At some point each member of the workshop was required to take center stage and present a dramatic presentation of how we became who we were. Through this process, we learned a lot about ourselves and each other. Our presentations brought shock, surprise, anger, tears, laughter, and joy. I was not the only one in the workshop who had been arrested and locked up for nothing. I definitely was not the only victim of educational abuse.

Like Woodie, Barbara Ann was certainly a college graduate, and she was not the only one. As time moved on, I was very surprised that so many participants were college graduates, and Brother Duane Jones held a Ph.D. in English. A few members of the workshop were high school dropouts, but status did not matter in the workshop. We were united as Black Militants, Black Warriors, Black Nationalists, Black Revolutionaries. With high energy and raised fists, we were determined to bring about radical changes for Black Americans and other oppressed people in this land.

At the time, I thought the Black Power raised fist symbol was introduced and instituted by The Black Panther Party. Years later, I was disappointed to learn that a raised fist or clenched fist is a symbol of solidarity and support, dating back to the ancient Assyrians, 1200 BC. Throughout time, and within many nations, a raised fist has been used as a salute to express unity, strength, defiance, and resistance. More than twenty different organizations in the Unites States have used the raised fist symbol to fight for justice, including: The African National Congress, American Indian Movement, Women's Liberation and Jewish Defense League.

Nevertheless, The Black Panthers were our raised fist originators, our heroes, and a source of motivation that empowered Black Americans to fight for civil rights and economic justice. In The National Black Theater, we wrote poetry and plays that killed off only the White people who were evil. As a source of encouragement, Barbara Ann frequently referred us to our African ancestry and suggested that we tap into the strength and power from those roots. During the slave trade, Black people were captured and sold from various areas in Africa. Barbara Ann contended that a countless number of slaves who were brought to America came from the Yoruba culture in Nigeria. She pointed out that our music and unbound rituals of worship, especially in Black Pentecostal churches, was traceable to our African origins.

Barbara Ann reminded us that theater was all around us, in the streets, in churches, and other institutions, and within ourselves. As performers and artists, our responsibility was to portray various characters in order to raise consciousness, inspire, and liberate the minds of others.

Participating in the workshop was liberating and frustrating. It was indeed frustrating trying to maintain balance between my newly found

Black militancy and all of my White friends. My coworkers were understanding of my social and political issues. Each of them could relate to oppression, especially Teddy, the Chinese activist. My work buddies and the patrons embraced my Afro and reached out to pat it. Teddy said, "You are beautiful no matter what."

Meanwhile, Midge and I talked on the phone and went to a jazz club when time and circumstances were convenient. She was still fuming over my arrest and embraced my Afro and militancy. She could best be described as, "A radical White girl." My gay friend Nikki easily empathized with me when we enjoyed a quick lunch one day. He said of himself and other homosexuals, "We are so oppressed, we can't even publicly admit who we are." Nikki loved my hair and insisted that we dash to our favorite photographer's studio for new head shots with my Afro. Nikki and I remained friends, but NBT had ruled out my participation in H.B. Studios. However, Nikki and I maintained the same answering service for commercials and print work.

When my new portfolio pictures were available, I distributed them to my favorite agencies. Between following up on modeling jobs and commercials, participating in NBT, reading Black history books and working The Living Room, I was very busy. A busy schedule with meaningful activities seemed to make time vanish quickly, and 1968 dashed into the past.

16

"A BLACK QUARTET" AND WOODIE KING, JR.

Occasionally, Woodie came to NBT, talked with Barbara Ann, observed our performances, and spoke to us about all facets of Black Theater. One day in February 1969, Woodie called and gave me the date and time for a meeting at Henry Street Settlement regarding the four one-act plays.

On the day of the meeting, a large conference room was filled with the playwrights, actors, and technicians. Some of the men were dressed in colorful African dashiki shirts with matching caps. I felt like applauding when the brothers exchanged the Black Power handshake. As people greeted and embraced each other, I presumed that they were already acquainted. The room vibrated with good energy, overlapping conversations, and laughter.

Woodie's secretary handed us a thick batch of 8 1/2 x 11 papers that were bound together like a jumbo workbook. I immediately started reading and realized that it was the script for the four one-act plays -- "A Black Quartet:"

1. Prayer Meeting or The First Militant Minister, by Ben Caldwell - "A hip Black burglar, a jive Black preacher and an outasight sermon."

2. The Warning - A Theme for Linda, by Ron Milner - "A Black girl who discovers her own womanhood and the meaning of Black manhood."

3. The Gentleman Caller, by Ed Bullins - "The wildly funny, murderously-edged revolt of the Black Mammy."

4. Great Goodness of Life - A Coon Show, by LeRoi Jones, aka Amiri Baraka - "A scalpel-like dissection of the soul of the Black Bourgeoisie."

Woodie introduced himself and the authors. Each of them presented a synopsis of their play. After they finished, Woodie said we're going to read these plays. He called our names to read various characters in the plays, and he made notes as we read. It was a process that entailed a few meetings and readings until it felt like all of the women had read all of the female characters and likewise for the men and male characters. All of us became acquainted with each character and their actions in all four of the plays. Consequently, we the aspiring actors, became acquainted with each other, and everyone that I bonded with was a college graduate, including Loretta Green, Louise Heath, and Anna Marie Horsford.

Therefore, it seemed most unlikely that I would have been cast in a leading role, but I was. Joy and fear almost overwhelmed me when Woodie told me that I would be playing the part as "Linda" in the Ron Milner play, "The Warning - A Theme For Linda."

After many, many weeks of cast meetings and endless rehearsals, "A Black Quartet" premiered in Brooklyn, July 1969. On November 2, 1969, we opened off-Broadway at Tambellini's Gate Theater in Manhattan. While we had been reading the plays, I had empathized with the Linda character. Although she was a naive, seventeen-year-old virgin, I identified myself in her character.

The character had to take pain pills for her monthly cycle. She had two younger sisters, and she did most of the household chores. Linda, her two sisters and their mother lived with maternal grandmother. This coming of age play reflected mother-daughter and grandmother drama. It spoke of good for nothing men and how they became that way. Grandmother hated her "ex," but Linda loved and adored him. Grandmother explained that she hated him because she had to leave their three daughters in his care while she had gone to get more pneumonia medication for her sick baby.

Grandfather had been too drunk to go, but he could not stay awake long enough to give their two-year old daughter her remaining dose. After taking the bus and waiting hours for the medication, she returned home and found her baby dead on the bedroom floor. The incident occurred when Linda's mother and sister were young children.

Revealing the baby's death was the most emotional scene in the play, and real tears flowed down my face during every performance. Pain and suffering from my childhood had provided a reservoir of tears and emotions to extract from. Barbara Ann Teer and everyone from The National Black Theater came to see the plays and provided many encouraging comments. I almost melted like warm butter when Barbara Ann said, "You're doing a great job of allowing the character to use your instrument."

Like all good theater, the plays in "A Black Quartet" evoked a range of emotional, social, and political responses from viewing audiences and the critics. Whenever the critics wrote a glowing review about the playwrights, actors, directors and technical support, we accepted it as validation. If the review was unfavorable, we retorted with statements like: "White folks have not walked in our shoes, and they do not understand our struggles."

I was astonished and humbled by all of my glowing reviews like this one from 'The New York Times,' July 31, 1969: In part, Richard F. Shepard wrote, "Vikki Summers radiates warmth and ingeniousness as the girl who learns that she must be a strong woman." However, the best validation came from my one and only slashing review by Clayton Riley, who wrote a lengthy, denigrating article in 'The New York Times,' "Adjust Your Binoculars, Uncle Sam," August 3, 1969. In part, he wrote: "Vikki Summers is not able to do anything well in 'The Warning,' and the play is seriously impaired by her poor sense of timing and lack of stage presence. The sister is simply not up to playing the part, mostly, I imagine because she is so inexperienced and so young." Ironically, Clayton Riley was a Black critic.

Joseph Julian wrote a rebuttal letter To The Editor. A White Writer Argues: In part he wrote: "The outrage committed by Clayton Riley in his article, "Adjust your Binoculars, Uncle Sam," must not go unanswered. His are the binoculars that need adjusting. If they were in focus, he could not possibly have described Vikki Summers as flat, monotonous, and completely lacking in stage presence. Could he actually have been watching and listening? She is one of A Black Quartet's greatest strengths. If Mr. Riley was unable to relate to the simple honesty, the very deep humanity and beauty of Miss Summers' performance, he indeed has a problem."

I ignored Clayton Riley's cutting words as I laughed out loud and danced around. "So young!" At the time, I was twenty nine years old and only four months away from turning "The Big 3-0." He perceived me as being too young and inexperienced to play the part of a seventeen year old virgin. That bitter critic confirmed that my portrayal of the vulnerable protagonist was truthful and convincing. My performance mirrored Linda as "so young, inexperienced" and uninformed, because that was true for the character. Furthermore, Linda daydreamed and fantasized over a seldom seen boyfriend who represented unrequited love, which also resonated within me. All of those elements were an intrinsic part of Linda's character.

Honestly, it was rather scary being on stage, making sure that I was standing in the correct spot, delivering my lines clearly, with great volume and without yelling. Voice projection was required before individual cordless microphones became the norm. One night my mind raced ahead of the production, and I dropped an entire scene. Panic raced through me, and time stopped! I could hear my fellow actors running up the back steps to the stage. Louise Heath played the part of Linda's taunting cousin, Nora, and Loretta Green played the part of Linda's sister, Joan. I could hear the stage manager mumbling something, and things were bumping around backstage.

All I could do was cry. My pounding heart pumped hot tears down my face. Minnie Gentry, a powerfully talented and accomplished actress, commanded the stage as Linda's grandmother. She delivered an off script monologue to Linda that sounded like part of the dialogue. She inserted actual lines from other scenes like, "I know you don't know nothing 'bout no love." She ad libbed lines like, "You don't know nothing bout life, period!" Minnie ad libbed and lectured to Linda about no good men and life challenges, long enough for the other actors to get in place. Then she took us back on script. Louise and Loretta entered the stage with wide-eyed curiosity and delivered their lines with more energy and intensity than ever.

Linda had the closing line in the play where she spoke to her boyfriend, Donald, and said: "Don't come unless you can give me as much as I can. Please, Don, please..." The stage lights faded to black. Bright lights rose with the entire cast on stage for curtain call. Although most of them knew that something had gone wrong, the audience cheered, clapped, and gave us a standing ovation with all praises due to Minnie Gentry's spontaneous monologue.

Woodie called an immediate cast meeting. I tearfully apologized for dropping a scene. My fellow actors cheered me up by telling funny stories of their own performance blunders. Woodie encouraged me to stay focused and to keep up the good work. He complimented Minnie for dramatically "milking the scene." He praised Louise and Loretta for their quick reactions and outstanding performances.

Dropping that scene rattled my confidence as an actress, and I wondered if Clayton Riley had been right. No way! Clayton was wrong, and my confidence was greatly restored by this review from 'The Nashville Tennessean,' on Sunday November 16, 1969, after the writer had visited New York and reviewed "A Black Quartet." The critic, Clara Hieronymus wrote in part: "Using her whole body in splendidly disciplined emotionality, Miss Summers created a character that exceeds much of the play's dialogue in impact and power to move. She is a remarkable actress."

Miss Hieronymus's empowering words and "Ingeniousness" from Mr. Shepard's review were huge compliments, but the process of portraying Linda obviously required a lot of work, including constant rehearsals and incorporating stage notes and critiques from our producer and director, Woodie King.

Speaking of work, due to my budding acting career, I was no longer working my night shift. My co-workers at The Living Room had wished me well and cheered me on. Before ending my employment there, my false arrest case had been assigned to I. J. Rabb, a young attorney. I had sued

New York City in the amount of $100,000 for defamation of character, harassment and psychological damage. Attorney Rabb empathized with me and explained that it would be a long, drawn-out process. The case was indeed drawn-out, but some years later I received a settlement check for approximately $800. I was satisfied that my voice had been heard, and I accepted the check as an apology from the NYPD.

Meanwhile, I was ecstatic with my budding acting career but do not recall how much I was paid for my "starring role." It did not matter. I felt fortunate to be earning any money as an actress, and the role brought my guild cards: American Guild of Variety Artists, Actors Equity Association, and Screen Actors Guild. Of course, we had to pay monthly dues for our guild cards.

Continuous work as a waitress enabled me to afford acting. After leaving my night job at The Living Room, I began working a day shift at The New York Hilton Hotel. It was within walking distance from my apartment. Working at The Hilton allowed me to earn money during the day and perform at night. We also performed matinees on Saturdays and Sundays. Since the Hilton had more servers, there was someone to cover my shift whenever I needed to take off.

I had valid reasons for taking off. The production was going well with good reviews and appreciative audiences. Following an unknown number of performances in Tambellini's Gate Theater, we became a touring company and took the show on the road to upstate New York, Boston, and Los Angeles.

Every performance was a fantasy that came true, but the reality of returning to Los Angeles as a New York actress was absolutely magical. The minute I found out, I called all of my topless dancing buddies and friends from The Playboy Club. All of them sounded very excited and promised to attend. Some of them teased, "Can't wait to see you perform with your clothes on."

During the first week of February 1970, "A Black Quartet" opened at The Inner City Theater in Los Angeles. Opening night, the theater was packed with enthusiastic people, including local critics. Their reviews of our production and performances ranged from favorable to exalted.

As I recall, we performed in Los Angeles for two weekends. My friends came and praised me for moving to New York and achieving my dreams. In spite of rehearsals and performances, I found time to hang out with my friends and gush over how much their kids had grown. If time flies when you're having fun, my life was in fast-forward. All too soon, "A Black Quartet" concluded at The Inner City Theater, and our production company returned to New York City. "A Black Quartet" closed in 1970, but I can not confirm the exact closing date. However, I can confirm that I had met a tall, dark, Black militant warrior in the National Black Theater in

1969. Known as El' Jabber, he was highly developed in Martial Arts. His lean, muscular body and massive Afro-hair made his six-foot, four-inch frame appear even taller.

El' Jabber was frequently told that he looked like Malcolm, except, "light skin, dark skin," and they wore similar eyeglasses. El' Jabber had personally known Malcolm X and served as a bodyguard, although they were referred to as "Foot Soldiers." He left the mosque following conflicts between Malcolm X and Elijah Mohammed. El' Jabber fit the description of "tall, dark and handsome" with a full beard and mustache. His warrior image made him very popular with the "Sistas" in the workshop. Even so, after we became friends, he mentioned that he was somewhat self-conscious of being cross-eyed in his right eye, because kids had teased him when he was growing up. His mother told him that she did not know why his right eye was turned outward when he was born. Later in life, El' Jabber channeled those frustrations into Martial Arts. He did not practice Martial Arts in a commercial studio. There were only six warriors in the class, and the instructor, Dwight, trained them in his totally unfurnished living room. They were "underground warriors" who could reportedly kill people with their bare hands and specific body maneuvers.

El 'Jabber's life experiences and athleticism drew me towards him, like a moth to flickering flames. He was attracted to my strong and enduring spirit. Born and raised in Harlem, he lived across the street from Columbia University, but he did not attend. Since we were both single, with no kids, and no partner, we became good friends and enjoyed hanging out together. He introduced me to stretching, strength training, and physical fitness. I was elated to have him in my life. He certainly knew his way around New York, and we rode the train and walked places I never would have gone alone. When time allowed, we went to jam sessions to hear Nikki Giovanni, "The Last Poets" and others read their consciousness raising poetry.

We made it a point to go wherever "The Last Poets" were teaching and preaching. With African drums pounding, Felipe Luciano, Gylan Kain, and David Nelson rhythmically spoke politically charged messages and historical facts that made us jump up and shout, "Teach! Preach it, and Right on, Right On!" They were undoubtedly the premier rappers. Their words and drum beats definitely raised our Black awareness and infused us with pride that kept us charged up for the revolution, so that we could bring about some positive changes in our own lives and in our nation.

As time moved on, El' Jabber and I became inseparable. He was totally pleased with the doorman and my apartment building. He enjoyed cooking delicious meals for us, and when time allowed, we invited his mother. Regardless of my Black freedom and revolutionary attitude, my southern and midwestern upbringing did not allow me to "shack up" with a man. Therefore, we quietly went to a Justice of the Peace, got married in January

1970 and celebrated my 30th birthday. His 26th birthday was coming up in July. El' Jabber held a modest paying clerical job with the federal government, which enabled him to pay his portion of rent with his mother in their huge, rent controlled apartment complex where he had grown up. With him moving in with me, his mother had to relocate to a one bedroom within the complex.

Having my own "Black Knight" was comforting. He anxiously awaited my return when "A Black Quartet" had been on the road. Affectionate and protective, he did not drink or smoke, did not eat pork, was not abusive, possessive, or jealous. No need to sleep with a sharp butcher knife under my side of the mattress. Although I was thrilled with my "Black Knight," the closing act of "A Black Quartet" left me feeling downhearted. Conversely, I happily filled the void by seeing as many plays as possible, attending forums, rallies, jam sessions, and participating in The National Black Theater every Saturday morning. I also maintained telephone contact with Woodie regarding upcoming theater projects.

Meanwhile, I worked three days a week at The Hilton, and two days a week I made rounds for print work and commercials. El' Jabber worked 9 to 5, five days a week, but he was very restless with his "slave" job. He wanted Black Power and green money. His favorite phrase was "Black Entrepreneur," and he was determined to become one. El' Jabber had two close friends who were married to beautiful women, but they were not members of The National Black Theater. They were busy becoming entrepreneurs. John was a teacher, and William was an attorney. Both of them were involved in a multi-level marketing program.

In the program, the person who brought in the most people made the most money and received a percentage override on all of the new people that his people recruited. On paper, it was an endless pyramid of cash flow. The product was Holiday Magic Cosmetics, and distributors were located on the ground floor of the Empire State Building. As we became involved, our Holiday Magic business cards with the Empire State Building address was very impressive.

There were various entry levels based upon the amount of product one was willing and able to purchase. The most basic entry level was a Holiday Kit. It contained five of the basic skin care products. We started with two kits, and I soon became a top selling "Holiday Girl." I loved the products, went to meetings and learned a lot about facial exercises and skin care. People frequently commented about my beautiful skin and wanted to know what I was using. My Holiday Kit became an extension of my right hand.

My husband's job tolerance increased with the number of products he sold to his coworkers, but he was focused on recruiting people and working the marketing plan. We were provided brochures and workbooks that outlined the presentations. El' Jabber memorized the scripts and made them his own. He became a master presenter of the Holliday Magic marketing plan.

Shortly after El' Jabber's twenty sixth birthday, one of the presenters in the organization came into the Empire State Building bursting with new information. He was a recent graduate from an amazingly motivating, mind training program. The guy claimed that the training increased his memory capacity, taught him how to visualize, and how to tap into his psychic abilities to solve and prevent problems. He described the "mind trainer" as a little, short Mexican man with some mind blowing information.

17

JOSE SILVA MIND CONTROL

"The little, short Mexican man" was Jose Silva, a powerful human being who had tapped into human consciousness and was training people to do amazing things through the power of their own mind. Jose Silva, his wife and ten children, lived in Laredo, Texas. Based upon many years of scientific research and application, Mr. Silva had developed a course of study that became known as Silva Mind Control. During the 48-hour training program students learned how to utilize four basic levels of mind with their own controlled awareness.

Without even trying, the graduate was doing a mini presentation on Silva Mind Control, which became known as The Silva Method. El' Jabber and I were anxious to know more, but we had to wait a month for the next basic class. We sold enough Holiday Magic to pay for Mind Control, and we were highly anticipating the first day of class.

Day One:

Eventually, it was time to participate. The class was presented in a large hotel meeting room on Manhattan's west side. We arrived early with plenty of time to register and meet Mr. Silva, who preferred being called Jose. He was constantly surrounded by curious people, and I was one of them. Approximately forty excited students filled the room, and everyone was talking and speculating about Mind Control.

When it was time to start the class, Jose tapped his little silver bell until we stopped talking and focused on him. A young White guy stepped forward, and Jose introduced Harry McKnight. Harry was among the first five instructors that Jose had trained to teach the 48-hour course, which required two weekends, and both of them would teach different segments of the course.

Jose told us that he began researching human intelligence and mind activity in Laredo, Texas in 1944. He provided some background and personal information about himself and his family, and so did Harry. Students blurted out questions and voiced skepticism. Jose assured, "Don't worry, if you don't get it, I will refund your money, but I'm not worried because you already have it. We are here to help you use it."

In front of the room, there was a huge green chalkboard with a large, colorful vinyl chart hanging from the top of it. Jose explained that the chart depicted four basic levels of brain functioning. From top to bottom: The bright blue area represented BETA, the outer conscious world with brain activity from 14 to 21 cycles per second. The bright green area depicted the ALPHA level of inner consciousness and creativity, with brain frequency of 7 to 14 cycles per second. The bright red area was referred to as the THETA level, with brain activity of 4 to 7 cycles per second of deep inner consciousness. The base of the chart was black and exemplified the DELTA level, with brain activity of 4 cycles and less per second, also known as the unconscious level.

As Jose progressed in the presentation, I understood that we would learn how to tap into the ALPHA level and train our mind to function at various levels with controlled awareness. Jose explained that the basic course was structured into four segments, one for each day. He gave us a simple definition of conditioning and programming. He said, "We will tell you what we are going to tell you. Then we will tell you. Then we will tell you what we told you." His explanation drew laughter from me, El' Jabber, and most of the students. He further stated that we would learn from a relaxed position with eyes closed, while listening to a tape-recorded sound of a metronome.

Jose encouraged us to focus on absorbing the methods and techniques so that we could apply them to solve and prevent problems. He also stated that a growing number of people were interested in learning Mind Control, but he needed to train more instructors. He offered, "As you progress through the course, let me know if you are interested in becoming an instructor." Interested in becoming an instructor, I was doubtful of my ability to learn everything that he and Harry had mentioned.

Jose dismissed us for a very short break before the first relaxation exercise. Since El' Jabber and I were seated in the front row, I sprang to Jose and confessed that I had been labeled "uneducable," and was worried that I would not get it. Facing me, Jose gently placed his left hand on my right shoulder. As he pressed his right thumb in the middle of my forehead, he said, "They made a mistake. Forgive them. God made you a functioning genius, and this is so." As Jose pressed his thumb against my forehead, it felt like the energy from his thumb washed my brain free from all of the negative input from my childhood and life experiences.

At that moment I was absorbed into pure white light, which made me feel very hot and woozy. I almost fainted. Jose balanced me. He smiled at me and said, "Now that you know you are a functioning genius, enjoy the learning experience." Jose dispelled all of my doubts and replaced them with a level of confidence that I did not know how to imagine. The "short break" was extended by questions from other doubtful students who surrounded Jose and Harry. While still answering questions, Jose rang the silver bell until everyone was seated and attentive.

Lights in the room were turned down as the metronome sound calmed the atmosphere. Jose said, "Find a comfortable position and close your eyes." Some people stretched out on the floor with a pillow. Some sat upright in their chairs. El' Jabber and I sat upright but pulled up a second chair for our feet. My inner ears loved the metronome sound, which produced happy feelings throughout my body. Jose's corrective energy on my forehead made my spirit soar. As he instructed us to "Take a deep breath and go deeper," simultaneous sensations of being awake and asleep intrigued me.

Jose and Harry took turns teaching the class. Their programming sessions and lectures flowed rapidly. Space and time were boundless at the inner conscious levels. They gave us ample breaks and adequate time for lunch. After dinner and into the evening, the last session ended around 9:00 p.m. with the mantra, "Eyes open, wide awake, feeling fine and in perfect health, feeling better than before."

Concluding the first day, we had learned many controls and positive statements. We had received "Effective Sensory Projection for Our Success." I had clung to every positive word and phrase, but my constant "Beneficial Statement" became: "Every day, in every way, I am getting better, better and better."

My brain was on high alert from so much information that was rapidly absorbed. This was not about Black people, White people, Mexicans, or any other ethnic groups. This was all about brain, mind, and human intelligence. I could not wait to tell Midge, Nikki, Woodie, my friends from "A Black Quartet," Barbara Ann, all of my friends in The National Black Theater and The Living Room. I wanted my family, friends and the entire world to know about Silva Mind Control.

Day Two:

Meanwhile, I looked forward to day two on Sunday morning at 9:00 a.m. El' Jabber and I were energized from the class conditionings and excited about the next sessions. We arrived very early, and most students got there before Jose and Harry entered the room. We, the students, eagerly exchanged information about our experiences in yesterday's class. We agreed that we had collectively shed several levels of negativity and skepticism during the first class. Nonetheless, several students rushed and bombarded Jose and Harry with questions the minute they entered the room, but I was not one of them. I was elated and grateful for Jose's answer to my question the day before. Sunday's class format remained the same, and Jose brought us to order with one tap of his silver bell. He told us what he was going to tell us about "Self-Improvement." Throughout the day, he and Harry took turns programming us with new information.

All of the "Statements" were reinforced with every conditioning. One of my favorite "Genius Statements" was: "You are now learning to use more of your mind and to use it in a special manner." That was very encouraging and further cancelled out "uneducable." It also cancelled Aunt Nodee telling me, "You're dumber than cat shit," after I flunked an exam that Delores passed with a "C." The experience was extremely painful, because I had gone to class everyday, and Delores had cut class everyday, except the day of the exam. Daddy, Shortridge High School and all things negative were being corrected through Silva Mind Control training. My favorite "Preventive Statement" was "Negative thoughts and negative suggestions have no influence over me at any level of the mind."

The "Impression of New Material" was programmed at deeper, healthier levels, which enabled us to learn massive amounts with little time and effort. The second day of class ended with the metronome sound and conditioning, "At the count of 5, you will open your eyes, be wide awake, feeling fine, and in perfect health, feeling better than before..."

El' Jabber and I were excited about the third day of training, but we had to wait an entire week, because the class was taught over two weekends. During the week I continued working my day shift at the New York Hilton, and El' Jabber maintained his dreaded clerical job. Both of us sold Holiday Magic products everywhere we went and encouraged others to join our organization. Time dragged on until Saturday finally came around. Filled with energy and a new attitude, El' Jabber and I had high expectations from the third day of Mind Control training.

Day Three:

As usual, we arrived early in the hotel room and talked with fellow students about information learned in the two previous classes and how we had applied it. When Jose and Harry entered the room, most students smiled and greeted them like long-lost, loved ones.

Jose had to tap his silver bell several times before we stopped talking and sat down. He and Harry presented an overview of what we would be learning throughout the day and into the evening.

I especially welcomed the metronome sound and receiving new information. All of the "Positive and Beneficial Statements" were reinforced in every conditioning session. By the end of day three, we had mentally projected into the inanimate kingdom by mentally entering four different kinds of metal cubes. We mentally projected into the animal kingdom and plant life. In the plant kingdom, I had eaten my share of watermelons, but that was the first time I had ever gone inside of one. Astounding! Jose emphasized that those projections enabled us to establish points of reference in different kingdoms so that we could use those experiences to solve and prevent problems.

Harry continued by mentally guiding us to create a personal laboratory with two technicians who would help us detect and gather information for problem solving. Truly, this information was mind blowing! It felt like a mind control smorgasbord, and I wondered how much could I gobble down. I believed Jose and Harry, when they said "Don't worry about getting it." I readily accepted all of the "Positive Statements," and one of my favorite health phrases was, "I will always maintain a perfectly healthy body and mind."

Throughout every class Jose and Harry encouraged us to express our experiences and, "Ask as many questions as you like." All of us were bubbling with questions and comments at the end of day three. Collectively we wanted to know how did we project into plant life, and why did the copper cube feel warmer than the steel cube?" Even the skeptics who had come to expose Mind Control as "hocus-pocus," were actively involved.

We were so charged up, most of us would have gone on way into the night, but Jose sent us home around 9:30 p.m. with encouraging words. "Tomorrow we will do mental projection into human life. You will present problem cases to each other, and you will detect and correct problems through subjective communication." I really wanted to see how that worked!

Day Four:

Sunday morning most of the students arrived early, eager, and excited. A few expressed severe apprehension. We had neatly printed our case information on 5x7 index cards as instructed. Each student brought at least four different case cards, which contained the subject's name, age, gender, location, and the subject's problem. Everyone closely guarded their case cards and held them close to prevent information leaks.

I made a case card for my dog Trixie, Grandma Lizzy, Daddy and Grandma Mamie. After Jose and Harry completed the conditionings for problem solving in the Human, Animal, Plant, and Inanimate Kingdoms, we were separated into several groups of two so that we could tell each other what was written on those index cards. We were not allowed to work with anyone we knew.

How did we get the information on those cards? Student "A," took a deep breath and went to "deeper healthier levels of mind." The student used a mental screen to view and sense information. I was student "B" for the first exercise. I told student "A" that the subject's name was Othelder Williamson, Indianapolis, Indiana. Student "A" proceeded to tell me that as she scanned the subject's anatomy on her mental screen, she did not get any feedback. She said, "I sense that he is dead." She told me that he died from gunshot wounds. She told me, "This man had been very harsh to his children." She went on with more details. She also provided accurate information on both of my grandmothers. She wept while providing information on Trixie's life and death. How in the world did she do that? Unbelievable!

Even more unbelievable was the information that I provided when she presented her subjects. My heart pumped rapidly when it was my turn to be student "A." Nonetheless, after closing my eyes and relaxing, I felt calm and confident. I imagined my mental screen. Student "B" gave me the name and location of her first subject. I envisioned an eight-year old boy with a cast on his right leg. I sensed that the child's leg had been broken below the knee. I further sensed that the boy had been struck by a car while riding his bike. I also provided accurate and detailed information as student "B" presented all of her subjects. Where in the world was the information coming from?

Even so, our ability to gain information from unknown sources was not unique. All of the students sensed and provided some information on subjects presented to them from index cards. Every student was shocked and amazed, and all of us wanted to know "How" did all of those experiences occur?

Jose reminded us, "Don't waste your time and energy worrying about 'how.' You will get better results by applying what you have learned." He also cautioned, "Do not go back to your homes and communities and tell people that you are a functioning genius. No! No! Let it show through your actions."

As day four concluded, I understood how I had been able to see both of my grandmothers and my wonder dog, Trixie, after they had passed from this outer conscious world. Jose explained that children are more open and receptive. However, our western culture and educational system tends to eradicate our natural intuitiveness.

At the end of day four, every student who completed the course graduated from Silva Mind Control. Quiet tears of joy moistened my cheeks when Jose presented my diploma on August 9, 1970. It bears the signature of Harry Mc Knight, Instructor and Jose Silva, Director.

Since we loved the class and results so much, we decided to continue. Who could have guessed that I would receive another diploma from Silva

Mind Control in Laredo, Texas. El' Jabber and I had been excited about flying to Laredo, and participating in the intensive training, which took place during four consecutive days. There were a few women among the men. Collectively, we represented several potential instructors from various states where Jose had taught the basic course.

El' Jabber and I were the first African-American couple trained to teach Mind Control Methods. He focused on teaching the basic course to adults. I was excited about teaching the methods to children. On October 2, 1970, Jose signed and presented a diploma that certified every graduate to teach Mind Control. The graduate diplomas were also signed by Harry Mc Knight.

El' Jabber and I returned home from Texas, bubbling with positive expectations for teaching Mind Control. In order to teach a class, instructors had to advertise, generate interest, secure an audience, rent a hotel room, and present an overview on the benefits of Silva Mind Control. This was easier said than done. If enough people signed up to pay for the hotel, we would teach a class. Otherwise, they waited until there were enough students. We were aware that the subject matter in Mind Control would be greeted with skepticism.

Meanwhile, both of us were still employed, and fellow employees commented on our calm and different demeanor. Whenever El' Jabber and I were available on Saturdays, we went to be with our friends in the National Black Theater, and naturally told people about Silva Mind Control.

After completing Mind Control and becoming instructors, we were no longer angry enough to die while killing off only those White people who were evil. The good ones were helping us fight the revolution. No more chants of, "Kill Whitey." We accepted all of humanity and were proud to be Black reflections of The Creator. We were focused on human intelligence and spreading the benefits of conscious, positive, mind activity.

Challenging is an understatement in terms of spreading the benefits of Mind Control. People who knew us could not believe that we had become instructors in such a short span of time. Our friends and associates wanted us to do some Mind Control tricks and asked such questions as, "How much money do I have in my wallet? What did I eat for breakfast this morning? Can you bend a spoon with your mind?"

Similar questions were asked whenever we presented an overview of Mind Control to prospective students. In order to increase our chances of gaining more students, El' Jabber and I teamed up with another instructor to present the overview and co-teach the class, like Jose and Harry. Since 99% of the students were White, El' Jabber and I were suspiciously scrutinized. He dressed in contemporary suits and ties but wore his thick hair in a huge Afro. My Afro was covered in a colorful African head wrap that made me appear a foot taller than my actual height. Knee length, high heeled leather boots under my long dresses added to my height.

During the presentations, El Jabber and the other instructor presented snippets of the course, but I was the chosen one for the memory demonstration. My life experiences of having performed on various stages added to my confidence in presenting the memory demonstration. After a few words about Mind Control, I turned to the chalkboard and asked prospective students to give me 25 words, "nouns please," which I numbered from 1 - 25 and wrote them on the chalkboard. Using the Memory Pegs that we learned on day two of the basic course, I associated the first given word to a glass of "tea," which was number "1" of the Memory Pegs.

I instantly associated each given word to a Memory Peg and created a fun, visual image for easy recall. For example, if the first word given to me was elephant, I visualized a whopping elephant swimming in a small glass of "tea." Who wouldn't remember that? After the 25 words had been presented, I took a few seconds to mentally review.

Then I turned to face the audience and repeated each number and the word that I had been given. Some skeptics asked me to repeat the list backwards. Whatever word was given for "25," I hung it on a huge "nail," which was the peg word for "25." Potential students tried to trip me up by calling out random numbers. People were fascinated and puzzled by my "genius" qualities.

One time, during a presentation a skeptic became belligerent and accused me of cheating. He alleged that I had a hidden microphone or something under all of that material wrapped around my head. He thought El' Jabber was telling me the answers.

In an emotional and spontaneous response, I whisked off my head wrap and popped it like a matador in a bullfight. No microphone or anything fell to the floor. Bearing bright red cheeks, he apologized. Not only did the man take the class, he brought his wife, other family members, and some friends.

As the father of four school-aged children, he and his wife organized my first children's class, which I taught the second weekend of December 1970. Parents told their kids that the class was an early Christmas present. On the Saturday morning of class, I arrived at the hotel very early so that I could greet each student and instantly memorize their name. Approximately twenty White children arrived with their parents. The kids were ages six to seventeen years old, with a wide range of attitudes. Some of their parents had completed the basic course and some were participating in the adult class next door with El' Jabber and the other instructor.

Children were not interested in the background and research of Silva Mind Control. They were not concerned about my lack of formal education. They were not opposed to my chocolate complexion and fluffy Afro-hair. However, some of them were very curious and asked, "Can I pet your hair?" Permission granted; this was good preparation for projecting into all of the kingdoms: human, animal, plant, and inanimate.

What mattered most to the children was my memory demonstration, using the first 25 memory pegs. Every child was excited to learn that "mind trick." They jumped with excitement when I told them that I would teach them how to memorize 100 things in a few minutes. I told them the course had 100 memory pegs which they would learn easily and quickly.

I further explained that we had to complete several other experiences before learning the memory pegs on day two. At the beginning of class I warmly greeted the kids, called each one by name, and asked what they wanted to use Mind Control for? Quite a few of them shrugged their shoulders and said, "I don't know." The older kids wanted to improve their school grades. Some of the younger ones wanted to stop wetting the bed. One little girl wanted to stop biting her nails until they bled. A young boy wanted to stop sucking his thumb, and there were many other responses.

I thought about Jose and smiled when I told the kids what I was going to tell them. Children loved the idea of learning with their eyes closed, while sprawled out on the floor with pillows and blankets. The adults also used pillows and blankets during deepening exercises, but unlike adults, kids responded to the metronome sound by moving their heads, hands, feet, and bodies, or a combination of moves. Some of them emulated the metronome with their own vocal sounds. Even so, within a few minutes all of them were quietly and completely engaged in the process.

The four day class was basically the same for adults and kids, except the kids absorbed the information faster. Teaching the class was easy and fun, as I read the instructions from my teacher's manual. The kids loved "mentally" counting down from 10 to 1, but they counted out loud. Whenever I said, "Take a deep breath and go deeper," I laughed quietly when they sucked in air with all of their might and exhaled in slow whooshing sounds.

Without hesitation, they happily absorbed all of the "Statements: Genius, Beneficial, Protective and Preventive." For the children, every session was an adventure! With sheer delight, they went in and out of various forms of plant life, jumped into metal cubes, and floated through all of the kingdoms as defined in Silva Mind Control.

Truly, the kids were remarkable in their acceptance and creativity. The course provided a plethora of mental techniques that we could use to solve and prevent problems. Each participant selected their favorite techniques, including the kids. All of the children chose the memory pegs as one of their favorites. Each child was excited about doing a 25-word memory demonstration, and they provided the words for each other. The six-year old girl smiled with great pride when she did her memory "mind trick."

Adults did not have time do a memory demonstration for each other during class, because they were doubtful and talked more. Since I did not have to present lectures and answer endless questions, I was able to impress new material upon the children in a shorter span of time.

On the last day of class all of my young students brought four index cards with secret information written on them. Four or five adult graduates, mostly parents, came to assist me and the kids with presenting and perceiving information on those index cards. As you may already suspect, the children excelled! They imagined colorful visions and amazed themselves and each other with their mind power. Whenever they "guessed" inaccurate information, they did not get all choked up and stop, like some adults would. Kids responded with, "cancel that," and continued providing new information. On graduation day, each child received a diploma signed by Vikki Richardson, Instructor, and pre-signed by Jose Silva, Director. I emphasized to the children, "Please do not tell anyone that you are a functioning genius. Let it be known through your actions." The kids had also been given a packet of information on each day of class, including their cherished list of 100 memory pegs, which they placed in their Mind Control folder. Likewise, adult students were also given the same abundant information.

As time progressed, the feedback from my young graduates was swift and positive. Collectively, they stopped bed-wetting, nail-biting, thumb-sucking, bad dreams, unfavorable behavior and poor grades, to name a few. Reportedly, when an eighth grade White girl improved her test taking from "F" to "A," her White teachers accused her of cheating. Of course I flashed back to my own painful past and realized this kind of misconduct between the educational system, teachers, and students, greatly exceeded racism.

Race definitely was not the issue when the child's mother went to meet with the teacher. The mother explained that she and her daughter were recent graduates of Silva Mind Control. That teacher soon became a Silva graduate, along with other school personnel and some of the students.

Good results from the course spread through word of mouth. One of the graduate parents had a sister with three school aged children in Rochester, New York.

The sister and her spouse told their friends about Silva Mind Control and organized a class with sixteen kids. I was surprised and a little apprehensive to learn that I would stay with the family and teach the class in their home. The family lived in a large, fashionable home with a spacious basement. When I spoke with the parents by telephone and told them what I needed to teach the class, they purchased a huge green chalkboard on a tripod for the memory pegs. Later on, their kids appreciated it as a new home game for drawing, word games, and working through math problems, long before iPhones and video games were available.

I had taken the train to Rochester, and the parents picked me up on

Friday evening. Since I had never met the parents, they were very impressed when I walked up and called them by name. Silva Mind Control was off to a very good start. Knowing that kids are rapid learners, and two consecutive weekends in Rochester was not practical, I condensed the material into two very long days. We started after breakfast, around 9:00 a.m., and finished around 6:00 p.m. with ample breaks for playtime, snacks, and lunch. Each of the student's parents brought a homemade dish for lunch and snacks.

Some of the parents really wanted to sit-in on the class, but their own children opposed and insisted that they go to an adult class. However, at the end of day one, I invited the parents for the very last deepening exercise with the metronome sound, which motivated them to take the adult class.

At the conclusion of class on Sunday evening, the room was packed with parents, relatives, and friends. All of the sleeping bags, pillows, and blankets had been replaced with matching folding chairs, which transformed that basement room into a mini auditorium.

My excited, graduating students jumped up and down to demonstrate the memory pegs. I always allowed the youngest child to be first. To keep them engaged, I would say, "First one to tell me the number written on this paper will be next." When a child called out the number, I would hold up the paper for all to see. They also "guessed" colors and objects in a like manner. The children wonderfully impressed us and marveled over their individual learning experiences and acquired abilities. As time moved forward, they applied the memory pegs and their favorite techniques in school and everywhere, as needed.

Teaching opportunities became more frequent, and things were going well for me and the children's classes, even though some people complained about the cost. I do not recall tuition amounts for the children's or adult's classes, but the majority of people claimed that the course gave so much for so little.

The other instructor decided that he could teach the basic adult course by himself, with the help of testimonials from graduates. Teaching solo increased the cost of securing students, because El' Jabber had to pay the entire out-of-pocket cost for a hotel room to present an overview of Mind Control, and sometimes not enough people would sign up to justify a class. Disappointed but not embittered, El' Jabber made a conscious effort to focus on our African-American community. Although there had not been an outpouring of interest from friends in the National Black Theater, a few had attended our seminars on Mind Control. El' Jabber went to his life-long neighborhood in Harlem and distributed flyers to business owners, churches, schools, organizations, and individuals.

There was a spark of interest from a few people but not enough to teach a class. Finally, El' Jabber connected with a Black ophthalmologist. He was not troubled about El' Jabber's lack of academic credentials. He was more concerned about the benefits of the course. As a somewhat overweight father of a teenaged son and a seventh grade daughter, he looked forward to Day Two for "General Self-Improvement." The doctor and his wife invited approximately twelve adults to take the course in their home. The family lived in Queens and generously converted their living and dining rooms into a comfortable learning environment with a chalkboard.

Since there were no bitter skeptics in class, the positive course information flowed easily. Most of the participants were professionals and excited about applying Mind Control. They relished at . . . "Deeper, healthier levels of mind." Like everyone who completes the course, that small class in Queens amazed themselves and each other with their application of Silva Mind Control. After "testing" the course material for themselves, those parents were anxious for me to teach their children. In the same location, three weeks later, about sixteen predominately Black kids astonished themselves and sparkled with pride when I handed them their Silva Mind Control graduate certificate.

Teaching the class in Queens had been a windfall for both of us and was especially encouraging for El' Jabber, because future classes were forthcoming. The eye doctor and his associates appreciated the benefits of Mind Control and brought their relatives and friends to experience the course. Things were going great! El' Jabber and I had every reason to believe that classes would continue for both of us.

To ensure future classes, El' Jabber handed out flyers on the streets and subways. We approached community groups and various schools. School personnel rejected Mind Control because it did not fit into the curriculum.

Undaunted, we contacted one school in Brooklyn where the principal was receptive to Mind Control. The exact date flew by without documentation, but it was a wonderful day in early 1971 when we went to meet with school personnel. The African-American principal and his assistant were excited to greet us and hear the course overview. I could not resist doing the memory demonstration for the two of them. He and his assistant provided the words, which I wrote on an 8 1/2 x 11 sheet of notebook paper. After I associated all of the words to the memory pegs, I gave the list to the principal. With eyes closed and focused upward, I recalled the list of words from 1 - 25. When I opened my eyes, the principal and his assistant were staring at me with their eyes and mouths wide open, in disbelief! Their facial expressions made me laugh out loud with delight. I gave them the opportunity to quiz me on the words by any number and order, which they did with glee. All of my information was correct, and each answer added to their amazement and amusement.

The principal explained that he could use some allocated "extra curriculum" funds to pay for the kids who were interested. The allocated funds would not nearly cover the standard cost of Mind Control for the children's course, but that did not deter us.

It was an alternative school, known as a "600 School." Kids who were enrolled in "600" Schools had been expelled from regular public schools due to rebellious behavior or other problems beyond their control. The children were victims of physical abuse, neglect, lack of supervision by drug addict parents, imprisoned parents and other unfavorable circumstances. The children's consequences resonated within me, and I looked forward to their positive end results from the course.

The second week after initially meeting the principal, I arrived at the school around 8:30 a.m. on a Tuesday morning to teach Mind Control. The class would be taught in a regular classroom with twenty five desks and a large chalkboard. The principal had informed me that twenty boys would be attending. There were no girls in the class.

Nonetheless, twenty-two young men eventually swaggered into the room, with an age range of eleven to seventeen years. After arrangements had been made for the class, the principal briefed the students on what to expect. For the first day of Mind Control, he was there to greet me and the students. When the last child entered, the principal introduced me and left the room. The class was scheduled from 9:00 a.m. to 2:00 p.m. with ample time for breaks and lunch.

After greeting each child and memorizing his name, I asked, "Would you like to learn with your eyes closed and no homework?" Every hand raised! I announced, "I'm going to do a 'mind trick,' and I will teach you how to do the same thing." Some of the boys were busy talking and fooling around. I proceeded and asked the students to give me words that were nouns. "Nouns! What's that?" I explained, "Make sure the word is a person, place or thing, something you can see, like table, cup, shoe. . ."

The boys became very animated with their choice of words. They spoke the same language as Daddy and Grandma Lizzy. I rejected all vulgarity and asked for a better word. When I turned my back to the chalkboard and gave them the words, some of the boys sighed, "D-a-m-m-m-m!" Others cheered and whistled through their fingers.

Ticking sounds from the metronome brought a variety of responses, including some kids who vocally emulated the sound. The metronome continued, and I began with "Controlled Relaxation." They devoured the "Genius Statements" and all of the positive phrases. When the time came, they dazzled themselves and each other with their memory demonstrations. After that, other students were clamoring to join the class, but we only had one more day. I was allotted fifteen hours to teach the course, which was five hours a day, minus breaks and lunch, on Tuesday, Wednesday and Thursday. I crammed in all of the visualization techniques and projections into the four basic kingdoms.

Like the upper middle class children, the "600" students were indeed

"Functioning Geniuses." Throughout the class I emphasized, "You cannot change what has already happened to you, but you can use your mind and your actions to bring about positive results now and into the future." Silva Mind Control caused the most obvious transformation upon the "600" students. The course gave them expanded consciousness, mental tools to work with and hope for the future. They were "functioning geniuses" who needed guidance.

18

THE NATIONAL BLACK THEATER
AND NYU

My future was looking very bright. I was happily married and fascinated with teaching Mind Control. Even so, ambivalence tugged on my outer conscious mind, because I had moved to New York to become an actress. Due to Mind Control and work, I did not know the last time I had made the rounds or sought any acting jobs. I missed Woodie and my acting friends. El' Jabber and I always looked forward to visiting The National Black Theater, but our involvement with Mind Control made those visits infrequent.

Nevertheless, one Saturday in February 1971, we were warmly greeted by the sound of African drums, Barbara Ann, and fellow members of NBT. A few people were very curious about the positive benefits of Mind Control. I shared with them that the techniques I had learned made my diverse life experiences feel connected and corrected. Revisiting the workshop was a joyous experience as participants read poetry, spoke on various issues and provided information.

There was a tremendous amount of information to absorb on civil rights, Black economic power, the theater, and possibilities for Silva Mind Control. Life proceeded at a rapid and productive pace with all of the above.

Like a leap through time and space, by summer 1971 El' Jabber and I had moved from Manhattan to Hartsdale, New York. A potential burglar had attempted to break into my apartment on two different occasions. I was unwilling to give him a third chance. Even though I had paid a locksmith to install a deadbolt lock when I moved in, I fully realized that it could be broken. When I reported the first incident to the apartment manager, I asked him, "How can a burglar get into this building with a doorman standing down there?" With his heavy Brooklyn accent, he said, "This is New York." Additionally, Manhattan's congestion and lack of green lawns with trees and flowers further motivated my move. Living in Manhattan had required El' Jabber to walk me through Central Park frequently so that I could breathe. I loved the beauty of Central Park and wished that I could live there.

Although I loved the excitement and high energy of the city, I welcomed the tranquility and charm of Hartsdale, which was a quaint little village. One of the most heartwarming features of the village was a beautiful manicured park with lovely flowers and interesting statues of various breeds of dogs and some cats. The park was on the far end of Hartsdale Avenue, opposite the train station. When I noticed a lady crying and hovering over the statue of a miniature poodle, I looked up and read the arch shaped, sculptured sign, "Hartrsdale Pet Cemetery." The sign was naturally decorated and somewhat obscured by a winding vine, blooming with lavender bell shaped flowers.

Our fashionable apartment building was in the 100 block of Hartsdale Avenue, a couple of blocks from the train station, which was only twenty miles and a thirty-five minute train ride to Manhattan. My small apartment in Manhattan felt like a distant dream from the past. Our Hartsdale apartment also had one bedroom, but the place was huge by comparison. Earthy colored, hardwood floors gleamed in the dining area and every room, except the walk-through kitchen and bathroom. There was a large nook at each end of the kitchen, one was the dining area and the other was bonus space. The bathroom was almost the size of our Manhattan bedroom. We lived on the second floor of a three story building, and the view from our balcony was invigorating. I could see the sky, trees, the ground with grassy spots and some flowers in the courtyard, which our balcony faced. Major beauty was provided by green thumbed neighbors who grew multiple color flowers in terrace boxes on their balconies.

Our balcony did not have any blooming flowers, but I had accumulated several large green plants, which had helped me breathe in the Manhattan apartment and kept me connected to nature. Four tall plants stood at the end of a plum colored area rug in the living room, in front of the terrace door. A lighter shade of plum curtains covered the terrace door. The matching chairs with three legs were reupholstered in crushed brown velvet. The gold velvet sofa, red velvet Italian provincial chair, throw pillows, glass end tables and green plants made our living room colorful and comfortable. Also, there were two big plants in the bedroom, and I bought a brass head board, sky blue area rug, and matching drapes.

Our comfortable lifestyle required funding, and some of it was coming from my savings accounts. We purchased monthly train passes to reach our weekday jobs. My manager at The Hilton had been totally understanding and allowed me to work a day or night shift if requested. El' Jabber barely tolerated his clerical job while looking forward to building bigger classes. The notion of building a large organization in Holiday Magic had faded as we became involved with Silva Mind Control.

There was an ongoing request for children's Mind Control classes. At the time, I was the only children's instructor in the area. Most of the instructors were male, and all of them taught the adult class, because tuition for kids was considerably less. Therefore, I took the train to a few cities upstate, stayed in various homes, and taught an average of twelve kids per class. One time I rode the train to Buffalo and taught a class of twenty- four kids. I stayed with a family but taught the class in a hotel where our room was next door to the adult class. Some adults wanted to join our class, because we were having more fun and laughter than they were.

Everyone who took the class received the benefits, some more than others, contingent upon attitude and application. All children absorbed the information and responded without critical analysis. The children and I loved learning. Frequently I had visualized myself attending NYU and learning more.

Like a kid, I was totally thrilled beyond words when I received an official letter which stated that I had been accepted as a full-time student at New York University for fall semester 1972! Wow! I laughed, cried and danced around the apartment, clutching the letter tightly and waving it above my head.

The path to NYU had begun in February 1971 during one of our infrequent visits to The National Black Theater. On that day some of the information had been provided by Duane Jones, an English Professor at NYU. My ears had perked up and my brain processed every word when Duane announced that New York University had created a scholarship program in honor of Dr. King and his belief in higher education. He further stated that the scholarships were specifically for students who had been unsuccessful in high school but longed for a college education. Duane concluded, "If you are interested, see me afterwards for more details."

When the workshop ended, I almost levitated to Duane! New York University had structured a program just for me! I vibrated with energy as Duane gave me the address, names and phone numbers. Knowing that I was ready to enroll immediately, he smiled and said, "Slow down, you would be enrolling for fall semester 1972." As an English professor at NYU, Duane was the best insider and support system imaginable. According to Jose Silva, the phenomenon had placed me in the right spot at the right time! I had provided and received details through phone calls, met with my individual student counselor and provided my birth certificate where my name was misspelled as "Vesna And Williamson," which did not match any of my previously known names.

Fortunately, after arriving in New York I had gone to the official location to have my name legally changed to "Vikki Summers," and Midge was my witness, which was a criteria. I had to bring my birth certificate, and a signed letter from Mother indicating that she had named me 'Vessye Ann Williamson.' I filled out some forms and paid a fee. After waiting for a very long time in a huge room with a lot of people, my witness and I were finally called up, and I was sworn in as "Vikki Summers." The attendant rubber-stamped the form bearing my legal name, handed it to me and said, "Next!"

I took all of my name documents and marriage license to my counselor and was enrolled in NYU as Vikki Richardson. The counselor showed me my Shortridge transcript and assured me that the program would provide academic counselors and tutors to help with all of our subjects. I had relished in the enrollment process and orientation with the other students. I had felt validated by the welcome committee in the Student Union Building. I especially enjoyed the super-sized punch bowl filled with sangria in the reception area. Fruit in the sangria was sweet and bountiful, and there was plenty of finger food. The area was decorated with colorful ribbons and balloons, which made us feel welcomed.

Adding to this long desired miracle, my tuition was totally paid, and I received a stipend fund. Whatever the amount was, I considered it a fortune!Based upon our past, poor academic performance, the program did not allow us to carry more than 12-units. The program's structure allowed time for us to attend tutorial sessions, prepare assignments, and work. Some of the students were young parents.

With the application of Mind Control techniques, at the end of my first semester, I was a straight "A" student and placed on the Dean's List at New York University. Most unlikely! After making the Dean's List, the astonished program director called me in for a conference regarding my academic transformation. Professors, including Duane, tutors, and everyone involved in the program, were in attendance and puzzled over my progress.

Duane was not one of the teachers in the scholarship program, but he was a consultant. I do not know how many students were in the program, but it was confirmed that I was the only one who earned a 4.0. I summarized my remarkable progress in three words, "Silva Mind Control."

My captive audience was in awe as I candidly spoke about the benefits of Mind Control. I offered to teach a weekend class to my fellow students and everyone else who was interested in learning Mind Control. Many reasons prevailed and prevented me from teaching Mind Control at NYU. There was a lack of funding. The course did not fit into the curriculum, and there was the disconcerting notion of the uneducated teaching the educated.

Meanwhile, El' Jabber had been getting enough students to "Keep hope alive." He had concluded that a stable teaching location in an influential area would increase the probability of gaining more students.

The location selected was a two bedroom, three-bath apartment in Lincoln Center, which we referred to as our teaching studio. The unit number was 31-H, with a balcony overlooking Manhattan.

We took occupancy in May 1973. The plan was for El' Jabber to teach adults in the spacious living room. I would teach the kids in the master bedroom, and the other bedroom would be the office. We furnished the place with a chalkboard, some folding chairs and a couple of plants on the kitchen counter. The place came with wall-to-wall carpet and window blinds which completed the furnishings.

Walking into the apartment was breathtaking as the view engulfed us through the thick glass terrace doors. Venturing out on the balcony was like stepping into outer space. Gazing down upon Manhattan from 31-floors up in the air made me hold on to the balcony rails. Thoughts of ten or twelve energetic kids jumping up and down and leaning over the balcony sent chills down my spine.

A few weeks later when I taught a class of eleven kids, I did not allow them to step out on the balcony. They excitedly pressed their faces against the glass terrace door and stared out. They also enjoyed leaning their bodies against the windows in the bedrooms and peering down at the tiny people and cars on the streets.

On the ground, in the air, people could learn Mind Control anywhere. As usual, the graduating children amazed themselves and each other with what they had learned. There was a constant flow of positive feedback from graduates. School grades and attitudes improved. Diseases and disorders disappeared. Collectively, there were thousands of graduates and each one had a successful Mind Control testimonial.

I was happy to be among them with my academic testimonial. I also made the Dean's List for my second semester at NYU, which ended in June 1973. Filled with hope and anticipation, I yearned for my next semester of the four-year scholarship program, but I would have to wait until September 1973.

With school ending, there would be fewer classes for me to teach, because people would be gone on vacation. El' Jabber was teaching, but the classes were small, not enough to cover expenses. He believed that more people would be attending classes, because he had made some promising contacts with a few companies and organizations. He also tried to get a grant so that I could teach the methods to inner-city children as com munity services.

However, those future possibilities did not help with the current expenses. Early on, El' Jabber had acquired lines of credit and credit cards, which he freely used to purchase expensive attire so that he could look sharp and professional when he presented the Silva Mind Control overview to prospective students. El' Jabber taught a few students in June, but I did not have any future classes scheduled.

Even with positive visualizations and affirmations, I sensed financial disaster. We could not afford Hartsdale or Lincoln Center, not to mention both! El' Jabber said, "We can give up the apartment in Hartsdale and save that money by staying in Lincoln Center and sleeping on the floor. We hastily moved from Hartsdale in July 1973 before rent was due. With some strategic arranging, we placed all of the furniture and rugs in our office room and in the large closets so that we could maintain teaching space in the living room and master bedroom.

Late one summer night near the end of July 1973, I was standing on the balcony at Lincoln Center looking out at the dazzling New York skyline. My stomach swirled around as I felt us financially crashing down from 31-H. I stepped back and leaned against the wall. El' Jabber joined me on the balcony. Knowing that we could not financially recover and drastic actions would be required, El' Jabber said, "You have good friends and connections in Los Angeles. Let's move back out there." He was anxious to get away from persistent creditors who wanted their funds repaid.

My savings were melting away, and I was not generating enough income to restore them. In New York I was earning less and spending more. My employers had been very generous in allowing me time off without pay to pursue my dreams. I did not regret pursuing my dreams, beautiful furnishings, expensive locations or Silva Mind Control. Certainly, I would highly regret not being able to continue my scholarship program at NYU! The thought of not attending NYU sent me into temporary panic mode, but I used a relaxation technique to focus on the positive, even if we could not remain in New York.

El' Jabber had quit his low paying job after he started borrowing money. He clearly understood that he could not borrow himself out of debt, but he would borrow money on one credit card to pay another. We had paid the rent for May, June and July, but August would not be paid.

We did not have any immediate options for staying in New York, and we did not have any concrete plans for survival in Los Angeles. I knew the cost of living was less, but what would I do with all of that furniture and stuff that I could not afford to ship to L.A?

I called Nikki because I knew he would have some ideas on how to sell the furniture. He gave me the names and phone numbers of a few buyers and told me what price to sell the items for.

I called, and the buyers were very responsive. I sold the items to buyers who made offers that matched Nikki's asking price. I gladly accepted offers that exceeded the asking price. Those items included the Louis XV desk, Italian provincial chair, and the thick glass tables from Belgium. After two or three days, I had received a small fortune for all items sold, even though my fortune was a fraction of what I initially paid for them.

I used part of that fortune to ship our many music albums, books, some art work, clothing and other items by Greyhound bus to Los Angeles. I called Bunny Fran and told her that my husband and I were moving to L.A. She was very happy about my return and stated that she would notify all of our friends so that they could plan a party, but first we had to get there. We were anxious to vacate 31-H, because rent was not paid for August. We gave away plants and household items to El' Jabber's mother and to some of our friends. There was so much to do!

No time for farewell parties. I called Duane and tearfully explained why I would not be attending NYU's 1973 fall semester. He assured me that the Dean's List would help me transfer to a university of my choice in the Los Angeles area. I called Woodie, Barbara Ann, my friends from the theater and The Living Room. Midge was sad, and she cried because I was moving back to Los Angeles, even though we rarely saw each other.

Vikki Richardson

19

A HYSTERECTOMY IN LA
AND BANKRUPT

Los Angeles was calling. Time had run out for us in 31-H. It was an eventful day near the end of August. Around 10:00 a.m, El' Jabber and I would leave that location for the last time. We each carried two pieces of luggage for our flight to Los Angeles. We sat our bags on the floor near the elevator and anxiously waited.

When the elevator finally stopped on our floor, two law enforcement officers stepped forward and walked towards our apartment to serve us with an eviction notice. We entered the elevator and watched as one of the officers knocked hard on the door of 31-H. The elevator door closed and descended to the lobby. When the elevator stopped in the lobby, we picked up our luggage and walked towards the exit. The doorman held the door for us as we ventured out on the streets of New York for the last time. We caught a taxi to Kennedy Airport.

Boarding a flight is always an exciting event, but El' Jabber was especially eager because he loved flying, and he paid for the tickets with a credit card. As the jet flew west, I stared out the window and wondered what kind of work would we do to survive in Los Angeles. I could not help reflecting back on my first move to Los Angeles in 1965. What an amazing difference eight years had made in my lifestyle. How ironic that I arrived in the month of August on both occasions.

Since there were no disruptions or national events, the exact date passed by undocumented, but it was the last week of August 1973. Late afternoon sun welcomed our arrival to LAX. We collected our luggage and took a taxi to the Holiday Inn on Hollywood Boulevard, an area that I had once been familiar with. El' Jabber used a credit card to pay for the room. Armed with a 'Los Angeles Times,' I sat on the bed and immediately began our search for an apartment in Hollywood, within walking distance of the hotel.

A couple of days later, September 1, 1973, we settled for an unfurnished and less costly studio apartment on Wilcox and Hollywood Boulevard. The apartment was on the first floor. It was clean with a modern kitchen and bath, but the dull green carpet was not pretty or luxurious. Nonetheless, we would be sleeping on it. Good thing I had learned to accept the benefits of sleeping on the floor.

Shelley made things somewhat better by driving us to pick up our stuff that I had shipped on Greyhound, including sheets, blankets, a couple of decorative pillows, clothes books and music albums. I bought a couple of small green plants and some spiritual candles to furnish our one room apartment.

As I sat on the floor sorting through our books and arranging them in alphabetical order, it felt like I had crashed and was moving backwards through life. From my first luxurious apartment, to Hartsdale, to Lincoln Center to no furniture at all -- wish I could wake up from this bad dream. Unbelievable! Now what? My financial mind said, "You are a trained character actress. You can play the part of a topless dancer again." However, the thought of my husband and political consciousness ruled out toplessness before I took action, so "back to square one."

The 1973 fall semester had begun when we hastily enrolled in Hollywood High School Adult Education. I took typing and office management. El' Jabber enrolled to complete his high school education. We applied our Mind Control learning tools and excelled in our classes. Within a few weeks I was typing 80 words per minute.

Employers who sought temporary employees had someone post their job opportunities on bulletin boards near our classrooms, and teachers would announce available jobs during class. Before the end of September, I was working as a temporary receptionist-secretary in a law firm in Hollywood, but I was crying in my pillow every night, because NYU would be starting without me.

After all of those years of longing to attend college, finally I had been accepted to a top university on a full scholarship but could not continue. Even with the positive benefits of Mind Control, I was devastated, but not suicidal.

Filled with regret and conflict, I argued with myself, "If it wasn't for Mind Control we would not have financially crashed, but if it wasn't for

Mind Control I would not have been transformed from uneducable to honor student."

My most favorable option was to imagine positive end results and come to terms with the here and now. I purchased a monthly bus pass so that I could go where the jobs were. In Los Angeles, the rapid transit system was not at all rapid, and I wished for New York's speeding subways.

Soon, I came to terms with the tiny apartment and working temporary office jobs. El' Jabber filled out job applications and shopped on his credit cards, because they were his only financial source. My temporary work paid the rent and provided our basic needs. In spite of frequent flashbacks to my New York lodging locations, I affirmed, "Every day in every way, I am getting BETTER, BETTER and BETTER."

By December 1973 our situation had gotten better after I accepted a permanent position as a legal secretary with the State Bar of California, located on 3rd and Bixel Street, near downtown Los Angeles. It paid a fortune compared to temporary wages but a pittance compared to being a Bunny or working topless. Fortunately, the State Bar provided medical and dental benefits for me and my spouse, which the former employers did not.

My spouse did not find any work, but he did find a Martial Arts class to participate in as part of his curriculum at Hollywood High. He located a women's gym for me where they focused on stretching and strength training. I was astonished to see that one of the instructors was hugely pregnant, totally flexible, and able to do all of the moves that she instructed us to execute.

Meanwhile, time dragged at the State Bar. As secretary to a young attorney, my office was just across the way from his larger office. I also typed documents for any of the other attorneys as needed. The exact number of attorneys and secretaries who worked there was unknown.

Compared to some larger companies I had temporarily worked for, like Southern California Edison, the State Bar was a small workforce where I developed a friendship with Patty and Susan. Both of them were also personal secretaries. Susan typed 90 words per minute, and Patty typed 100. The three of us became known as "The Whiz Kids."

We were always chosen to work on special and tedious projects. One of the most tedious assignments was typing over words in state measures and bills whenever a law or proposed law was ratified. The process required striking over each letter in every word to be removed, by using the dash symbol on the typewriter, then typing in the new words of the ratification, alongside the stricken words.

Oh joy! Not at all, but typing ratifications was no worse than our "Top Secret Assignment." Equipped with headphones, we had the under-whelming task of transcribing "The Nixon Watergate Tapes." Working for the State Bar of California frequently reminded me of time served in the state of Indiana, The Intangibles Tax Division. Unfortunately, I did not have another glamorous, fairy tale escape route in mind.

Even so, the positive benefits from Mind Control prevented depression and propelled me forward. Looking forward enabled me to enjoy the little things in life instead of looking back and crying over the past. Truly, I enjoyed visiting and hanging out with Fran and all of my friends from Playboy. My old buddies and El' Jabber were pleased to meet each other. Seeing all of the kids was heartwarming and hard to believe their rapid growth and beauty over the past six years.

Another little thing of great value was our medical and dental insurance. After the imposed waiting period, we were eligible for medical and dental exams. I had not gone to a doctor for a general checkup since I had transferred to the Hollywood Club. When I initially transferred to the club in 1965, Fran and Hope referred me to Doctor Warren Sheeley for a general checkup. He was fondly known as "The Bunny Doctor." He was an elderly gentleman with a full head of thick, snow white hair, who presented a caring grandfatherly image.

Fran confirmed that Dr. Sheeley was still going strong in his same location near Hollywood Boulevard and Highland Avenue. One weekday near the end of March 1974, I called, spoke with his receptionist and made an appointment for "Bunny Vikki." Dr. Sheeley was delighted to hear "Bunny," and we spoke for a few minutes. His office was closed Sundays and Mondays, but he saw patients every other Saturday, 9:00 a.m. to 1:00 p.m. The following Saturday, I arrived early for my 11:00 a.m. visit.

He greeted me with a big hug and "Great to see you again." It was comforting being in his presence. We briefly spoke of our life events over the past six years. Although he was over 80 years old, he was not planning to retire anytime soon. After the exam, Dr. Sheeley said, "You appear to be totally healthy, but I want to see you in six months." He was concerned that I had been consistently taking birth control pills for the past eighteen years to control the pain from dysmenorrhea.

"The pill" had provided monthly comfort and allowed me to function. I could not imagine getting through life without it. My life was starting over in an unfavorable way, from New York University to Hollywood High School. Nonetheless, Hollywood High had restored my typing skills and prepared me to work for the State Bar.

In June 1974, El' Jabber graduated from Hollywood High with honors and beamed with pride in his cap and gown. He was also proud that the cross-eyed condition of his right eye had been corrected. His eye no longer turned outward, which improved his vision and appearance. Starting over was challenging, but medical coverage was comforting, and something we did not have in New York.

Medical benefits were certainly appreciated when I went to see Dr.

Sheeley for my follow-up appointment the first week of September. After the exam, I sat on a chair near the exam table, and Dr. Sheeley sat facing me. He said, "Young lady, I suspect that you have fibroids growing in your uterus, because that little bump in your tummy is not a pregnancy." I practically yelled, "Fibroids!" What are they, and how did I get them? Did birth control pills make them grow?"

Prior to the appointment we knew the lump was there, and El'Jabber had said, "You need to increase your sit-ups." No amount of sit-ups and stretching made it disappear. I stopped eating bread and butter and reduced my intake of sweets, but the little lump in my stomach did not go away. Fibroids!

Dr. Sheeley explained that fibroids had been a health problem long before women started taking birth control pills. I was anxious to know how to get rid of them. He said, "Removing them requires a hysterectomy, with entry through your abdominal area." I shrieked, "Hyster-what?" You mean, cut my stomach open! That really would wreck me!"

Suddenly the room felt very small, hot, and stuffy. My body automatically slumped in the chair, and my face fell into both hands. Tears flooded through my fingers, and my body shook like a 6.3 magnitude earthquake! Dr. Sheeley sprang from his chair and stood beside me. He attempted to calm the quaking by gently patting me on my back and shoulders. He spoke comforting words and assured me that it was not the end of the world.

The procedure would not destroy my womanhood, and the surgical scar would heal. He smiled at me and said, "You are beautiful now, and you will still be beautiful after the procedure. Plus, you are really physically fit, and that will help you recover faster." Dr. Sheeley focused on the good points.

Random discomfort from the tip of my protruding uterus in the vaginal tract would be permanently eliminated, and I would not have to take any more birth control pills. It felt like I was whirling in a vortex. Suddenly, I remembered to take three deep breaths and apply some Mind Control techniques to stabilize myself.

Speaking with a soothing tone, Dr. Sheeley explained all aspects of the procedure. He referred me to one of his colleagues, Dr. Miller, a gynecologist and surgeon, whose office was nearby. Dr. Sheeley called him and scheduled an appointment for me a couple of days later.

When I rushed home and told El' Jabber what caused the little bulge in my lower abdomen and the ensuing surgical procedure, he was thunderstruck! He verbalized all of the Mind Control methods we could use to eradicate it. We applied all of them. El' Jabber suggested a raw juice fast. Our juicer was the first thing I had shipped from New York. We had been consistent juicers since 1969. He made fresh carrot, apple, and celery juice two times a day. He believed that pure juice, Mind Control, and exercise would flush out the growth in my abs.

El' Jabber went with me to the appointment with Dr. Miller. After completing his examination, he confirmed that the growth was still there. He provided an overview of the procedure and the consequences. He presented anatomical graphs of tumors growing inside the uterus and the uterine wall. He explained that I had endometriosis, which was the culprit that caused unbearable monthly cramping.

I asked Dr. Miller what would happen if I did not get the surgery? He said that the growth would continue, and over time it would likely invade everything in my abdominal area. "You would look like a woman nine months pregnant, and the growth may be was scheduled for surgery at Hollywood Presbyterian Hospital on Vermont and Sunset. When I reluctantly disclosed the information to my co-workers, they were equally shocked. My Bunny buddies could not believe it! All of them offered empathy and reassuring words.

On September 11, 1974, El' Jabber and I arrived at the hospital around 7:00 a.m., and Dr. Sheeley was there waiting for us. A surgical nurse and anesthesiologist were ready to do their jobs. El' Jabber kissed me goodbye, and I was prepared for surgery. Dr. Sheeley stayed by my side. I did not recognize Dr. Miller in his scrubs. After the anesthesiologist put that tube over my nose and mouth, I did not care about recognizing anyone or anything as I drifted into deeper, healthier levels of mind.

There was no conscious awareness of time or space for several hours, during and after my surgery. At some point I woke up in the recovery room feeling thirsty, and I had to pee. I raised up from my pillow and noticed a narrow intravenous tube inserted into my right arm. The little tube was attached to a bag of clear fluid, hanging upside down on a skinny, silver pole with four tiny wheels. No problem, I could easily roll it along to the bathroom.

My midsection felt like it was missing, but my left arm was working to move the sheets, so that I could get out of bed. Before attempting to swing my legs out, I noticed a pencil size tube at the end of my hospital gown. The tube flowed into a clear plastic bag attached to the foot of my bed. The bag was about the size of a volleyball, and it also contained some fluid, but that fluid was not very clear.

A nurse magically appeared and asked, "Do you need something?" I said, "Yes, I need to get out of bed and use the bathroom." She said, "You are attached to a catheter, and your urine automatically drains into that little bag," as she pointed towards the end of my bed. She also focused on the obvious "IV" tube in my right arm and said, "So just settle down and rest."

Under my hospital gown, my abdominal area was bandaged and taped. I was anxious to know exactly what body parts had been removed or what remained. While rubbing over my bandages and wondering what was underneath, Dr. Miller walked in to confirm my progress. He explained that he removed my uterus, because six little tumors had grown and entangled themselves in my uterine wall.

I blurted out, "Six little tumors!" My heartbeat rapidly increased! While taking birth control pills over the years, I had jokingly said, "Someday I'm going to get married and have six kids all at once, and this is my fertility pill." During those times, I had laughed and amused myself that people would help us financially with multiples, but no help at all with six single births.

Dr. Miller's lips were moving, but I did not know what he was saying when my voice interrupted him again, "Six little tumors!" I told him about my multiple birth jokes while taking the pill. With highly raised eyebrows, he looked at me and slowly said, "Very interesting." He continued to explain that my ovaries and all other organs were healthy and functioning properly. He gave me a printed sheet of instructions for recovery and follow-up.

After Dr. Miller left my bedside, a little while later I was transported to a regular hospital room with two beds and draw-drapes around them. I wept and wallowed in sorrow, because it was final. I would never be able to have a baby. Having a baby had not been a desire during my Playboy Bunny and topless lifestyles, although several of my Bunny and topless friends were happy parents. Mother had repeatedly stated that having children was the worst thing that could happen to you, and Daddy had demonstrated how much he hated having us. Even so, after El' Jabber and I were married, I was thinking of starting a family after I graduated from NYU and he became financially stable.

Unstable best described our present situation. My life flashed before me in frames. Not so long ago, it felt like I was on top of the world and moving upwards with my modeling and acting career. Suddenly I was sleeping on the floor and missing out at NYU. I sobbed, "Now I can't even get out of bed to use the bathroom." Before torrents of tears totally swept me away, a gentle hand was patting on my chest. I looked up into Dr. Sheeley's kind and concerned face. He granted me the right to cry and consoled me that everything was going to be alright.

Dr. Sheeley's words were encouraging and uplifting. He pointed out that every woman on earth is not destined to bear children. He assured me that my womanhood and sexuality had not been destroyed or diminished by the surgery. He told me to focus on recovering and enjoying a bright future.

As Dr. Sheeley was speaking of leaving, El' Jabber rushed in carrying beautiful flowers and a container of freshly made carrot, apple, celery, and pineapple juice. I was very happy to see him, the flowers, and juice. He was anxious to know how I was feeling and what had been surgically removed. His body responded with subdued shock when he stared at the tubes attached to me.

I assured El' Jabber that I was comfortable, and everything was getting better and better. Although he and I had been very disappointed that we did not psychically remove the fibroids with Mind Control as we expected, we did not give up on the methods. We expected positive end results, no matter what. El' Jabber and I agreed to double up on our favorite techniques for rapid healing. We planned to use the same techniques at specified times throughout the day.

Time was standing still in my hospital bed but not for long. A couple of days after surgery, a nurse detached my catheter and escorted me out of bed for a walk. When I finally managed to stand up, I could feel my internal organs rushing around, trying to fill the void created by my missing womb. I groaned from pain and cradled my abdominal area with my left hand, but I could not stand up straight.

Looking like a little old lady bent forward by osteoporosis, I held onto myself and rolled along my "IV" pole, while the nurse held onto me and slowly walked me to the bathroom. Using the bathroom would have been a terrifying experience if Dr. Miller had not informed me about excessive bleeding after surgery. He had told me, "Don't worry about it. It's the last period you'll ever have."

"The last period" was a rewarding thought for my future. No more bloody surprises on white jeans and unsuspecting bed sheets. My thoughts wondered if my future would return me to New York University somehow. Though my immediate future was focused on the daunting task of getting out of the bathroom. The nurse held onto my left arm and ushered me back to bed with the promise of a longer walk tomorrow. How many tomorrows would I have to endure? How fast could I heal? Not fast enough, but visitors made time more bearable. My Bunny buddies came to visit and brought delightful flowers and cards. I was truly shocked to see Patty and Susan during their lunch hour. They brought a big flower basket and a funny "Get Well" card signed by everyone at the State Bar, and there was lots of cash in the card. Tears of gratitude quietly rolled down my cheeks as I thanked them profusely.

El' Jabber came to visit everyday and brought a container of homemade juice. Fresh pineapple juice reportedly contains massive healing enzymes, and I loved it! I could feel my body gradually healing as pain and soreness dissipated.

I don't know what day the bandages were removed, and I saw the incision for the first time. There were no open ghastly wounds. The area was obviously swollen and revealed a full-length, vertical scar from belly button to top of bikini line. I don't remember how many days went by before Dr. Miller removed the stitches, but I do remember the stinging sensations.

Drinking juice, positive thinking, and following instructions finally got me released, after approximately eleven days. My objective had been to remain in the hospital until I was totally healed and back to normal. Amazingly, Dr. Sheeley had come to visit every day. When I mentioned his kindness, he had smiled and said, "No problem, I have a couple other patients here, and there is always somebody new coming in. I just make the rounds." Fran had come to visit several times, and she drove us home.

Before surgery, one day I was talking with the apartment manager, and she told me about her friend who was going to have some kind of surgery. She also mentioned her own surgical procedure, and I told her about my impending surgery. She was a kind woman who worshipped her grandchildren.

Surprisingly, when I arrived home from the hospital, she had provided a twin-sized bed for me to sleep and sit on. She was very empathetic, because she had endured a hysterectomy a few years prior. She said, "A hysterectomy is bad enough, not to mention trying to get up off the floor."

I could get up off the floor, with some assistance. After a few more days of continuous juicing and healing, El' Jabber lowered me to the floor for my first post-surgery exercise. Having carefully placed me on my back, he aligned my arms and body. Then he said, "Take three deep breaths and see yourself as you wish to be." I repeated the deep breathing process for awhile. A few minutes later he said, "Raise your hands above your head." Slowly, I slid my arms on the padded floor, moving them towards my head.

Before my hands were within touching distance of each other, a pulling sensation shot through my stomach, and I relaxed my arms. El' Jabber stood behind and lifted me from the floor. I easily walked to the bathroom independently. Strength training and stretching from the gym appeared to be paying off. I was not totally healed, but when I went for my post-surgery checkup, Dr. Miller was amazed with my progress, and he encouraged me to keep up the good work.

Lying on the floor, touching my hands above my head and getting up became a daily exercise. We added on simple floor moves as I became stronger. With my back flat, El' Jabber lifted my legs several inches above the floor and held on while I attempted to carefully bend my knees and move them towards my chest, without ripping something. I did not rip anything, and I certainly became stronger.

Vikki Richardson

20

BACK TO WORK AT
THE STATE BAR OF CALIFORNIA

Two weeks after surgery, my co-workers welcomed me back with balloons in my office. My body and fingers were moving slower than before, but I was getting faster with time. In order to restore my typing speed, I practiced typing drills everyday from my 'Standard Typing Drill Book,' which I kept with other informational books in my office.

Before long, my typing was up to speed, but I had to get up and move around more frequently to avoid stiffness and back discomfort. Fortunately no pain medication or hormone supplements were required. I loathed swallowing pills, especially big ones.

Further discomfort was prevented by not riding the bus to work initially. El' Jabber asked a friend to drive me to work. They dropped me off before they went to school and picked me up afterwards. Both of them were students in Los Angeles City College. El' Jabber and I had enrolled for fall semester 1974, and classes had begun near the end of August, day time for him, evening classes for me.

My childhood friend Odeana was a keypunch operator, and I was also looking forward to finding time for learning the keypunch machine. It was a punch-card data entry machine, and keypunch operators made more money than regular clerical staff.

In the meantime, I was thankful to be earning enough money to pay rent for a one bedroom, nicely furnished apartment, utilities included, and we moved from Hollywood and Wilcox on November 1, 1974. Our new three story building was located in the Wilshire District, 160 South Virgil Avenue, Los Angeles.

The facility was newly built and filled with amenities inside and out. Inside there was a nicely furnished recreation area, which looked like a huge living room with an electric fireplace. A full-sized kitchen, bar stools at the counter, dining space, sofas, tables with lamps and a pool table completed the party room, which was free to use with a reservation. Through the doors from the party room were the women's and men's saunas, and two bathrooms.

Outside, beautifully landscaped plants, trees, and flowers decorated the courtyard. A cascading waterfall invited tenants into the huge, bubbling jacuzzi. A large swimming pool was just a few feet away. There were several comfortable lounge chairs around the pool. Eight to ten tables with umbrellas and chairs placed around the courtyard made me feel like I was living in a resort area.

In every apartment unit, the kitchen, dining area, and living room was designed just like the party room. Our unit was on the second floor, facing Virgil Avenue. It provided a spectacular view of the Wilshire District and downtown. The night view called me to sit on our large balcony and gaze into the dancing city lights of Los Angeles.

The bedroom was big enough to have space remaining around the queen sized bed and mirrored dresser. I was delighted with the two-part bathroom design. Part one contained the sink and wall-to-wall mirrors above the generously long counter. A wall-to-wall closet with three sliding doors faced the mirrors, which made the room appear larger than it was. Part two had the shower, tub and "throne," and the user could close the door for total privacy, while the other one used the sink. It was like having two bathrooms. El' Jabber and I were very happy with our new apartment and surroundings. It felt like a combination of everyplace we had lived in New York. Knowing that we would be living in our new apartment long term, I had a phone installed, and people soon started calling El' Jabber immediately. We lived in the "213" area code, which was reminiscent of our "212" area code in New York. Our Virgil Avenue apartment also had a well-managed laundry room in the basement, and all of the machines worked. Fortunately, every place we had lived provided a pleasant laundry room, and Lincoln Center had several.

Those conveniences made life easier. Our new location was closer to work, and I could get there in less time. Things were going well at work, and El' Jabber was doing great at Los Angeles City College. He had become very involved in student affairs and school politics. He was also working as a peer counselor, very busy, but not financially productive.

When surgery had become evident, filling out drop cards for my classes never occurred to us. Therefore, I was still enrolled and returned to class a week after returning to work. I had also enrolled in a grammar class that included creative writing. I was confident that Mind Control would help me catch up with the class work, and it did.

Sometime during the month of October 1974, one of El' Jabber's school friends knew of a 1960 Studebaker Lark for sale. It looked like an old Rolls Royce with shiny chrome grill and massive chrome bumpers, front and back. There were chrome strips that formed a horizontal line on each side of the car. Starting at the headlights, the chrome strips extended all the way around the car, like one continuous line. The car had a silver body and black top, like my 1965 Mustang, which I had wished for frequently.

The car was "priced to sell." The seller told us some of the repairs that the car needed, but he did not tell all. Using our Mind Control projection into inanimate objects, El' Jabber and I knew that the car needed more work than the seller disclosed. When we told the guy about our findings, he was so stunned, he lowered the price. I do not recall the exact "bargain" amount, but I paid the small amount in cash.

As repairs moved into the future, we realized that the seller should have paid us for rescuing him from that car! First thing fixed was the starter, and I was happily driving back and forth to work and school.

Painfully wishing that I was in NYU, I remained enrolled in Los Angeles City College. NYU to LACC was a downward move, but it was a move up from Hollywood High. I loved learning, and I knew that things would get "Better, Better and Better."

However, lots of visual imagery was required to perceive things getting better. By December 1974, El' Jabber's creditors had somehow located him, and they were among the most frequent callers. After we moved to Los Angeles, credit cards were his only method of paying for things, until each card were taken at point of sale.

Creditors wanted payments by any means necessary. They did not care that I was not the one who created the debt. I was his wife and considered equally and legally responsible. When they started calling me at work, threatening to garnishee my wages, I asked a couple of the attorneys some "What if" questions regarding bankruptcy.

Based upon their general answers, I took action. I closed my savings account and stashed my "egg money" in the bottom of a Kotex box that sat on a shelf in the closet. Grandma Mamie's advice from my childhood had paid off. Whenever she sold butter, cream and eggs in Jackson, she referred to her profits as "Egg money," and she always said, "Baby save yourself some egg money." To stop the sharks, I paid each of them a minimum payment to prevent garnishee proceedings.

At work, the State Bar Library welcomed anyone who took time to use it. Everything I wanted to know about filing bankruptcy papers was readily available. I read the instructions on how to file my own bankruptcy papers instead of paying an attorney. I went to a legal bookstore and purchased the bankruptcy kit with a workbook and all of the needed forms.

Filling out the forms was very detailed and specific. I had to list every debt owed, some I didn't even know about, but El' Jabber did. He gladly provided all needed information. The forms required a detailed list of every asset: bank accounts, stocks, bonds, jewelry, coins, stamps, everything that a person could possibly own.

I utilized the worksheets and verified accuracy before typing approximately twenty-five pages to be submitted to the bankruptcy courts. This was indeed a "Do It Yourself" filing, but instructions required me to use the term, "In Pro Per." By the end of December 1974, I paid a filing fee, and our bankruptcy forms were professionally prepared and filed In Pro Per, with covert assistance from the State Bar of California.

After our case was filed, it was given a case number. After that, every calling creditor was given the bankruptcy case number, and they stopped calling, but our phone did not stop ringing.

El' Jabber had run a successful campaign and won the election as student body president at LACC. He had become very popular, especially among his female supporters. They always presented valid reasons for calling. Those reasons kept him very busy with outside activities, which created distance in our relationship.

Being student body president with an entourage gave him a new attitude, laced with arrogance. His lifestyle had radically changed since he moved from Harlem. He appreciated living in Los Angeles, the weather and the many benefits. Medical insurance had corrected his eye problem. Dental insurance provided permanent teeth instead of wiggly, removable bridge work. Moreover, he had learned to drive and received his first California Driver License. He absolutely loved driving the glitzy Studebaker whenever it felt like running.

His popularity and importance gained him invitations to various events and parties, where he was the fashionably dressed star with a New York accent. He definitely had "a gift for gab," and the ladies loved it. They giggled, commented on his accent, and kept him talking. At those events, he engaged in lengthy conversations with everyone and danced with several ladies, but I was not among them. Guys attending the events knew that I was El' Jabber's wife, so they mingled, flirted and danced with other girls, which left me standing or sitting alone, watching everyone else having fun.

There was no fun at all existing inside of a distant relationship within the same apartment. It was sort of like living with a roommate but not quite.

All of my prior roommates had paid their share of the rent and living expenses. El' Jabber argued that attending college would prepare him to get a better paying job in the future, but his distracted and disengaging behavior towards me did not feel like a firm foundation for our future.

Whenever we had heated discussions, I blamed surgery for his distance. He vehemently denied the allegations. I agreed that it was not just the surgery. I was still the same "beautiful" woman that I had been before surgery. Other than the unsightly scar on my abs, I still had my "Bunny body." Although my body was thinner, I was strong, thanks to stretching and strength training exercises at home on the floor.

Working during the day and going to LACC in the evening did not leave any gym time, especially since the gym was in Hollywood, and we were not. I could not prevent my thoughts from wondering how my peers were doing in NYU, as I visualized myself entering UCLA. Taking classes at LACC kept me connected to learning and the energetic student environment. There seemed to be no end to advancing levels of grammar and writing classes, and I enrolled. I also took public speaking.

In June, at the end of the 1974 school year, I received a beautifully printed plaque bearing these words: "This is to certify that Vikki Richardson has been elected to Who's Who Among Students in American Junior Colleges in recognition of outstanding merit and accomplishment as a student at Los Angeles City College, 1974." I also earned an "A" in every class.

School was out for summer, and I expected El' Jabber to find a job of some kind, but he went to summer school instead. He claimed that by attending summer school, he would have enough credits to get his Associate Degree in Political Science. LACC had allowed him to carry all of the classes for which he had time. Mind Control methods enabled him to power through the course work. He "tested out" for some of his classes and received credit without class time. He earned an "A" in most of his classes. An occasional "B" was his worst grade.

When El' Jabber finished summer school in 1975, he excitedly confirmed that he was going to New Delhi, India for two weeks. He had mentioned the possibility several months prior, but the trip was contingent upon funding for him and three other honor students. They were scheduled to visit some universities, agricultural, and diverse cultural areas.

Funding was provided. He and his fellow students flew off to India. After a couple of weeks, El' Jabber returned from India filled with great importance and philosophical concepts on Eastern Religion and meditation, but no immediate intentions of getting a job.

While arguing over the issue he asked, "Would you live in a place like this on your own?" I snapped, "I certainly would!" He said, "So what's the difference whether I pay any rent or not?" My ears could not believe what they heard!

His growing importance and busy schedule had destroyed our relationship, and he was not interested in repairing it. Time to go our separate ways. No cursing, yelling or slamming items around, it was simply time to move on.

El' Jabber had met a wide variety of interesting people as student body president at LACC. When we split up, he moved into a very large home in Northridge. From his description, the place sounded like a compound with a combination of Eastern Religion, meditation, chanting, and Martial Arts. Reportedly, he would earn his keep by teaching Martial Arts. Good for him and the Studebaker. We went to DMV, and I registered the car in his name. What a relief!

21

ACADEMIC SCHOLARSHIP
TO UCLA

Relief came in various forms, and things were getting better and better. One remarkable day in August, I received my acceptance letter for the 1975 fall quarter at UCLA! I screamed, hugged the letter to my chest and did a happy dance. I danced through every room and out on the balcony!

I had mentally replaced NYU with UCLA when El' Jabber and I crashed out of New York. Reality told me that I would not be returning to NYU, no matter how much I wished. I did not know how or when I would attend UCLA, but I held onto the visual image. Shortly after moving to Virgil Avenue, I had called UCLA Admissions and obtained much needed information. Through it all, I had visualized myself in UCLA and followed enrollment instructions. It was a lengthy process, but I had nothing better to do. Nothing could have been better for me than finally becoming a UCLA student.

My thoughts whirled back to being a topless server, when customers teased, "What's a nice girl like you doing working in a place like this?" I had coyly answered, "I'm working my way through UCLA." Scenes flashed back to the topless dance I had performed for the UCLA physics professor's 50th birthday party in a Malibu home. As a Playboy Bunny, I recalled the cherished trip to campus with Ron, the Black busboy who was a UCLA student. My words and thoughts about UCLA nine years prior had become a reality. Wow!

Five attorneys from the State Bar helped make UCLA a reality for me by writing embellished letters of recommendation. Three of them were UCLA undergraduates and two of them had obtained their Law Degree from UCLA.

Fortunately around that time, the State Bar was upgrading office typewriters to the more modern IBM Selectrics. Selectrics had a little round ball that contained all of the typing symbols, and the ball rotated with every key strike. Rapid, rhythmic typing turned the ball into a blurry whirl.

Since the office had to get rid of the older electric typewriters we had been using, I offered to adopt one. They actually gave me the typewriter I had been using since working there. I was also given a heavy wood, dinosaur-type desk that had been replaced with a modern streamlined version. The heavy desk had a pop-up lever under a typewriter-sized wooden tray that the typewriter was placed upon. When the typewriter was not in use, it could be lowered under the desk top and concealed by closing the little swing-out door, attached to the left hand side of the desk. There was a huge top drawer and three large side drawers for storing stuff. My coworkers teased that I would need plenty of space for the books and endless homework required by UCLA.

There was a lot more to do before books and homework. I made a copy of my acceptance letter and kept it in my purse. At my earliest convenience, one Saturday morning, I walked almost a mile from my apartment on 1st Street and Virgil Avenue to Wilshire and Vermont and rode the bus marked "Westwood-UCLA." When I thought the bus was approaching the campus, I said to the friendly driver, "Please don't let me ride past my UCLA stop." He flashed a winning smile and said, "Don't worry. It's the last stop and the end of the line." There were two or three buses parked with drivers on their rest break when he drove up and parked behind them.

Thrilled to be on campus, I smiled at the driver, "I'll be starting classes this September, and I came to find my way around." Pointing towards my black high-heeled platforms, he chuckled, "You gonna do all that walking in those things?" They were six inch heels, but the cushy, toes out, platform design with ankle straps made them comfortable for me. I was determined to appear tall and muscular.

After all, I had carried and served very heavy trays while wearing spike-heeled pumps in The Playboy Club and danced topless for hours wearing very high-heeled shoes and boots. My feet were trained well, and the excitement of being on campus almost made me take off running! With a campus map from the bus stop area, I started walking towards campus. The first building I came upon was Murphy Hall. Next, I marveled over the size and structure of Powell Library. According to the map, that area was known as "The Quad." From there I toddled down "Bruin Walk" to the student store.

After practically examining every item in the store, I bought a T-shirt, an ashtray and a drinking mug with UCLA's sparkling symbol on each item. When I finally wrestled myself out of the student store, I accepted the Janss Steps challenge and walked up the 87 steps. From there, I hiked my way to North campus and gazed upon the University Research Library, fondly known as "URL." That was just the beginning of buildings and gardens to see on the 400 plus acres of UCLA, but not all on the same day.

Time flew by faster than ever, and late afternoon was upon us. I walked to the parked bus and waited for the driver to return from his or her break. When the driver approached, I couldn't believe it was the same guy who drove me to campus. Sitting in the driver's seat he did not look that big. But standing up, he looked like a football lineman. He was African-American, approximately five feet, eleven inches tall, a head full of dark brown curly hair and bright brown eyes with ultra thick lashes. His complexion and hair suggested some other ethnic mixture in his background. He started laughing when he recognized me, and he teased, "You been out here all this time in them shoes! Did you buy the place or what?"

We both laughed and introduced ourselves. He said his name was "C.W." I said, "C.W.! That's it?" He laughed louder and said, "Well, that's what everybody calls me." I sat behind the driver's seat, and we engaged in general conversation as he drove, and passengers got on and off the bus. He wished me well at UCLA. When I got off the bus at Wilshire and Vermont, he said, "Be safe. See you next time."

As time moved forward, I received a letter inviting me to campus for orientation and to meet my financial aid, peer, and academic counselors. My academic counselor asked, "What are you planning to major in?" I replied, "I don't know yet, maybe Psychology." After looking over my transcripts and asking several questions, she told me that I would be enrolled in the UCLA College of Letters and Science.

My financial aid package would reportedly provide a full academic scholarship, based upon my Dean's List accomplishment, and UCLA accepted me as a transfer student from NYU. They also accepted credits from my English classes at LACC, which made me an official UCLA freshman with some credits.

The financial aid counselor had warned me that I probably would not receive any funds before classes began. Therefore, I worked until the last minute before school started. At work, Patty and Susan planned my "Back-To-School" potluck lunch with cake and a card stuffed with cash. Regardless of their "stuffed shirt" reputation, the State Bar staff was very generous and supportive of me. I could not thank them enough for their encouragement during my surgery and for their UCLA support. The general information and legal knowledge that I gained while working there was priceless.

My last State Bar paycheck covered rent and phone, which were my only expenses after filing bankruptcy and escaping the cash-consuming Studebaker. I did not get any immediate scholarship cash as the counselor had warned, but I did receive a monthly bus pass during orientation.

My academic counselor advised me to wait until my class enrollments were confirmed by "Hal," the campus computer, before buying the textbooks. She also told me about the UCLA Learning Laboratory where they taught students how to learn. I thought, "That will be my first class." My peer counselor informed me of student activities and campus events. After "Hal" verified enrollment in my first three classes, I used "egg money" to purchase textbooks, a UCLA book bag and needed supplies.

First day of class fall 1975, adrenal energy woke me up with the birds. I don't remember what time my first class began, but I left home around 6:00 a.m., which allowed time for walking to Wilshire and Vermont in my platform shoes. Traveling on Wilshire Boulevard, I lived approximately ten miles from UCLA, but it took forever to get there on the bus.

I saw the UCLA "Express" bus roll into the boarding area and stop. The doors swung open and, C.W. smiled and said, "Good morning Miss UCLA." I bounced up the steps and sat behind him. As passengers crowded into the bus, I began reading some UCLA brochures. The express bus made designated stops. When C.W. rolled past local stops, I could see waiting passengers waving the finger, yelling and cursing at the driver for passing them by.

I arrived early and waited for my first class, Cultural Anthropology. Finally, it was time for class and the room was filled with eager students, some were hopeful of enrolling in the class. The professor introduced herself and said, "If you have an enrollment slip, please come and present it as you receive your syllabus." The syllabus presented the course of study and included dates for the midterm and final exams and the professor's name and office hours. It also listed the textbook and five additional books for suggested reading.

My professors in English 10A and Latin American History 8A presented similar syllabi with a list of suggested reading. On the first day, all of the professors presented a brief overview of their course, pointed out the homework assignments, and dismissed us to go purchase our books. An endless number of students rushed to the Student Store, where we could hurry up and wait for the line to eventually move inside the store. I bought the three textbooks and planned to use the library for the twenty suggested readings. My peer counselor had told me to buy used books because they cost less, and good used ones had highlighted information presented on the midterm and final exams. She also told me that 'Cliff' Notes were tiny paperback books which summarized the reading material.

A White male student working in the used books section had caused laughter when I purchased my books, because he had "USED" stickers all over his face and the back of his hands. I had been very happy to see two Black students working in the student store. One was a beautiful girl with dark brown skin, and the other one was a good looking brother with a beige complexion and a serious attitude.

As time rapidly progressed into the quarter, I had been looking around campus, hoping to see the few Black students from orientation. I had seen a few other ones rushing across campus at a distance and smiled to myself, "Well, there goes one." I had been "the only one" and alone on many occasions in my life, and I considered myself, "Tough and ready." I was totally thankful and crazy busy, reading, cramming, writing papers, and scrambling across campus from one class to the next.

One of the enchanting features about being on campus was the resonating sound of tolling bells. The bells started resounding a few minutes before the hour, every hour. Students ran like rabbits in all directions, determined to reach the lecture hall or classroom before the bells stopped tolling.

Utilizing Powell Library, I prepared most of my homework in its splendor, but there was still more to do at home. If there were any convenient lockers on campus, they were secrets. Therefore, my book bag and I became one. Like a flash flood, midterms were upon us. I earned a "B" in each class. I was totally disappointed and visualized myself earning three "As" as final grades.

Diligence became my constant companion, and I kept up the good work. Campus felt comfortable, and I loved the country-like atmosphere, wide open space, with lots of green grass and trees. There was plenty of walking for sure, but the distances were much shorter than walking home to the log cabin from Neeley Elementary School in Denmark, Tennessee. Plus, there were no angry mules or snakes to chase me on campus.

Certainly, I had come a long way from Neeley Elementary, and becoming a UCLA student had been most unlikely, especially on an academic scholarship. Nonetheless, I was a "young coed" in a top university. Overall, UCLA students were friendly and helpful, and I joined a study group for each of my classes in order to improve my grades for the finals.

In spite of all of my efforts, my final grades for Fall 1975 were "B" in every class. Not one single "A," which rendered me missing in action from The Dean's List. Grateful to have earned good grades, I was not critical. Adjusting from the semester structure to the quarter system was justifiable, and I would improve with time. The quarter system was so much faster than the semester structure, it almost made me dizzy - start - midterms - finals - finished - take a deep breath and do it again!

Vikki Richardson

22

DIVORCE - IN PRO PER
AND UCLA

During the quarter break, I dashed to a legal book store and purchased the divorce kit with all needed forms. Filing for divorce was elementary compared to preparing the bankruptcy documents. The divorce was filed for "Irreconcilable differences." We did not have any children, pets or property to fight over.

Winter quarter 1976 would have been very discouraging if I had not met Denise (Class of 1978) and Kathy (Class of 1977) in the discussion session of my English 90 class, a study of William Shakespeare's greatest works. I cut my Shakespearean teeth on 'King Lear.' I almost bit off more than I could chew. There was a lot to ingest, and I almost choked, but the audio tapes in Powell Library saved me, and I took my textbook to read along.

All of Shakespeare's Works, and the Works of many others, were on audio tapes in Powell Library. "The Tragedy of King Lear" was on audio from introduction to the closing words of Edgar. Edgar was the legitimate son of Glouster, a powerful man in the kingdom, but Edmund was Glouster's bastard son, which created conflict and plot progression. Edgar speaks the last words in 'King Lear:'

> The weight of this sad time we must obey,
> Speak what we feel, not what we ought to say.
> The oldest hath borne most: we that are young
> Shall never see so much, nor live so long.

King Lear, by modern terms, suffered from dementia, which caused him to make some irrational decisions, like dividing up his kingdom, which caused chaos. His three daughters, Goneril, Regan, and Cordelia could not agree on the best plan for their father. He was not cooperative, and there was no mention of Mrs. Lear. Furthermore, King Lear practiced favoritism among his daughters, and everyone in the kingdom did not live "happy-happy ever after." It was tragic!

Sometimes while listening my way through Shakespeare, I would fall asleep and become interactive with the characters. One time I jumped up and screamed loudly from a sword fight. That woke me up, along with everyone in the library! Sort of embarrassing, but much more hilarious! We had to read three or four plays, short stories, poetry, including sonnets, and we had to write a sonnet.

The final exam was soooo hard! For example, we had to identify a small passage from any one of the plays. Name the play, identify the act and passage. Name the speaker, identify to whom the character was speaking, and how was the passage essential to the play? By then, all of Shakespeare's "Sir speed you," ('King Lear') and "Come hither Fellow," ('Julius Caesar') had merged into one. Even though I was disappointed with my grade, I loved Shakespeare! He helped me survive and thrive at UCLA, and life in general when he spoke through Edgar in 'King Lear,' Act IV, Scene 1:

> The worst is not.
> So Long as we can say,
> This is the worst.

The professor, James Condren, presented interesting lectures on Shakespeare to approximately three hundred students, who wrote rapid notes. Later, I scheduled an office visit with him, and he offered encouraging and helpful information on a paper that I was working on. When he said, "Young lady, you are brilliant," I burst into tears. Surprised by my outburst, he chuckled and said, "Most people would take that as a compliment." I laughed and told him that my high school principal had labeled me uneducable. He apologized for the errors of others and spoke reassuring words to me. He did not know that he provided great healing from past negative input. His words also endowed me with much needed courage to survive UCLA.

Most literary lectures were presented in Rolfe or Royce Hall, but students were assigned to a teaching assistant who was known as a "T.A." They were earning a Master's Degree or Ph.D. in English. Students were divided into groups of approximately twenty, and we met with the teaching assistants in various classrooms for discussion of the subject matter.

When the campus bells stopped ringing, a perky young lady introduced herself as Linda while passing around a clipboard with little squares on a sheet of white paper. She said, "Please print your name in the square, and sit in the same seat until I remember all of your names. Then, you can sit anywhere you like."

Noticing that the bubbly, beautiful blond sitting next to me was Kathy Williamson, I reached over, shook her hand and said, "Hello cousin." She appeared very amused and said, "Well, hello cousin to you too," as she vigorously pumped my hand up and down. Both of us laughed out loud. I said, "My last name is Williamson; well that's my birth name." We became instant friends.

Denise was also seated next to Kathy. Denise and I had a similar appearance, but she had cute dimples. My hair was Afro; her hair was pressed and curled, and we also became instant friends. As time progressed, the three of us became study buddies and vowed to be friends for life. Friends for life were needed at UCLA, and meeting Kathy and Denise was comforting, and we encouraged each other. We talked about our classes, professors and required coursework. Both of them were English majors.

English was not enough. To meet my language requirement, I chose Elementary French instead of Spanish. At the time, I had visions of living in Paris someday. Learning my first French words at UCLA was a huge challenge. I was the only student with no prior French classes. Most students already had four years of high school French, and some of them had spent time in Paris practicing the language.

Moreover, I could not believe that the T.A. taught the class in French from day one! I practically moved into the French lab. Headsets with audio tapes, workbooks and drills consumed me. We had to read a novel written in French and answer questions about the story, and of course all of the exams were written in French, and we had to speak it.

My midterm grades were scary! I wondered if Mind Control was still working. Finals grades created doubt. "C" in English 90, "C" in Elementary French, a "B" in History 8B. When my grade cards arrived in the mail, tears of disappointment poured over them. Making bad matters worse, later on my financial aid counselor informed me that my scholarship amount would be reduced because my grade point average (GPA) dropped below 3.0, and I applied for a student loan. My saving grace was knowing that I had done my best and believing that I would do better next quarter.

In Winter Quarter 1976, I was walking into Campbell Hall to meet with my English mentor, Steve, when I encountered two Black female students. Gale was six feet tall, lean and perfectly beautiful (Class of 1977, Political Science). Tammy was very attractive with engulfing green eyes, and she did not appear to be a Black woman, but her speech patterns and political awareness shouted, "Soul Sister," (Class of 77, Psychology). When they saw me approaching, Tammy exclaimed, "Look Gale, another Black student," and the three of us became instant friends for life. Tammy and Gale had been friends since Junior High.

The three of us spoke rapidly about life and UCLA. When the subject of grades came up, tears formed in my eyes over my last grades. When I expressed my disappointment over the two "Cs" and a "B," they looked at each other, then stared at me. Tammy said, "And you are crying over that?" Gale went on, "A lot of students are praying, give me a "C" and set me free." Both of them chimed, "Girl you are doing great in UCLA!" They made me laugh and reassured me, but that was not the last tear I would shed over my grades.

Spring Quarter 1976, my final grades were: B, B, A. Things were getting better and better. My academic scholarship funds were restored, and I also accepted student loans. I had some friends on campus and fun activities could not be ignored. Spring rapidly led to summer. School was out, and it was time to find a job. Unfortunately, the State Bar did not have any temporary positions, but my former coworkers were pleased to hear from me and proud of my progress.

Apple One was an agency specialized in providing temporary staff to various companies. I was immediately hired as a receptionist-secretary in a law firm on Wilshire near Vermont. When the Apple One agent gave me the work location, she did not understand why I was so tickled. I told her, "My life seems to revolve around Wilshire and Vermont."

Whatever the job paid, I managed to cover my expenses and save some "egg money." Over summer, I read Shakespeare for fun and entertainment. Buying a TV was not a thought, but I did own a little stereo where I could play my albums and dance like a Go Go Girl. I never stopped dancing!

When I was recovering from the hysterectomy, I made up a dance called, "The Hysterectomy Strut." I placed my left hand on the wall or counter for support, crept along slowly and rhythmically waved my right arm to the beat. I carefully danced my way back to total healing.

While school was out, my Bunny friends came to visit. They loved my apartment. We basked in the amenities and enjoyed being together. Fran and Shelley were especially proud of me and were very encouraging.

Summer was brief, and the UCLA process started in August. I knew what to expect and was excited about returning to campus. When I got on the UCLA express bus on Wilshire and Vermont, guess who was driving? C.W. and I laughed like school kids. It was like seeing an old friend again. There was a passenger seated behind him, and I sat nearby until the guy got off the bus, and I occupied the seat. C.W and I talked about UCLA and things in general until we arrived on campus and I dashed off.

I was excited to meet with all of my counselors and happy that my full scholarship amount was restored with my "A" and two "Bs" earned in the

Spring Quarter. From Tammy and Gale I was introduced to the Freshman Summer Program (FSP), located in Campbell Hall, which was relatively close to Royce Hall. FSP was responsible for facilitating the enrollment of most Black and other students of color. Everyone welcomed me wholeheartedly to FSP, and I was hired as a peer counselor in Fall 1976.

Fall 1976 was very encouraging. My sister El' Nora became a UCLA student! She had been inspired by the possibility of attending UCLA and had moved from Indianapolis with her gorgeous daughter, Mauricia, eleven years old. El' Nora was living in Long Beach where she had a dear friend who was politically connected and could help her find employment. On campus our paths were like two parallel lines, but it was heartwarming knowing that she was there somewhere, and we looked forward to quarter breaks and visiting. I especially looked forward to seeing my little niece, Mauricia.

As the quarter progressed, I met Tammy's sister Linda, a graduate student who held an executive position at FSP. I met Sandi, Sheldon and his brother Kenny, Rhabin, Robert, light-skin John, brown-skin John, Dr. Quazzi, Tony, James, Milton aka "Big Mac," and many other Black students. We later became known in the Freshman Summer Program as "The Soul Patrol." Meanwhile, I had to select my classes and complete the enrollment process. Focused on completing core classes, I chose Astronomy to meet my physical science requirement, fall quarter 1976.

I was giddy with excitement and looked forward to exploring the universe. The universe had always been captivating and a source of wonderment since childhood. When we lived with our grandparents, the night sky was our source of entertainment; we did not have a TV or telephone. Granddad pointed out the Little Dipper, the Big Dipper and the Milky Way. He explained why the moon changed from one size to the next, and how the earth rotated around the sun.

When Robert and I were little kids in the log cabin, we thought the sun went down behind the thick trees and sank into the ground. Living with our grandparents, we were free to play, and we frequently outran the moon and counted all of the stars, but the most exciting event was chasing a falling star down the dark, dusty road.

Meanwhile in UCLA, the huge lecture hall was on South Campus, and packed with three hundred or more students. I sat in the front row directly in front of the podium. When the campus bells stopped reverberating, the professor stepped on stage and introduced himself, "I am Dr. Stephen P. Maran, a visiting professor from NASA." He told us what material he would cover during the quarter and referred us to the syllabus. He said, "It's not a requirement, but do take advantage of the Hubble telescope here on campus." I listened to every word and wrote them down as fast as possible. Class ended and I ran to see the Hubble telescope. Whichever building it was in, I found it but could not dash in and gaze through the lens. There was a waiting list with several students ahead of me. I had to select a view date and time by writing my name and class number in a slot on the sign-up sheet.

After waiting approximately two weeks, it was my turn to peer through the powerful lens of the Hubble, around 7:00 p.m. There was a future astronomer, a graduate student, waiting to guide me through my Hubble experience. I peered in and saw a 'Through the Looking Glass' reflection of my HUGE face and teeth, which made me squeal with amusement. When I looked through the lens the student said, "It's already tomorrow in China." The sun had gone down in the United States, was rising in China, and I was looking at it in real time. That was truly amazing!

I was anxious to see the moon and everything Granddad had pointed out when we were children. As I gazed upon various forms out in the universe, I waved my arms, wiggled around, and made a wide variety of vocal sounds. At times, I had to hold on to myself, because it felt like I was flying through space. The student was amused with my reactions. The Hubble gave me an expanded level of consciousness and was the most educational amusement ride ever.

Fall 1976 was totally engulfing. I was a happy camper with a little cash flow from peer counseling. I was succeeding in my classes, and all was well. My midterm grades were acceptable. I was carrying four classes, and I had a "B" in three of them. I was also expecting a "B" in Astronomy, even though I took the class for a passing grade. So, I would get a "P" instead of a "B."

When the T.A. returned my midterm exam, the first page was completely covered with a HUGE red "F!" I shrieked and clutched it to my chest. My body felt like it had been shot, stabbed, or suffered a serious traumatic injury, which temporarily left me speechless. Tears ran down my face without permission. I felt very queasy and used Mind Control to balance myself.

Next day after the midterm, when Dr. Maran finished his lecture, he hopped off stage and sat beside me as I was lifting up my book bag. He said, "Young lady, I can tell that you were not successful on the midterm. Come to my office when you have time. I think I can help you." His office location and hours were printed on the syllabus, and I went at my earliest convenience.

When I went to see Dr. Maran he said, "You were bright and sparkling before the midterm, then your lights went out." I gave him an overview of my educational past, and he apologized for the lack of insight by past educators. He looked at my answer selections from the multiple choice exam and said, "Here's your problem." He explained, there are four choices, and one is blatantly wrong. One is wrong when you read it carefully. One has some validity, but that one is the "sucker" answer. The best answer is the one with the most validation.

I was astonished when Dr. Maran told me that he was one of the people who did the math that launched rockets into outer space, and he showed me some examples. The math was trigonometry, something I had never seen before. Then he gave me a stack of exams topractice on and showed me how to avoid the "sucker" answers. I took the exams with me, followed instructions, and followed up with two office visits before the final exam, and he checked my answers.

To my surprise, some of the practice questions were actual questions on the final exam. Sweet! More importantly, I had learned to avoid the "sucker" answers. Astronomy presented my first multiple choice exam, and I had never taken a standardized test.

Dr. Maran was one of the most impressive people I have ever met and one of the most empathetic. I called him, "My Astronomy Angel." My final grades for Fall Quarter 1976 were: P, A, B, B. I looked forward to continued progress as time leaped forward. Also during Fall Quarter 1976, English had claimed me as a major. Kathy and Denise were thrilled that I had become an English major, and they laughed, "Welcome to bedlam."

The three of us enrolled in the same classes whenever possible. All of us loved William, and we enrolled in every Shakespeare class available. The three of us sparkled and earned top grades in the study of Chaucer and his 'Canterbury Tales,' taught by the wonderful Professor, Florence Ridley, but I had to endure the painful study of John Milton on my own.

Fall Quarter 1977, Fundamentals of Creative Dance provided two units, tremendous fun, and fitness. Dance classes and aerobics embraced me, and I took as many as my schedule allowed every quarter. Meantime, I became a contestant on The Gong Show with Chuck Barris in October 1977. 'The Gong Show' coordinator had warned that we would be waiting a long time and to bring a magazine or something to read. I went with my companion, William. I was enrolled in Shakespeare's Later Plays, English 142-B, and I carried my UCLA book bag. It was a very long wait, and I crammed in as much study time as possible.

Finally, the stage director called me for warm-up. I had choreographed a two-minute routine that included three head-rolls on the floor. I wore an orange leotard and white denim short-shorts. My knee socks had a horizontal design in bright orange and white stripes, and I wore tan platform heels, same design as my black platforms.

My black hair was styled in shoulder length cornrow braids, called extensions. Over summer Fran had introduced me to her braider. Braiding required long hours of chair time, but time well spent. Just wash and go for two or three months, then repeat the process. Braids provided long hair with more stability than wigs. Even though I had graduated from wearing wigs, I was ready to whip my braids around.

For my dance routine, I chose "Staying Alive" by The Bee Gees. The music presented a rocking beat, and "Staying Alive" had become one of my theme songs at UCLA, academically and physically. Chuck Barris had the most reassuring mannerisms, and he made contestants feel calm and happy. He was fondly known as "Uncle Chuck." When it was time for my routine he said, "Ladies and gentlemen, this young lady is a UCLA English major, and she sure knows how to wiggle her verbs around."

Lights, camera, action! I entered center stage genuinely laughing at his introduction and rocking to the beat. The Go Go Girl emerged with her bumps and grinds, and the audience howled! My muscle memory adhered to the choreographed steps, and my feet knew when the routine should have ended, but the music played on, and I continued dancing. When the Bee Gees voices finally trailed off with the high tenor, holding "Staying Alive..." I threw kisses towards the audience and accepted their thunderous applause, as "Uncle Chuck" said, "We'll be right back with more stuff."

Backstage, I said to the stage manager, "The music played longer than two-minutes." With an impish grin on his handsome face, he said, "I know." The next contestant was a male singer who was soon gonged by the judges. I was a finalist with second place. Some little old couple won the competition doing the fox trot, and we all received prizes for our efforts. I don't know what their prizes were, but I won a carpet steamer, lava lamp with purple lava, and a collection of fragrances and sundries were shipped to my home address.

Back on campus a couple days after the show, my Shakespeare professor was the first person to say, "I was shocked to see you dancing on 'The Gong Show.' I responded, "I'm shocked to know that you watch 'The Gong Show,' and we enjoyed a good laugh together. I became known as 'The Gong Show Girl' in a minuscule circle of UCLA's 30,000 students.

UCLA seems to have some inherent vibrations that cause students to thrive under pressure. However, opposite extremes occurred when some despondent students plunged to their death from the tallest buildings after midterm and final exams. Those area were soon cordoned off and monitored. From early childhood, I had a tendency towards homicide rather than suicide.

After adjusting to the quarter system, pressure worked well for me. I was carrying four classes instead of three, working a few hours a week, participating in unavoidable campus activities, like rallies and demonstrations. My final grades were: "A-, B+, B, B," and I could live with that.

Coursework was my first priority, but UCLA professors and Teaching Assistants were very stingy with "A" grades. I did my best at all times but also made an effort to participate in fun activities. One of the most fun activities involved working with Tammy, Gale, Sheldon, "The Soul Patrol," and many others to produce the annual African Cultural and Arts Festival.

Spectacular, colorful and cultural, human beings of all descriptions came to campus for the Saturday event and enjoyed authentic African dishes and various foods from other cultures. There were African drummers, a variety of dancers, singers and speakers who represented numerous people of color.

Who knew that producing fun could be so intense. I was on the entertainment committee, and my job was calling artists to see if they were willing to participate. Some of them were "stars" unto themselves and presented lofty attitudes. Others were unavailable, but the artists who did participate were well worth my efforts. That experience served me well working in the Freshman Summer Program (FSP), with Tammy, Sandi, Sheldon, Kenny and "The Soul Patrol." I had become a counselor and English tutor for the program.

Over three summers, we lived in the Sproul Hall dormitory with a group of incoming students who were enrolled in UCLA's summer school. FSP was structured so that incoming freshmen from urban schools could acclimate to UCLA and avoid total cultural shock and academic demise. As counselors, we met and prepared a budget for needed funds, and we always aimed high, because there was no time for budget revisions. We wanted our students to have the best experience possible, and everything required funding. Like the incoming kids, I was very excited to be in a dorm. It was a new experience for me. There was an 8 1/2 x 11 clipboard with a pad of lined paper and a pen attached to my door, so that students could sign up for personal tutoring. All of the tutors had clipboards on their door for student appointments.

Academic assurance was our first priority for the students, but we were also responsible for their well-being. Additionally, we planned field trips, which entailed getting waivers and having various forms signed by university administrators, and we verified insurance coverage. We were accustomed to working our way through the chain of command, and received forms rubber-stamped with "APPROVED" for everything needed.

At the end of each summer program, we provided a venue for a talent show, where the students and counselors could showcase their talents, or present someone who wanted to participate. Regardless of frustrations, the end results always amazed us on performance night, when proud parents and friends packed the audience and cheered.

23

UCLA PERFORMANCES
AND GRADUATION

Some of my most fulfilling performances and fun activities consisted of participating in several productions with the UCLA Black Dance Association. We were a group of approximately twenty-five students who loved to dance but were not dance majors, except for Lula Washington and "Boom-Boom."

Lula was known for her ocean-like waves in dance movements, and she choreographed powerful pieces for Black History Month. Her presentations told stories about slavery, freedom and houses of ill repute. I always looked forward to dancing with her. We spent weeks and weeks working for a five minute dance routine. Lula frequently spoke about opening her own dance studio when she graduated from UCLA.

"Boom-Boom" also danced in Lula's productions. She was a lead dancer who filled up the stage alone. When she danced, her body said, "Boom-Boom!" When she was not dancing, her body said "Boom-Boom!" She was about my height, huge breasts, a tiny waistline, and her derriere looked like two basketballs underneath her clothing. Her legs and thighs were sculptured, and she made high leaps appear effortless. She and several other dancers also choreographed. Producing an hour-long production required several dancers and choreographers. For those of us who loved to dance, the sacrifices were worth our efforts.

Time was moving fast and did not extend itself so that I could do everything, but I certainly enjoyed the endeavor. In spring 1977, I had taken

Radio and News Journalism, which was informative and fun. It entailed working in the UCLA radio station and broadcasting the news two days a week. I interviewed random students and found campus news to report. A ticker-tape instrument in the broadcast room constantly fed in new information. My job was condensing it into a two-minute report.

Fellow students were very encouraging when they saw me on campus and said things like: "Hey, I liked your report (on whatever the subject had been). That was really interesting. You sound good on the radio." For all of my running around and reporting expertise for UCLA Radio, my final grade was a "B."

The Stunt Work class in fall of 1978 left me breathless. We had to learn how to gracefully fall off of the stage, fall down on stage and roll over in a fight scene. We also ran several inches up the wall and flipped around. We were required to form a line, run, jump up and shoulder-roll over a four-wheel padded cart, land on our feet, run around, get on line and do it again. The cart was covered with long black flowing material, which the instructor pushed around the room while we ran and flipped over the cart, and he was pushing it a lot faster than I thought he should.

We were expected to flip our feet up in the air and walk with our hands, which I could not master. One day I flipped up and over so fast, the impact left me breathless, and the lights grew dim. Two fellow students lifted me from the thickly padded mat, and I started breathing again. The instructor said, "Let's try that again." It was worth it for my final grade, an "A."

During the Fall Quarter of 1978, I played the part of a newscaster in a One-Act play. The characters were politically charged, and my character was almost trampled attempting to report the story. I think the theater group did one play each quarter, and the productions were called 'The Noon Miracles.' The plays were always presented at noon, and it was a "miracle" that they were able to produce them in ten weeks. There was no grade, no credits, just my love for the theater.

At some point in the fall of 1978, I decided to take in a roommate. There was never enough money to enjoy entertainment at UCLA, like The Alvin Ailey Dance Troupe and many others, not to mention outings in Westwood Village. Since I was married to UCLA, I did not spend a lot of time at home, especially while living in the dorm with the Freshman Summer Program. Moving out of my apartment was not an option, knowing that I would eventually graduate from UCLA.

I wrote a descriptive ad for my apartment and posted it in the Student Union Building where many other ads and notices were posted. I had studied until Powell Library closed, and I ran to catch the last bus leaving campus. The bus engine was running. The door was open. I entered, took a seat and began reading. When the driver stepped up in the bus, I looked up and saw C.W.'s smiling face. Although I rode his bus to UCLA almost everyday, he was shocked to see me on his last run and asked, "What are you doing out here so late?" I told him about the roommate ad. He exclaimed, "I was just getting ready to move!" Then he asked, "Male or female?" I responded, "It does not matter, as long as they pay their half of the rent." I had made the bedroom available for the roommate, and I was going to sleep on the floor in the living room, which I frequently did anyway. I had learned to love sleeping on the floor. It seemed to provide more rest in less time.

When I gave C.W. my address, he knew exactly where I lived because he had watched the construction while driving a bus route on Virgil Avenue. We had exchanged basic information during our brief chats but not phone numbers, and I felt more comfortable with him than I would have with a complete stranger from UCLA. The next day I removed the ad, but several people had written down the information and my phone number. My phone rang for quite sometime with potential roommates who sounded totally disappointed that the place was not available.

Over the weekend C.W. moved in, paid the entire rent amount, plus an additional $100.00 "for UCLA stuff." Noticing the flabbergasted expression on my face, he smiled and said, "That's the least I can do as hard as you're trying to get through UCLA." I burst into tears and gave him a big "Teddy Bear" hug. He laughed and apologized for making me cry. Later on we went grocery shopping in his 1972 blue Cadillac and put my empty refrigerator to work.

Winter 1979 was enthralling. My Women's Study class was packed with every ethnicity of womankind on campus. It explored the exploitation and oppression of women. There was an Egyptian woman who made us wince and weep with the graphic details of circumcising young girls by cutting the clitoris and without the aid of anesthetics. Each student was asked to volunteer some information and explain how it impacted our life. I presented my Bunny experience in The Playboy Club and spoke of working topless.

An attractive White lady in a sharp business suit presented information on how she moved from being a prostitute to a business woman. She was earning her Master's Degree in Business Administration, while working as an executive in a local company. She smiled proudly and said, "I know how to handle men." That was one of the most relevant classes for me, and I earned an "A." It was my best academic quarter: A, A, B+, B.

Time was winding down, and I was looking forward to graduating in June 1979, but the Spring Quarter was waiting to be completed. While standing in line to purchase books and supplies in the student store, I noticed a display rack stocked with paperback books with the title, "A Black Quartet." I dashed towards the rack with a loud, "Oh my God."

I could not believe it! I snatched up a book and opened it. Sure enough, there I was, four pictures of me and cast members on pages 98 and 99. All four of the plays were there, just as we had performed them. My reactions caused other students to look at the books and buy them, as I spoke out loud and pointed to the photographs without conscious effort. I bought ten of them for family and friends.

There was one other outstanding and confirming encounter during my UCLA journey. I was waiting in line regarding financial aid. The never-ending line extended out of the building and looped around. As I stood there half-heartedly reading some 'Cliff Notes,' I noticed this guy walking towards me. He was dressed in Levi jeans, cowboy boots and hat, wearing a red plaid shirt. I was admiring the turquoise on his belt buckle and on the little black string tie around his neck.

He walked straight to me and said, "Hello, my Cherokee sister," and gave me a big hug. I almost dropped on the ground as images of Grandma Lizzy flashed in my mind. I gasped! "How do you know?" He said, "Your cheekbones and eyes, especially your cheekbones." Tears poured as my heart fluttered! I told him a little bit about Grandma Lizzy, and he said, "She spoke truth." We hugged, wished each other well from the "plantation and reservation, to UCLA." We laughed, waved, and he rushed off while students waiting on line stared at us curiously.

Spring Quarter 1979 was indeed my last and most academically challenging. For starters, I had to read 101 books, which I scanned. Thanks to he Learning Lab, they had trained my eyeballs to move faster. This was accomplished with a device anchored above the reading material.

The instrument had a horizontal light that progressively traveled down the page. Readers had various speed options to choose from. If my eyeballs were not moving fast enough, the light would keep traveling and leave them in the dark. The light span was approximately one inch wide vertically and maybe seven or eight inches across. With pen and notebook available, I would set the light speed at my desired pace.

Stop the light, make notes, and continue reading. All systems were operating, Mind Control, The Phenomenon, Powers of The Universe, Almighty God and Jesus Christ himself! All of them were needed for me to read 101 books in ten weeks! One of my favorite classes for Spring 1979 was, "Black People in The American Theater." I was jumping with joy and pride over being enrolled in Professor Beverly Robinson's class. The course required a twenty-five page paper, which made me responsible for writing eleven papers within ten weeks. I thought, "I can do all things through Christ who strengthens me."

Frequently I wondered if the professors conspired on making all papers due at the same time, as a source of amusement among themselves. Time pressed me to write three or four papers simultaneously. My desk at home was covered with labeled papers in progress, and my typewriter hummed.

Thank you State Bar of California. My typing ability was truly an asset. I overhead fellow students speak about the enormous amounts they paid to have papers typed. Much time was required to research Black people in the American Theater, starting with the first known theater in America, which was not Black. It was built in Williamsburg, Virginia in 1716, not Broadway, New York, as perceived by the modern generation.

The first known African-American theater company was The African Grove Theater in New York City, around 1821, founded by William Henry Brown and James Hewlett. One day I was digging up information in the University Research Library and came upon a "Black Anthology of American Theater." It was a thick book that resembled a standard size dictionary. I thought, "This book must contain everything I need to know about Black people in the theater since the beginning of time."

As I read the table of contents, there it was, "A Black Quartet." I gasped and sucked in air, but I did not scream. The experience caused me to feel like I had traveled back into history and met myself.

Professor Robinson owned a copy of "A Black Quartet" in paperback that was in plain view when I went for an office visit. We were discussing the course when she referred to the book and said, "You feel familiar," and she pointed to my name and pictures in the book. Based upon my reactions, she jumped up from her chair and so did I. She embraced me in a hug and said, "I saw your performance at The Inner City Cultural Center, and I thought you were brilliant and honest." She showed me a theater program from the event and pointed to my name. I melted into a puddle of tears and so did she. The connection was overpowering! I received an A+ on my paper and as a final grade, because I earned it the hard way. My UCLA adventure was coming to an end. I had attended and listened to on campus recruiters from various companies, offering job opportunities and graduate school personnel seeking new students.

Still, there were multiple things to do. I met with the academic counselor in The English Department. He informed me that I was graduating in the upper one third of my class and congratulated me on a job well done. It behooved me to select an appointment slot for my senior pictures and order a graduation yearbook. Ordering my cap and gown was of utmost importance.

True to plan, and 'The Powers of the Universe,' graduation day arrived in Pauley Pavilion on June 15, 1979. Excitement and energy swirled around the thousands of us who were graduating. Speeches of congratulations and encouragement were genuinely applauded and appreciated. Graduation caps rose in the air like flocks of low-flying blue birds with golden beaks. Screams, hugs, kisses, tears, laughter, balloons, flowers, and tons of pictures were warmly expressed and accepted.

My photo album was provided by Fran, who had become an accomplished photographer and film editor. Bunny buddies and UCLA friends came to my graduation, but some of them were lost in the crowds, and there were no cell phones and texting. Mother booked a flight from Indianapolis. She was immeasurably proud of my accomplishments. My young nephew Derric and his sisters, Cathy, and Caressa, Audrey's darling children, were visiting from Indianapolis at the time, and all of them stayed with me and C.W., who drove them to graduation. My sister El' Nora and her daughter, Mauricia, came from Long Beach.

My life dream of graduating from a university had come true twenty years after I had graduated from Shortridge High School, where I never went to a prom and did not participate in a cap and gown graduation ceremony.

During my UCLA adventure, I did not make The Dean's List, but my overall accumulative G.P.A was 3.76, Magna cum laude equivalent. Now what? Maybe I will marry my "Teddy Bear," go to law school, teach English, work in Social Services, return to an acting career? Whatever I choose, life and UCLA had prepared me with "a coat of armor" and academic skills to endure and succeed. C.W. gave me a brand new, 1979 orange and beige, stick shift Toyota as my graduation gift to help me get there.

A New Beginning.

Vikki Richardson

ABOUT THE AUTHOR

BOOKS REFERRED TO:
1. A Black Quartet by Ben Caldwell, Ronald Milner, Ed Bullins and Leroi Jones - Copyright 1970
2. Mind Control Meditation, by Jose Silva - Copyright 1970
3. The Complete Signet Classic Shakespeare, by Harcourt Brace Jovanovich, Inc. - Copyright 1963
4. The Holy Bible, King James Version - Copyright 1909
5. The Internet - All historical dates and data provided through Google and Cyber Space

ARTICLES:
1. The Indianapolis Star - 10/10/1962
2. Jet Magazine - 7/28/1966
3. New York Daily News - unknown date - 1967
4. The Wall Street Journal - 5/9/1969
5. The New York Post- 7/22/1969
6. Ebony Magazine - unknown date - 1969
7. The New York Times - 7/31/1969
8. The New York Times - 8/3/1969
9. The Nashville Tennessean - 11/16/1969

vrun4jc@hotmail.com

Made in the USA
San Bernardino, CA
17 September 2018